DATE DUE

DEMCO, INC. 38-2931

SCAM DOGS AND MO-MO MAMAS

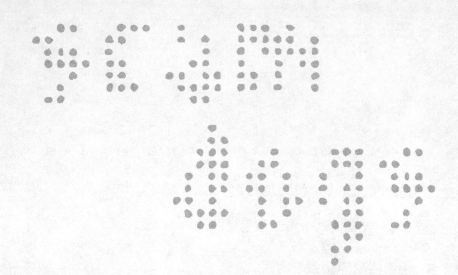

SCAM

DOGS

AND

MO-MO

MAMAS

INSIDE THE WILD AND WOOLLY WORLD
OF INTERNET STOCK TRADING

JOHN R. EMSHWILLER

HarperBusiness

An Imprint of HarperCollinsPublishers

HarperCollins books may be purchased for educational, business, or sales promotional use. For information please write: Special Markets Department, HarperCollins Publishers Inc., 10 East 53rd Street, New York, NY 10022.

FIRST EDITION

Printed on acid-free paper

Designed by Lindgren/Fuller Design

Library of Congress Cataloging-in-Publication Data
    Emshwiller, John R., 1950–
      Scam dogs and mo-mo mamas: inside the wild and woolly world of Internet stock trading / John R. Emshwiller.—1st ed.
        p.   cm.
      Includes index.
      ISBN 0-06-019620-3 (hc)
        1. Electronic trading of securities.   2. Day trading (Securities).   I. Title.
    HG4515.95 .E47 2000
    332.64'0285—dc21   00-025344

00 01 02 03 04 ❖/RRD 10 9 8 7 6 5 4 3 2 1

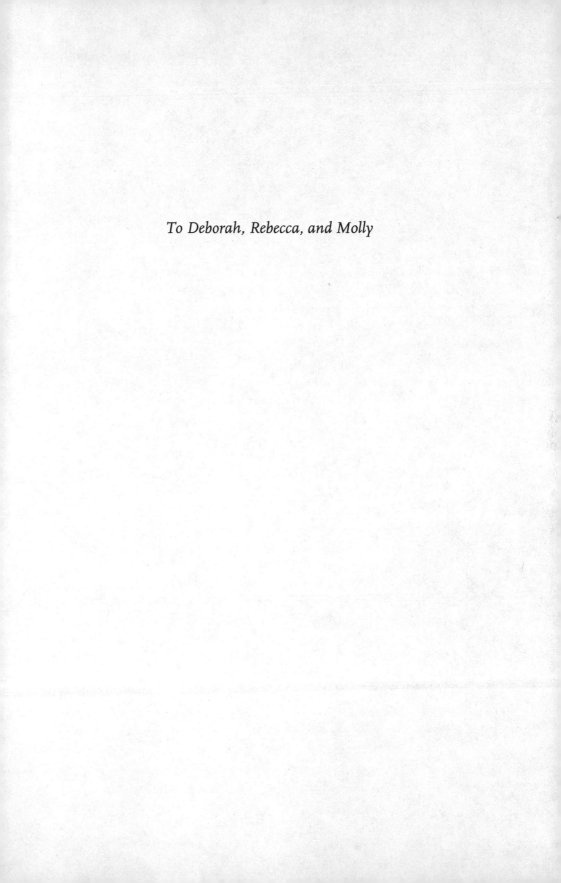

To Deborah, Rebecca, and Molly

ACKNOWLEDGMENTS

SINCE THIS IS MY FIRST BOOK, I'm tempted to give a thank you to everyone to whom I owe a debt of gratitude. Unfortunately, Harper-Collins only agreed to publish one book-length tome from me. So, I will have to leave some people out.

On the list of thanks, I might as well start at the very beginning with my mother. She deserved an easier life but never complained about not getting one.

Next, in roughly chronological order, comes Michael Miller, who has been my friend longer than anyone else. Not necessarily a notable accomplishment, but at least he gets points for endurance. Michael read a draft of the manuscript and has been very encouraging and helpful throughout this project.

To Don Bruckner, the first great journalist who ever befriended me and one of the people who—through no fault of his own—inspired me to get into the reporting racket.

To Chuck Camp, who taught me more than a few things about being a newspaper reporter and actually made working in Detroit fun. Plus, he is the only person I've ever met with the fashion courage to wear a two-tone red leisure suit. And tie. (However, it was the '70s.)

At my employer, the *Wall Street Journal*, managing editor Paul Steiger was kind enough to say yes to my request for a book leave and even kinder to say yes to my request to come back after the leave. Los Angeles bureau chief Peter Gumbel, who is my current boss, was extremely supportive of this project from the beginning. Besides offering some extremely valuable early advice, Peter read a draft of the manuscript and made suggestions that improved the text in important ways. Andy Pasztor, a longtime friend and *Journal* colleague, also read a draft, provided very good advice and, at one point in the reporting, some very welcome companionship. Though I didn't stick *Journal* colleague Alix Freedman with a manuscript draft, I did talk to her a lot about the project. Her encouragement managed to hold up even under the slagheaps of angst I kept dumping over the phone.

Geri Thoma has been my agent for most of the 1990s. She is also a very good editor, who has helped improve just about every scrap of writing I've ever sent her way.

Given the horror stories that other reporters/authors had told me about the modern publishing world, my editor at HarperCollins, Dave Conti, turned out to be a very pleasant surprise. Dave was easy to work with and had very valuable editing suggestions, which made the book much more coherent and readable. (Hopefully, you will think it is coherent and readable). I am also grateful to Dave's assistant, Devi Pillai, who helped in many small and large ways.

I'd also like to thank Tom Collins and Kate Fagan. Tom freely offered me his encouragement and considerable research and editing skills. Kate was kind enough to transcribe some of my taped interviews and actually make sense of them.

Then, there is Jonathan Kwitny. Jon died of cancer in 1998 before this project was even born. He was the greatest investigative reporter I've ever met. And to find a truer friend, you'd have to travel even further than Jon did in his global pursuit of stories. More than once while writing this book, usually late at night, I'd be tired and frustrated and about ready to give my computer a forceful introduction to a wall. Then I'd remember how Jon got up at 4 A.M. to write his books and still put in a full day at the *Journal*. I'd think about his incredible energy and optimism. And I'd keep typing.

Last, but hardly least, on this cavalcade of acknowledgments are the three most important people on the planet: my wife, Deborah, and my daughters, Molly and Rebecca. I cheerfully admit to being completely prejudiced in this evaluation. On this book—along with just about everything else in my life—they've helped me in more ways than I can count and probably more ways than I even realize. Deborah, especially, made so many contributions to the completion of this book that I should probably make her the co-author.

While all of the people mentioned above helped shape and improve this book, the remaining flaws are the sole possession of the author. Under federal copyright law, I think I get to keep them for a good long time.

THE INTERNET STOCK GURUS

A. **TOKYO JOE**, a.k.a. Yun Soo Oh Park, a.k.a. Joe Park, a.k.a. TokyoMex, a.k.a. Joe Matsudaira, a.k.a. Tmex, a.k.a. Tyrannosaurus Mex, a.k.a. . . . well, you get the idea. He just might be the most famous—or, if you believe his critics, infamous—stock picker on the Net.

B. **BIG DOG**, a.k.a. Mike Nichols: This six-foot-four-inch, 370-plus pound former textile coating salesman howled his way to wealth and prominence in the silence of cyberspace. He bought a new house, a new car, and a lot of rounds for his new friends at TJ's bar. He became successful enough that it nearly wrecked him.

C. **ANTHONY@PACIFIC**, a.k.a. Tony Elgindy: A Chevy salesman turned stockbroker, not necessarily a step up. He sailed through the sewers of Wall Street before emerging as a force to be reckoned with in the not-always-shiny new world of Internet stock trading. He attracts controversy the way certain fabrics attract lint.

D. **JANICE SHELL**, a.k.a. Janice Shell: Despite the quaint, pedestrian habit of using her own name, Shell has been known to drive certain cyberspace men wild. She either lives in Milan, Italy, or Clute, Texas, or Sacramento, California. Or somewhere else.

E. **GA BARD**, a.k.a. Gary Swancey: He is a poet, a trader, a cyberspace stock philosopher. He can also repair your heater or air conditioner and in a pinch pretend to be a blind beggar.

F. **JEFFREY S. MITCHELL**, a.k.a. Jeffrey S. Mitchell: A friend of Janice Shell and fellow member of the AML (Anti Moniker League.) One of the Net's merry pranksters, who sometimes prefers fictitious companies to real ones.

G. **SI JILL**, a.k.a Jill Munden: Probably the nicest judge and jailer you will ever meet in cyberspace.

H. **FLOYDYIE**, a.k.a. Floyd Schneider: You may call him The Truthseeker.

I. **PLUVIA**, a.k.a. Steve xxxx: You may not call him Keyser.

J. **CAVALRY**: His Internet battle cry isn't "Charge!" but "iChargeit!"

K. **THE INTERNET**, a.k.a. cyberspace, a.k.a. the Net, a.k.a. El Dorado: A large, amorphous something that probably isn't organic but definitely is lively.

PROLOGUE

DURING THE FIRST WEEK of the second month of the millennium's last year, not far from the intersection of Rodeo Drive and Wall Street, in a place called cyberspace, the usually dead-as-a-stone stock of JB Oxford Holdings, Inc. becomes a gold-plated, revved-up rocket that blasts into the financial heavens.

For a few dazzling days in February, Oxford outshines General Electric and General Motors, IBM and Microsoft, along with thousands of other publicly traded stocks of equal or lesser repute. It outshines them all.

Fuel for Oxford's remarkable run comes from newly minted electronic metropolises with names such as Yahoo!, Raging Bull, and Silicon Investor. In these communities, there are no towers and a word is never spoken. But there is lots of babble.

The early, silent mutterings of Oxford's coming wild ride had flickered on computer screens around the world in the dog days of January, when hopes for the new year mingled with hangovers from the old. The messages came from strangers, their identities wrapped in pseudonyms, writing in a language that usually resembled English. What they lacked in clarity they made up for in exclamation points.

    "JBOH WILL FLY!!!!!"[1]

ventured an e-mail message at three minutes past noon on January 18; the message referred to Oxford by its four-letter stock symbol. At the time, Oxford stock was hovering near the ground, at a tad over $2 a share.

```
"The stock is so cheap!"

"4000 long and more on day trades . . . GO JBOH!!!"

"I'm loooooooooonnnnnnnngnggg."
```

Presumably this was a description of a stock position and not a boast from a dachshund preening at its keyboard. In stock-trading parlance, being "long" means owning stock on the presumption that its price will rise. Someone goes "short" if he or she expects the price to fall.

```
"Stock is going to soar. Say you heard it from me first."

"I bought quite a bit of JBOH today . . . I frankly
haven't investigated the company a great deal."
```

Then, perhaps, an abridged Oxford history is in order. Incorporated in 1987, the company has gone through several names, including Otra Securities and RKS Financial Group, before becoming Oxford.

Oxford is a stock brokerage firm, one of the several thousand licensed brokers in the United States. To say it isn't exactly up there with Merrill, Morgan, and the other titans of finance would be overly generous. Even Oxford's headquarters is a long way from Wall Street, a continent to the west in Beverly Hills, California—just a short stroll from Rodeo Drive.

Now, having a figurative foot on the nation's premier financial thoroughfare and a literal one near one of its most famous shopping boulevards isn't as incongruous as the map coordinates would indicate. For each locale, in its own way, is built upon the same deep and abiding faith in the awesome economic power of nothing.

How else does one explain why a bag with a Gucci label on Rodeo Drive sells for hundreds of dollars, while essentially the same bag, sans label, can be had for a fraction of the price a few miles away? Or why the stock of Amalgamated Baloney and Consolidated Drivel (not a real corporate name, at least not yet) sells for $5 in the morning and $6 in the afternoon? Even on its best days, the company probably doesn't produce enough extra baloney or drivel to make it worth 20 percent more in just a few hours.

Unfortunately for Oxford, being so near two meccas of nothing power hasn't really seemed to inspire the firm for much of its history. In the previous four years—during one of the great periods of prosperity in American history, especially on Wall Street—Oxford has managed to register steadily declining earnings, except for 1998, when it had a $1.8 million loss. Oxford's headquarters is in a box of an office building, with all the pizzazz of a Peoria high-rise. The furniture at Oxford isn't exactly threadbare, but none of it appears to be auditioning for *Architectural Digest*.[2]

Oxford did make one move that would prove pivotal in the frantic days of February 1999. Back in September 1994, it started an online brokerage operation to service the then-aborning world of trading stocks over the Internet. Customers could use their personal computers "to trade equities and options, obtain quotes, retrieve account information and obtain research," according to an Oxford document from that period.

Initally, at least, it wasn't a noticeably successful step. Oxford hasn't been among such burgeoning big names of online brokerage firms as Charles Schwab and E*Trade. It is, according to a Dow Jones News Service story from early 1999, one of many "marginal" online brokers trying to make a mark.

But when the power of nothing takes hold, marginal can be transformed into mega pretty quickly. And in early 1999, that force was hungrily seeking anything that carried the cachet of the Internet.

By the last week of January, the crowds around Oxford's stock were swelling.

"TALLY HO, JBO!!!!! . . . "ROFLMAO!!!!! EOM"

(Partial Translation: Rolling On Floor Laughing My Ass Off!!!!! End Of Message.) (Have to leave "Tally Ho" to the anthropologists.)

"JBOH IS WAITING FOR THE RIGHT MINUTE [to] TAKE OFF."

"JBOH will be at $10 by this time next week."

"Yahoo message board has psychopath(s) on it."

". . . If it bothers you, kill it."

"SELL"

(II:2I A.M.)

"BUY"

(II:23 A.M.) (Two messages, same writer.)

"'Online trading craze' will last . . . JBOH is a company with lousy finance but in the right business at
the right time. Go JBOH!!!"

"Rumours! . . . JB Oxford & Sons has rejected a $1.1bn
takeover offer . . . said the $75-a-share and other
proposals were 'not adequate.'"

(Must have been the idiot "sons" of Oxford who turned down
seventy-five bucks for a stock that was trading at two and change.
Presumably, the offer is about as real as the kids.)

"Buuuuuuuuuuuuuuuuuuuuuulllllllllllllssssssss."

Shortly after midnight, January 28, the aliens arrive.

"Oh my god . . . there is LIFE out there . . . "

"PEOPLE OF EARTH. MERGER TIME IS NEAR."

"TO ALL ZIRCON PROTRACTORS!! THIS STOCK WILL HIT
$2.9375 TOMORROW."

"CITIZENS OF EARTH—PREPARE FOR BATTLE! . . . PREPARE TO
FIRE DESTRUCTO-BEAM!!! . . . WE HAVE SAVED EARTH! . . .
PEOPLE OF EARTH. BUY MORE JBOH!"

And they do.

Monday, February 1, 1999, dawns—as it does every day—
bright and clear or cloudy and cold, depending on where one
stands. But wherever one stands on the planet, the sun is shining
on JB Oxford.

On the previous Friday, Oxford's stock closed at a little over
$2.50 a share on a volume of 911,000 shares traded. At the close of
trading Monday, it has climbed to $5.56 a share. More than 20.6
million shares trade that day—roughly equal to Oxford's trading
volume for all of 1998.

"BREAKINGGGGGGGGGGGGGGGG OUT!"

"A NO BRAINER!! JBOH to $20."

"JBOH GOING TO 100."

"JB OXFORD—GOING TO 10000000000000."

"Post JBOH on every board possible!!!!"

"Merrill Lynch buying JB Oxford."

(Wrong.)

"THIS STOCK IS KA KA."

"BLAH BLAH BLAH there are investigations . . . "

Oh yes, the investigations. Here is an excerpt from the August
20, 1997, issue of the *Wall Street Journal:*

BEVERLY HILLS, Calif.—Federal agents raided the offices
of JB Oxford Holdings Inc., whose fast-growing brokerage
unit has been the focus of controversy for at least two years
and already is under investigation by the Securities and
Exchange Commission. . . . Agents of the Federal Bureau of
Investigation arrived with search warrants yesterday morning and carted away various documents. . . .

The *Los Angeles Times* of the same day added, "Sources call action the beginning of a wide-ranging probe by federal agents into Oxford and consultant Irving Kott."

Oxford hired Kott as a consultant in the early 1990s. His tenure at the brokerage firm merited a 1993 front-page story in the *Los Angeles Times* and subsequent long articles in the *Wall Street Journal* and *Time* magazine. After all, it isn't every day that a licensed broker-dealer hires one of the world's better-known securities swindlers.[3]

A Canadian in his late sixties, Kott generally calls Montreal home. But over the past quarter century, he has been chased in several countries and two continents by law enforcement officials. In 1976, Kott was convicted of stock fraud in an Ontario provincial court and fined $500,000. The Ontario Securities Commission, in a 1988 decision upholding a cease-trading order in a stock it believed was connected to Kott, described him as "well and unfavorably known" to the regulators.

Kott reportedly also has had problems with enforcement officials of a different ilk. In 1984, two Toronto organized-crime figures pled guilty to arranging a string of violent crimes, including a 1978 attempt to murder Kott by blowing up his car. Fortunately for him and his future employer, he wasn't near the vehicle when the bomb went off.

Why would Oxford hire a man with Kott's history? "Kott is brilliant in marketing" and the firm was using his "expertise" to help reorganize its operations, a senior Oxford official told the *Wall Street Journal* in 1995.

In that same year, Oxford shares had a little warm-up to the trading frenzy of '99. Volume, which for much of 1995 had been under 50,000 shares a day, soared to as high as one million shares daily. The stock's price shot up to $2 a share from about 75 cents a share.

Oxford officials at the time said that Kott's duties didn't include promoting the company's stock. Kott did not return phone calls seeking an interview.

In 1998, new ownership took over Oxford. They announced the departure of Kott and his son, Ian, who had been a top company official. The new management said that as far as it knew, the

Kotts had nothing more to do with Oxford. Of course, it's often impossible to know exactly who lurks in cyberspace.

```
"BUY BUY BUY."
```

```
"SELL . . . SELL . . . SELL . . . SELL . . . OVERBOUGHT."
```

```
"Don't ejaculate too early, HOLD!!"
```

```
"SQUEEEEEEEEEEEEEEEEEEEEEEEEEEZ!!!!!!!"
```

Oxford's stock takes a relative breather on Tuesday, February 2, 1999. Its price drops by about a buck though its volume is still a hefty 7 million shares. All that just sets the stage for Wednesday and Thursday.

On those two days, the stock goes from $4.75 to as high as $25.75 and trades over 33 million shares each day. By contrast, the trading volume of mighty Microsoft averages a mere 20 million shares a day over the same period. Even more astonishing, Microsoft has over 2.5 billion shares outstanding. Oxford has about 14 million. Traders are passing around the brokerage firm's shares faster than the dinner tab at a table of Scrooges.

```
"UP, UP AND AWAY—SEE YA ON EVEREST!!!!!"
```

```
"Oh pulease. 'Broker Rafi Khan Manipulated Prices, U.S.
SEC Says.'"
```

Besides Irving, there is Rafi in Oxford's history book. The tenures of Kott and Khan at the brokerage firm overlap. Khan insists that he didn't approve of Kott's presence there. A stockbroker and part owner of Oxford when it was known as RKS, the Pakistani-born Khan is widely known on Wall Street. He is a colorful character with a talent for picking stocks that subsequently soar in value.[4]

The SEC had decided that Khan's stock picking has been aided by stock manipulation, and in 1998 sued him for securities-law violations. He fought those charges. Later, in July 1999, he would plead guilty to a criminal charge of filing a false tax return and promise to provide information in "other ongoing investigations," according to a press release from the U.S. Attorney's office in Los Angeles. Khan's attorney and the authorities declined to identify the other investigations. Oxford wasn't charged with any wrongdoing in either of those cases. A company official says current management has nothing to do with Mr. Kott or Mr. Khan and doesn't have any reason to believe that Oxford or its current management are under investigation.

(On February 15, 2000, Oxford and the U.S. attorney's office in Los Angeles announced that the firm had agreed to pay the government $2 million to resolve the criminal probe into the company. Oxford didn't admit to any wrongdoing and reiterated that its curent management wasn't under investigation. The U.S. attorney's office said Oxford also agreed to cooperate in the government's ongoing investigation of "individuals and other entities." In an interview, assistant U.S. attorney Christopher Painter declined to identify those suspects. Also in an interview, Oxford chairman C.L. Jarratt said the firm has returned to profitability and looks forward to growth in the future.)

One of Khan's trademarks was research reports about stocks that feature large, bold headlines and phrases not found in the typical analyst's tome. One Kentucky life insurance company was "FINGER LICKIN' GOOD??!" while a technology company exuded "MAGNETIC POWER!!" Of course, when those missives were written in the early 1990s, such creativity was still largely confined to paper. As they say, that was then.

"HOLD YOUR SHARES!!!!! THIS IS FLYING!!!"

"Jboh, total scam, don't be conned."

"Its tempting to sell but DO NOT SELL!!!"

"I'm not TOO GREEDY to sell!!!"

"CNBC TALKING ABOUT JBOH!!!"

(CNBC is a cable channel dedicated to financial news.)

"JBOH! ! ! JESUS CHRIST! ! !"

"Cant read messages fast enough."

"I hear some very BAD THINGS ARE COMING down the
pipeline on JBOH . . . like Govt agencies and stuff
. . . Yikes!!!"

"Translation —> Please god make the price go down so I
can cover my short. Please Please Please Please."

"HUGE PUSH AFTER LUNCH. GET IN NOW!"

"ONLINE TRADING IS ADDICTIVE! CLICK, CLICK."

By the end of the week, the fury has subsided to a gentle roar,
though Oxford doesn't quite go back to being the sleepy stock that
it once was. In the next few months, it generally trades around $10
a share—sometimes in the high teens, sometimes scraping mid-
single digits. Its daily volume goes above a million shares, sometimes way above. A little fairy dust apparently sticks from those
magical days of February.

Other little online brokerage firms also see their stock prices
and volumes soar that first week of February. News stories and
observers largely attribute the rush to the new legions of online
traders, who chat on the electronic chat boards and buy and sell
stock through their computers—sometimes making dozens of
trades a day. "Internet mania," pronounces one story on the trading
in Oxford and the others. "Euphoric gains" fueled by "intense speculation," declares another story. "Internet fever," adds a third.

As 1999 rolls along, it seems that almost daily some new
Oxford or group of Oxfords—usually Internet-related companies—
catch the fancy of traders. Avalanches of e-mail and wild stock
activity follow. Some of these companies are big and well known,
others small and obscure. Many are legitimate business endeav-
ors, though not all of them are yet successful enough to have
such incidentals as profits. Others are outrageous, almost comi-
cal, frauds.

Of course, Internet fever is hardly the first time that mania
has marched through the securities markets. Indeed, even a light

tap dance through the last half millennium of stock marketing pro-
duces at least one observation: the process is very much like a
merry-go-round. Wait a little while and the same horse, not always
a pretty one, will come around.

More than 350 years ago, the Dutch had their now-famous
Tulipomania where they went a little crazy bidding up the price of
tulip bulbs—a sort of stalk market frenzy that served as a warm-up
to later stock market frenzies. By the mid-1700s, investors in England and France were throwing their money at dubious schemes to
exploit the eighteenth-century equivalent of the Internet on the
bright and shiny investment scale: the New World. Sadly, though
not for the last time, investors discovered too late that the schemes
ranged from far-fetched to fraudulent.

By the time of the American Revolution, the New World—or at
least the cities of Philadelphia, Boston, and New York—was developed enough to have its own securities trading and financial frolics.
Before the dawn of the nineteenth century, Wall Street had seen its
first financial panic, the first effort by federal intervention to stem a
panic, and the first market highflier to go to prison for his flying.

Over the next two hundred years, a few things, too numerous
to mention, transpired in the financial markets. On the whole,
events were pretty bullish. After all, the Dow Jones Industrial Average—an index of thirty major stocks and the world's most famous
stock market indicator—has managed to rise from 40.94 at its
debut in 1896 to over 11,000 in 1999.

There have been a few ups and downs along the way, to be
sure. On the upside, there was the mania for canal stocks (my personal favorite being the Dismal Swamp Canal Co.), the mania for
railroad stocks and, in the 1920s, the mania, seemingly, for any
stock that breathed. Each had similarities to the great Internet rush
of the late 1990s in its hopes and hype and outrageous conduct.

However, perhaps the most weirdly similar mania to what's
happening online at the end of the twentieth century is the one that
put an exclamation point on the end of the nineteenth century. And
it had nothing to do with stocks. On July 17, 1897, the steamship
Portland arrived in Seattle carrying a boatload of men from a wild,

rugged region to the north where the great Yukon River intersects with a lesser tributary known as the Klondike. A local newspaper story reported that the men from that wild outback were carrying with them "more than a ton of solid gold."

Though nineteenth century communications were nothing like today's, that golden phrase flashed around the world within a few days and set off one of history's great rushes of greed. Legions of men and women almost literally dropped their lives and set off for the Klondike to seek their fortunes.

Certainly there are differences between that gold rush and the one that followed a hundred years later. While Internet mania is viewed by many as heralding a new era, the story of the Klondike essentially ended another. It was the latest, and perhaps craziest, of the great gold rushes that sent wealth seekers to places as far afield as South Africa and Sutter's Mill during the 1800s.

And unlike the Internet gold rush, the one to the Klondike could not be done from the comfort of a living room. Indeed, the paths to that region around the Canada/Alaska border were difficult and dangerous in the extreme. Many died in the effort to get there, and not just men. One tortuous path of boulders, cliffs, and bogs was dubbed "Dead Horse Trail" because of the thousands of pack animals that perished along the way and "rotted in heaps," to borrow Jack London's description.

While there is relatively little physical privation from trying to mine the Internet stock-trading world, there are dangers and they seem to grow as time goes on. There are the risks to finances and psyches. Besides sometimes losing large amounts of money, Internet junkies talk of losing their bearings and nearly their minds as they are sucked deeper into the online world. As proved by a madman in Atlanta who murdered nine fellow Internet stock traders in July 1999, death and insanity can also be found in cyberspace.

For whatever differences exist between the manias of the Klondike and the Internet, there are some remarkable similarities— beyond the obvious presence of greed. The participants in each evolve their own codes of conduct and their own lingo. The language of the Klondike included "stampeders," "sourdoughs," and "cheechakos." On the Internet, "scams" and "dogs" and "POS" share space with "mo-mo mamas" and "ten-baggers." (See Glossary at the end of the book.) The Klondike had "Liar's Island," where men spent long winters telling each other tall tales. A century later, electronic islands float in a universe where there are no seasons but travelers still tell tall tales into the wee hours of the morning.

The miners of each generation take new names, as if their old, given ones somehow aren't up to the new quest. The Internet has TokyoMex, Big Dog, and the Georgia Bard. The Klondike had the Malamoot Kid, Cock-eyed Shorty, and Swiftwater Bill.

Swiftwater Bill struck it rich in the Klondike gold fields and became a legendary figure, in part for his alleged proclivities towards the prodigious. One story had it that in order to impress a certain "comely strumpet," Bill went around the mining mecca of Dawson buying up every one of the hardest-to-get commodity in town, fresh eggs.

Of course, Swiftwater Bill would be better known to the modern reader by his real name: William Gates. Though Swiftwater wasn't any relation to Microsoft's founder, some tell stories that today's Bill Gates also wants to buy up every egg in town.[5]

These two great rushes, a century apart, share at least one other thing: an ability to attract an incredible range of humanity. In the case of the Internet, professional stock traders and professional stock swindlers share cyberspace with legions of butchers and bakers and cappuccino makers—average men and women looking to make money, maybe transform their lives, and in the process, just possibly shake the foundations of the financial world.

Amidst this great onslaught is a guy named Joe.

CHAPTER ONE

As I walk through the Turtle Bay section of Manhattan's East Forties toward my first meeting with Joe Park, I already know enough about him to know that he isn't your average Joe. After all, how many other guys seem to be achieving fortune—certainly fame—while sitting in a lotus position, staring at a computer screen, naked?

My work as a *Wall Street Journal* reporter brings me to Park's apartment a few blocks from the United Nations in July 1998. As I walk, the morning isn't quite hot enough yet to make the buildings perspire, but I'm sweating.

The *Journal* and other big-time news outlets are beginning to gnaw hard at the phenomenon of Internet stock trading, like big, hungry dogs attacking a T-bone. But thanks to the magic of the media, each chomp just seems to make this bone grow bigger.

I've spent much of the previous decade at the *Journal* covering frauds and swindles, involving everything from stock scams to overpriced ostrich farms. This work has brought me into contact with a number of lively, less than trustworthy, characters. My bosses seem to think this is excellent preparation for writing about the world of online stock trading.

I stumbled across Joe Park thanks to two separate sources. One is Brad Dryer, co-founder with brother Jeff of Silicon Investor. Known as SI for short, Silicon Investor is an Internet stock-discussion operation, which works as a sort of electronic bulletin board where members can post messages. There are thousands of SI message boards. Most are dedicated to individual stocks. Others involve discussions about topics ranging from God to the cuisine of cannibalism.

Silicon Investor periodically puts out a list of its most "people-marked" members. A peoplemark means that one member has electronically tagged another member's moniker in order to track that person's e-mail messages. The more peoplemarks you have, the more people who are interested in what you have to say—because they think it's either valuable or influential or criminal or at least worth a good laugh. The system is a little like a Nielsen rating for the stock-discussion network.

Dryer told me about Silicon Investor's peoplemarks during a telephone interview in early 1998. He showed me where on the operation's website I could find the latest list of the 150 most peoplemarked names out of the tens of thousands of members. When I checked, the name at the top of the list was TokyoMex.

I also learned that TokyoMex in March 1998 started a Silicon Investor chat thread called "Tokyo Joe's Café." Within its first few months, it attracted thousands of messages from TokyoMex and hundreds of other writers. Silicon Investor officials tell me it's one of the fastest-growing threads of their operation's more than 2,500 active sites. The Café is so popular that it has even been the target of a hostile takeover.

I also heard TokyoMex's name from a source of mine on past stock fraud stories. This person—who, under a longstanding agreement between the two of us, shall remain nameless—called to tip me about a person whom he considers a major Internet stock crook and a "manipulating SOB" who "should be in jail." The person in question, my source added, goes by the online moniker TokyoMex.

When you're a newspaper reporter writing about fraud, you get lots of tips about alleged swindlers and almost as many assurances that the alleged lowlife is the biggest crook going. After all, who wants to bother hauling a small fry over to the Fourth Estate?

I've also found that when it comes to such information, even good sources often give bum tips. In some cases, the alleged malefactor turns out to be an honest enough guy who has simply angered the tipster. Others turn out to be willing enough to steal, just not very good at it. Like being a world-class athlete or a master musician, being a top-notch swindler takes both talent and practice.

Nonetheless, my first two encounters with the name of Tokyo-Mex left me intrigued enough to want to learn more. I started with basic information. Such as the name behind the moniker.

A computer database search turned up a January 26, 1997, article in the *Rocky Mountain News* that mentioned TokyoMex. That story identified TokyoMex as one Joe Matsudaira, who made a killing trading the stock of a little Denver-based Internet company. In the notes of my initial TokyoMex interview, done by telephone, I have him identified as Joe Matsudaira.

Later I ran across a July 8, 1997, piece in the electronic stock market news site, TheStreet.com, which said TokyoMex's real name was Paku Matsudai. The story added that he is also known as "Joe."

TokyoMex himself ended one e-mail message with the following menu of name options:

"Yun Soo Oh Park IV

aka Joe Paku

aka Joe Matsudaira

aka ex Asian Playboy

aka Jack kicker,,

aka a lover of humanity

aka poet literate en voyage"[1]

When I ask TokyoMex about his name, he says that he sometimes uses his late Japanese mother's maiden name, Matsudaira, or a variation, to honor her. Plus, he says, early on in his Internet career, "I didn't want to be well known at the time. I wanted to remain anonymous." He fairly quickly conquered his shyness.

His full name, he says, is Yun Soo Oh Park IV, the only son of an only son of an only son of an only son. Other names and assorted personas, he adds, come from a night at a London nightclub along with various adventures stretching from a Mexican jail to the beach at Unawatuna.

When the U.S. Securities and Exchange Commission in 1999 sends out subpoenas seeking information from online traders about whether TokyoMex has broken any or many securities laws, it refers to him as Yun Soo Oh Park. As the official guardian of the nation's stock markets for over six decades, the SEC is presumably investigating assertions by Park's critics that he is a serious securities scofflaw. I say "presumably" because the SEC doesn't comment on pending investigations. It usually won't even acknowledge that one is under way. Park says that while the SEC has his name right on the subpoena, the agency is dead wrong if it suspects him of any wrongdoing.

Online, Park has many variations of his TokyoMex moniker. Some he chooses, some are bestowed by others. He is also Tokyo Joe, Tmex, TM, TJ, Mex. One of his enemies sometimes calls him Tokyo Joke or Tokyo Hype. Perhaps the best variation, presumably given at least partly in jest, is Tyrannosaurus Mex.

As I walk toward his apartment in the gathering July heat, Park, by any name, is roaring on the Internet chat circuit. I and others in the media are doing our part to turn up the volume.

TheStreet.com's 1997 story called TokyoMex an online "legend" whose "personality tends to dominate" Internet stock-discussion boards. My November 1998 *Wall Street Journal* story would dub him an "Internet stock-trading star." A later piece in *Money* magazine, headlined "Smokin' Joe," anoints him as "arguably the most influential online market analyst and stock picker in the country." Though Park appears to have been little involved in the trading frenzy surrounding JB Oxford's stock in February 1999, his reputation was such that his name still popped up. *"If I had to guess why the run up is happening, I'd say it's on TMEX's list,"* wrote one Oxford message board poster.

He says he was born in Seoul in December 1959. Notes from various interviews I do with Park also show his birth date as 1956 and 1958. He says my notes must be incorrect.

Park's father was a poet and a professor of literature, his mother a housewife. While Park was growing up, the family split its time between Korea and Japan. By the time he was sixteen, he was itchy to see more of the world, especially Mexico. "I loved the colors of the paintings" there, says Park, who was an aspiring artist at the time.

But the teenager didn't have a visa to Mexico. He went anyway. His adventures getting there are grist for a story, perhaps the first great travel story of a man who would tell many. He retells his Mexico tale one day in an e-mail, which is full of his trademark commas, misspellings, and occasional profanities:

"I jumped the fence ,, a 9 ft high ,, San Diego to
Tijuana fence ,, got on a bus to south ,, went 30 KM
,, Mexican border patrol put me on a bus back to San
Diego ,, jumped the fence back to Mexico ,, you see I
really wanted to go to Guadalajara and paint ,, and
make love to senoritas,, This time ,, I hitch hiked,,
went for 2 hours,, and was caught and sent back to
Nogales , a Texas border town , well shit I crosse Rio
Grande again this time with a boy from New Jersey ,
who ran away from his home in his dad's Camaro ,, we
went as far as Hermosillio , another frigging border
control,, this time we were so far away ,, they locked
us up ,, in a room ,, 4 x4 ,, a broken toilet , with
mt. Blanc size dung on that broken toilet bowl ,, I
used my Van Heussen shirt ,, 4 x4 square to wipe my
dung ridden ass,, from one meal a day ,, rice and
beans and coffee ,, which was delivered by a village
epilaptic ,, who checked in to the Motel Hermosillo ,,
at midnight , and who spat on our food ,, the coffee
,, the beans and rice,, before he slid it under the

```
bar ,, 8 AM ,, every day ,,This went on for 6 days ,,
on 7th day ,, I could not take any more. . . . . so I
picked up the fucking ,, toilet bowl with all the Mt.
Blanc size ,,dungs and threw it against the jail house
bar ,, cops came running in ,, with half dozen Colt
45s ,, on my head,,I bribed them with all my earthly
possesions including a stupid Fisshing rod ,, ROFLMAO
, I was going to survive in Mexico."
```

He got out of jail, he spent nine months in Mexico, studying art and having fun. He returned home, went to law school, and became a lawyer for the next fourteen years, according to TheStreet.com's profile. *Money* magazine also reported that he obtained a law degree. Notes of one of my Park interviews show him describing himself as a "lawyer."

But as we talk more, Park tells me that he "hated" law school and "gave it up" before finishing. However, he adds, he used his knowledge of the law to work as a legal advisor to various companies.

In interviews with me and other reporters, he tells of working for various multinational companies in a multitude of locations around Europe and Asia. He is fair to fluent in six languages. He has tales from many places. There is even a fish story from Unawatuna, which he shares one day with his Internet traveling companions:

```
"I have moved over 120 times in my life time ,,, and
lived in some 2 dozen countries and islands,, from
Seoul to Unawatuna,,. . . . . . . . . One day when you have
a chance go to Unawatuna Beach in Sri Lanka ,, south
of Colombo and further south of Galle.. Unawatuna
means ,, valley of magic medicine,, a smal beach ,,
coming off a magic valley indeed,,, and was a resort
for Singalese kings for centuries..

I met a friend , Chandra Soma ,, who is the village
chief . . . it is a magical little place with a temple
at the edge of the rocks ,, and the best sunset in
whole of Indian Ocean ,, I played local doctor ,
```

treating infections ,, head aches ,, local suicides ,
until proper medical team arrived ,,

Chandra always let me have his master bedroom ,, right
on the beach ,, 12 ft from the water ,, and as I took
my morning swim ,, naked ,, his son ,, Talime ,, would
bring my chai in a glass ,, One day ,, as I was sitting at the hill above temple on the rocks watching
the glorious sunset ,, Talime was fishing ,, with bare
habds ,, lines wrapped around his hands,, at the edge
of the rocks ,, and suddenly ,, he was pulled in to
the water .. violently ,, And I saw his black head
full of curls ,, cutting the water , and screaming ,,
I ran back to the vilage ,, as hard as I could ,, and
told the villagers and his father Chandra ,, what was
happening ,, men rushed in the water on the canoe ,,
as they rowed ,, I saw Talime break the channel and
his head , now a dot in the cold steel black sea as
sun was dissappearing under the horizon ,, canoe also
dissappeared ..

Few of us elderly and women stood at the beach ,, for
some time ,, until we saw canoe showed up .. cutting
across the bay ,, we screamed and hollered as Talime
stood tall .. at the head of the canoe ,,, proud ,,
When they landed ,, he had a fish ,, 5 ft long .. 3 ft
high and 6 inches thick ,, and ugly as hell ,, Talime's hand was cut to the bones ,, by lines ,, a thicj
bloddless crevice ,,

I treated his wounds ,, bit he felt no pain ,, we
built the biggest frigging fire on the beach ,, dug a
hole ,, laud the palm leaves and cooked that ugly fish
,, for whole village ..

Moka De Ne Te ,,

It means ,, why not ? in Singhalese ..."

He tells reporters of two epiphanies that ended his corporate globetrotting in the early 1990s. One involved a chance meeting with a toilet salesman at the Rome airport. The other involved Park crying for several hours at a Buddhist temple in South Korea. Of course, both incidents involve longer stories.

Park met and married Misun Park. They had a daughter, Mimi Chloe. In 1992, the Park clan moved to Seattle, where in a relatively short time he managed to lose lots of money in the local real estate market and acquire a lasting dislike for this pearl of the Northwest. At one point, funds were so tight that Park says he applied for a job as a gas station attendant—and was turned down. "The gas station owner looked at me like I was a nut case," Park recalls. Perhaps driving to the job interview in a Mercedes and wearing a Rolex didn't help his image, he acknowledges. But, he adds, he needed a job and "I could be a happy pumper."

Luckless in Seattle, Park brought the family to Manhattan in 1993. He says he had about $50,000 in cash after selling his Mercedes. He figured he needed to find a business that would generate cash, and quickly.

He decided on the restaurant business, more particularly, the Mexican restaurant business with a subspecialty in burritos. Park opened an eight-hundred-square-foot eatery on the Upper East Side of Manhattan with $72 in the cash register and only a vague idea of how to use the register. He says he also neglected to hire any waitresses for the first day.

Fortunately, he did have customers and later opened other burrito outlets. Many of his patrons were Upper East Side investment bankers and securities traders who needed a little fuel—or at least gas. With his regulars, Park began talking about stocks while CNBC business news played on the TV over the bar. His eatery empire went by various names, including Tokyo Joe's Classic Burrito.

(Others also like the nickname Tokyo Joe, I discovered. A computer database search found that the moniker is mentioned in over 230 articles dating back to 1980. There is Tokyo Joe, a young Japanese singer who strummed a banjo at least once as a warm-up act for Don

"Tiny Bubbles" Ho, the Honolulu crooner. There is Kenneth "Tokyo Joe" Eto, whom a 1985 *Washington Post* story says testified about an alleged mobster before the President's Commission on Organized Crime while wearing a hood and a black robe—presumably to hide his identity rather than as a fashion statement. Other Tokyo Joes include a nightclub in London, a restaurant in Denver as well as another in, of all places, Tokyo. There is the 1949 movie *Tokyo Joe,* starring Humphrey Bogart. A boy from Narragansett, Rhode Island, shined in the Tokyo Joe Karate Classic in New Hampshire, according to a 1996 story in the *Providence Journal-Bulletin.)*

With his restaurant business established and some of his Seattle real estate finally sold, Park began exploring the Internet stock-trading world in 1996. He had been an investor in the past. In Seattle, he says, he had a brokerage account with Merrill Lynch & Co., the nation's largest brokerage firm. While Merrill no doubt has many satisfied customers, Joe Park isn't among that number. He says he lost lots of money following Merrill stock picks.

Like many new cyberspace voyagers, Park migrated early on to the Motley Fool. Founded by two very unfoolish brothers, David and Tom Gardner, the Motley Fool had by 1996 already turned into one of the best known and most influential stock-discussion sites in cyberspace.

Raised in the Washington, D.C., area, the Gardner brothers were schooled in the mechanics and rewards of stock market investing by their father, an attorney. After college, where both brothers majored in English, they started a monthly sixteen-page investment letter with an annual subscription of $48. The newsletter, of course, needed a name. While flipping through a book of quotations, David Gardner came across one from Shakespeare that caught his eye. It's from the comedy *As You Like It:* "A fool, a fool! I met a fool i' the forest, a motley fool." Later, in their book, the *Motley Fool Investment Guide,* the brothers explained that they chose the Motley Fool name because, "We'd always loved Shakespeare's Fools . . . they amused as they instructed, and were the only members of society who could tell the truth to the king or queen without having their heads lopped off."

Initially, the Gardners didn't have to worry much about losing any body parts by telling their version of stock market wisdom. This philosophy involves holding stocks of quality companies, investing in a few smaller, more speculative firms, and generally putting down the professional "wise men" of Wall Street while trying to keep a sense of humor about the whole exercise. Circulation of the *Motley Fool* newsletter never reached 500.

Of course, in those early days, the *Motley Fool* was carrying what might be called the Gutenberg Burden. In the age of speeding electrons, the newsletter was still coming out on paper.

The Gardeners' switch to cyberspace, however, seemed to be as much about luck as brilliant marketing insights. Tom Gardner was attending graduate school at the University of Montana and contributing articles to the newsletter. He sent his articles to brother David in Washington through the e-mail service of America Online. In 1994, AOL was on the verge of losing a customer; Tom Gardener had decided to use the e-mail system provided by the university. But he thought he would send out one final AOL message. It turned out to be a fateful one.

In the message, Tom Gardner told people about the *Motley Fool* newsletter and offered a free copy to anyone who asked. Just contact his brother, the message said. The next day a puzzled David Gardner, who hadn't yet been told about the e-mail, received three phone calls from strangers asking for a copy of the newsletter.

Three calls might not constitute much encouragement, but they were enough to convince the Gardners to take advantage of an AOL membership perk and start their own electronic stock-discussion board. Naturally, they called it the "Motley Fool." Soon AOL members were flocking to the site to discuss stocks. AOL made the Motley Fool an official feature, and buys 20 percent of the operation from the Gardners.

In 1995 and 1996, one of the biggest topics on the Motley Fool for Park and other traders was a company called Iomega. Iomega is a little computer-equipment company in Roy, Utah, that makes a product known as a Zip drive. The Zip drive allows a computer user to store an extremely large amount of information outside the computer on special diskettes. In 1995, Iomega was one of the hottest stocks on the Nasdaq stock market, rising from a few dollars a share to about $50 a share. Thousands of messages about Iomega were posted on the Motley Fool website at AOL.

In April 1996, the Motley Fool and Iomega hit the financial media big time with a cover story in *Fortune* magazine. The story's headline was "Investing in a Fool's Paradise." *Fortune* reporter Joseph Nocera wrote that the Motley Fool's Iomega message board had become probably "the single hottest forum in the commercial online universe. Every day thousands of small investors, some of them with a sizable chunk of their net worth in this one stock, log on to AOL just to find out what is happening on the Iomega board. 'Iomegans,' they call themselves, sounding as much like a cult as a group of hard-nosed investors."

Even in this huge flood of electronic verbiage, some of Park's messages stood out as unusual. One such message began and ended with references to Iomega (IO, for short), but detoured with a boat trip down the Nile. An excerpt:

> "It is a shitzel tag im New York and I had to post pone my golf till tw. Spent whole day going over the Emerald Research report line by line. I have never seen a report with more frank, honest and upbeat on a company. Like few post back about the 51/4 floppies, it truely is all comig together.
>
> Here is your bed time story I promised you on Egypt. . . . . . I found a real simple and most romantic and economic way to do Egypt while seeing all the things tourists miss. (Do it in Dec. Nile is mild and gentle due to dry season in Nubian Africa) To begin it is best to fly in to Cairo straight away catch domestic flt to Aswan the great dam and when you land hire a dhow (about 28 ft long arabic single sail boat used from the slave trade days and can competently sail coastal waters all the way to China) since it is best to see the sinking monuments and temples from the

water. You can sleep, eat and read on the dhow as it gently takes you from sight to sight and you can land at any shoreline. My boatsmen Ali in his forties and Yagoub had their cooking pots, tea boilers and array of provision including dates and nuts.

Spend two days exploring the area then catch the down stream flow and head north to Luxor, Thebes, Valley of the Kings and all along the way you will villages, farmers and less known cities of the past. Yagoub will wash your shirt everyday in the Nile and hang it up on the mast it would be fresh next day as largest golden sun rises in the mist of moisture from surrounding grennary near the Nile, children will be standing by the shore line and wave their hand Salam, Salam and as you bend the village from the minarets the chanting of the morning wake up Sallah, Ah ah ah ------- ah ah a haha ahah ah aaaaaaaa Alllah Akbar ----- aah h ah aa. It is the most heart wrenching sound to hear that will take you back instantly to the middle of the desert of the olden days when the Saracens, traversed these deserts all the way to Cote Ivor to bring back slaves to Makka. . . .

Walk around with belly sucked in, not in a Nike and not with a stupid Kodak dangling on your wrist. Dress up like the Casablaca and wear a Panama.

Have fun Fools

The key word is if IO pops Monday we dance if it drops we go to Banno.

Joe"[2]

Motley Fool co-founder David Gardner recalls Joe Park, though not so much for his travel epics. "I don't have many fond memories of that particular person." For one thing, Park's point of view seemed to be "antithetical to almost everything we stand for" at the Motley Fool, Gardner says. While the Motley Fool's philosophy leans toward long-term investing, Park seemed interested in jumping in and out of the stock daily, Gardner says.

Park also remembers the Gardners and the Motley Fool and Iomega. Initially, Park says, he lost some $200,000 buying Iomega stock. "I got in at 36 before it crashed down to 16. I was following the hype" surrounding the stock, he says. The Gardner brothers were big fans of Iomega. "The Motley Fool hyped it all the way. I was very disappointed with the Motley Fool," Park adds.

Other Iomega fans lost as well. One Motley Fool poster would eventually write that while Iomega "did have an awesome growth story . . . the Iomega saga would prove to be one of enthusiasm run amuck, of too many herd-like investors throwing money at a stock mainly because it kept rising."

Park says he eventually got his money back—and more—on Iomega. "I got it back by learning how to trade. Not by sitting and hoping it would come back," he says. He traded e-mails with other traders "day and night, learning how to short the S.O.B."

The brawling around Iomega whetted Park's appetite for more Internet action. He began prowling various parts of the chat circuit, posting messages and building a reputation.

He built it mostly at Silicon Investor, the stock-discussion operation started by the Dryer brothers. Park joined Silicon Investor in May 1997. He took the online name of TokyoMex and began pounding his keyboard. Much of his early typing and enthusiasm was reserved for a little Y2K stock called Tava Technologies, Inc.

Y2K, of course, is shorthand for Year 2000. It seems that millions of computers were built with a two-digit internal calendar. The worry was that when '99 kicked over to double zero, the computers wouldn't recognize that they had gone over to the year 2000 and instead would think they had gone back to 1900—when McKinley was still president and the only things wired were elections. Y2K pessimists feared that computers would go haywire and there would be a lot more chaos around the world than on an average day.

It isn't completely clear why the early computer wizards didn't better anticipate the Y2K problem. Maybe they just didn't think their work would last until the next century. Maybe they didn't think there would be a next century. After all, nuclear warheads blossomed well before Apples did.

Whatever the true seriousness of the Y2K problem, also known as the "millennium bug," the task of coming up with fixes became a bustling business in the years before 2000. This was particularly so in the securities market, where many Y2K stocks become hot items among investors. Dozens of companies were coming up with ways to reprogram old computers so the machines would glide into the twenty-first century with hardly a glitch.

Based in Denver, the company was known as Topro, Inc. until early 1998 when it changed its name to Tava. Topro/Tava specializes in supplying automation and systems integration services to industry. It is an important but not particularly glamorous line of business. As of mid-1997, the company's stock price was also decidedly unglamorous, around $2 a share.

Then in late June 1997, the company put out a press release announcing "a major new business initiative based on its new product PlantY2K One." Soon the stock market's version of Y2K flu was sending the trading temperature of Topro/Tava into the red zone.

By July 1997, the company's stock was beginning to appear regularly on the lists of the most actively traded Nasdaq stocks. Trading volume, which fell as low as 600 shares during one day in May, topped 4.8 million shares during one day in July. Topro/Tava's stock price also started rising, up 40 percent in one day.

All this action naturally attracted more stock traders. Joe Park began regularly posting messages on the Topro/Tava discussion board at Silicon Investor. He arrived as an unabashed bull. The company's stock symbol at the time was TPRO.[3]

> "As for the TPROs future price target its literally
> safe to say a ten bagger in my bullish opinion. Any
> announcement of a significant contract will push this
> over ten in 30 mins,"

he wrote in an August 3 e-mail, when the stock was trading at between $5 and $6 a share.

Besides cheerleading, Park also did homework on the company. He wrote of going—with his seven-year-old daughter Mi Mi—to a presentation that the company had in New York, attended apparently mostly by Wall Street types.

> "Meeting lasted from 6 PM to 8:30. Oderves and a full bar with a very charming barkeep was wonderful. This sob from Prudential kicked my daughters angle with his Florsheim . I gave him shit and made him apologise to my daughter. . . . . I liked the meeting very much. I told them that my daughter and I are representing MF tpro club and that we control 5 % of the float."

In between the errant Prudential shoes and the sounds of laughter, Park provided his readers with a long list of the things he heard about TPRO that he liked. There were promising dealings with giant Intel Corp and the possibility of the firm more than doubling its revenues by 2000. The bottom line, wrote Park:

> "I am buying more tomorrow."

As a mark of dedication to the company, he signed off as "Joe Topro." In a later e-mail, he informed readers that his attire for that New York meeting included shorts, and that just before the meeting he played a round of golf. Perhaps he should have signed off as Joe Tee-Pro.

In yet another e-mail, Park told of inviting the company's chief executive officer and chief financial officer to accompany him to Scores, a well-known Manhattan topless bar. The officials evidently had a previous engagement.

> "Oh well next time,"

Park lamented.

Such little touches as golf shorts and dancing breasts are sprinkled throughout Park's messages. On a day when TPRO'S stock price was down, it wasn't really a down day. It was really more like

> "a pit stop. Sort of like a LeMans race after leaving
> France before you cross over to Belgique heading over
> to mountains of Spa, you stop, refuel change the
> tires, change oil and wipe your goggles,"

wrote Joe Topro. He added a piece of advice to his twenty-four seconds at Le Mans, though his choice of beverage might have offended the French.

> "Relax have a Margarita on me and go spend some qual-
> ity time with your kids."

Sometimes Park's enthusiasm seems to get the better of him. At one point, another TPRO follower posted an e-mail chiding Park for saying that the company had raised several million dollars more from stock sales than it really had.

> "Be careful in your enthusiasm to not overstate the
> case,"

this person wrote.

Park promptly replied,

> "You are absolutely right. Hype is the last thing I
> want on TPRO. . . . . I call 8 next week. I love
> this story unfolding before very our eyes."

Not everybody was enamored with his frequent cheerleading of the company.

> "Lets see, yesterday you were saying 'buy buy buy,
> HUGE news coming, I loaded up, blah,blah,blah, big day
> tomorrow.' Didnt quite call that one,did you?"

taunted one poster.

> "You fool you will be kissing my feet in a week or so,"

replied Park.

As the weeks rolled along, Park kept up a running elec-

tronic dialogue with friend and foe alike. He wrote to a female
ally that

> "you gonna marry me !!! I am your match made in Nir-
> vana !!!! Joe Topro"

Foes received this online missile:

> "Phillistines, the dogs of the desert, the shitty 500
> buck a day scalpers. Those who dumped today were the
> a- h-s who were looking for 9 pop. I spit on their
> faces LOL and step on their scrotums. Look at the
> bloody volume !!!! open your schlitz augen (means
> slanted eye in German) Just had feed back from sev-
> eral MMs ----They friggin loved it !!! Enogh said. Of
> mice and men I say !!!!!!!!!!! Which one of you is a
> desert dung ???? Joe Topro."

Early on with Topro/Tava, he boldly predicted that the stock
would hit $25 a share by the end of 1997. It didn't come close to
that level. But it did top $14 by March 1998—some seven times its
price the prior June. That was high enough to boost Park's reputation as a stock picker in many people's minds.

But always, along with the pushing and shoving and biting
and predicting, there were stories from Park. Some were seemingly
aimed at calming the turmoil, both around Park and inside him.
Like this one:

> "Let me go in peace and enjoy my tranquility in sem-
> blance of TPRO bliss.
>
> Like the full moon night a long ago on the shores of
> Corfu, with silvery Grecian hills and white wind mill
> houses with lantern light shining through the smalll
> windows and a sillouhette of a melancholic femininity
> looking out to the sea, as it lapped gently through my
> toes.

Or was it on the road to the Mandalay as I recited
Kipling while I fanned my self with a banyan leaf, as
my Mu Mu sang gently his Burmese hymm of wanton loves
as we climed over the hill and looked down to the
Nesam river, wondering how much more to the village to
spend the night.

Or was it in Yap as I remembered Margarest Meads the-
sis on Yeppis, as how they believed that making love
will drive evil spirits from your body. As nights fell
and you readied for the bed, one or two very young
girls will come and silently lay beside you on your
bamboo mat. . . . . ."

The road went on. Through Goa and Dusseldorf and London
and Princess Diana's funeral and Won Hyo and Buddahood and
other stops, too numerous to recount, that all led to an apartment
not far from the United Nations building.

I FINALLY COME TO A STOP in front of Park's building on that July morning in 1998. I leave the summer heat and enter the lobby in Park's apartment building. The lobby is somewhat smaller than Carlsbad Cavern. I walk up to the security desk near the door. I ask for Mr. Matsudaira, partly to see what response I will get, partly because I'm still not sure of the real name of the man I am supposed to meet.

The guy behind the desk looks like one of those New York doormen who only smiles when a five-spot or better is headed his way. I am bringing him no joy today. He doesn't recognize the name Matsudaira. As he scans the tenant list, I mention the apartment number. "Ah, Mr. Park," he responds. He calls upstairs and then points me toward the elevators. If he wonders why I give the wrong last name for one of his tenants, he does an admirable job of hiding it.

I get on an elevator that doesn't seem to be in any hurry to get where I'm going. I exit at the designated floor and knock on the designated door, which is partially open. "Come in," yells a voice from inside. I enter a hall that leads to the left. "Come in, come in," the voice repeats. Only this time there is a body attached, walking toward me.

The figure coming at me is slim, about five feet nine inches tall. His black hair is cut short enough to stand at attention but looks to be marching in many directions. Small platoons of gray are gathering on each side.

Though Park says he often trades "buck naked," he's wearing white shorts and a white tennis shirt with a Burberry emblem on it. He is shoeless and unshaven. Park later confides, with a touch of embarrassment, that he hasn't had a chance to brush his teeth yet that morning. I tell him the same thing happens to me when I work at home all day.

As I get to know Park, I decide that he is paying me something of a compliment by meeting me even halfway to the apartment door. When the U.S. stock markets are open for trading (9:30 A.M. to 4 P.M., New York time) he almost never leaves his computer screens. He generally eats only one meal a day, after the markets close. The rest of the time his sustenance comes from sipping orange juice, smoking Marlboros, and sucking profits out of stock trades. He displays one downside of this regimen: a callus on his ankle from sitting meditation-style all day in front of the computers.

After our greetings, he invites me to pull up a chair next to him in his office, which doubles as his living room. He sits at a nicely finished wooden desk facing two computer screens that are busy with numbers, graphs, and news headlines. A third computer, a portable, lies dormant on the desk. Also within reach are bottles of aspirin, vitamin C, and children's vitamins—the only evidence I see that day of his young daughter. Nor do I meet his wife. I do, however, get to meet the family's small white Maltese dog. It stays close to Park, but doesn't seem to be doing any trading.

Across the room, a television set is tuned all day to CNBC business news. Park keeps the TV's remote control nearby and regularly changes the volume as whim or events dictate.

As I sit down, Park's eyes are already back on the computer screens. Park gives me a quick rundown of what I'm seeing. Some of the most important information, he says, comes from the screen displaying so-called Level II software. This is a package of information that for years had been largely used only by Wall Street professionals. Now, for a few hundred dollars or less a month, average citizens can get it.

Level II shows at what prices and in what quantities different brokerage firms are offering to buy or sell a given stock. An investor with Level II software can punch up such information on thousands of different stocks. Fans, such as Park, argue that this information is essential to helping determine price trends in a stock. Trading without this service, Park says, is like being "a blind man without a walking stick."

I know that Level II and other advanced market software are all the rage among many Internet stock traders. There are serious questions, however, about how many traders actually understand what is flashing before their eyes—and how many just think they do. One cynical Internet trader later would tell me that "giving some of these idiots Level II is like giving a three-year-old a stick of dynamite and a book of matches."

Level II quotes cover the stocks traded on the Nasdaq stock market. Brokerage firms that act as "market makers" in a given stock supply the quotes. As market makers, the brokerage firms offer to buy and sell shares of a given stock at prices that they post on the computer network. This is the information Park is looking at on his computer screen. There are often many market makers for a given stock. As market conditions change, market makers can change their "bid" and "ask" prices.

This same system applies to the so-called Bulletin Board, which is generally home to companies that aren't substantial enough to qualify for the Nasdaq. Some of the hottest, most volatile plays in the stock market can be found on the Bulletin Board, along with some of the most audacious frauds. The Bulletin Board has been a favorite hunting ground for aggressive Internet traders such as Park. Both the Nasdaq and the Bulletin Board are operated by the National Association of Securities Dealers, a private organization that's made up of the nation's brokerage firms and brokers and helps regulate their activities.

By contrast, the New York Stock Exchange uses what's known as a "specialist" system to trade stocks. Each Big Board stock is assigned to a specialist, who works on the floor of the exchange. Trading in a given stock, say IBM, passes through the specialist, who matches buy and sell orders and changes the stock's price as market conditions change. Both the market maker system and the specialist system have their fans that argue the pros and cons of the two approaches. Cynics argue that both systems give pros the chance to con the average investor.

"Oh, bloody hell," Park mutters as he watches the price of one of his stocks fall. Without taking his eyes off the screens, he explains that he's trading about half a dozen stocks at the moment. Juggle many more than that at one time and "my head goes crazy," he says. He lights a Marlboro and takes a puff.

His trading basket this day includes EGGS, the stock symbol for Egghead.com, Inc., an online marketer of computer products. "Egghead was at 9 last week. It's now at 29," says Park. He has been buying and selling EGGS along the way and currently owns 10,000 shares. "Go, baby, go!" he yells as the computer screen shows the price of EGGS rising.

He often talks to his computers, his only constant companion during the day. When Park wants to place a stock order, he clicks his computer mouse and calls up his brokerage account with E*Trade, one of the fast-growing new online brokerage firms. From his keyboard, Park punches in the symbol of the stock he wants to buy, how many shares, and the price he is willing to pay. Then he waits.

Sometimes he waits a few seconds. Sometimes he waits many minutes, not quietly. "Bastards," he mutters when an order for 10,000 shares of EGGS nabs him "250 lousy shares."

Part of the problem is that Park has specified a maximum price he will pay for the stock. This is known as a "limit order;" i.e., you limit the price you will pay. Park could have placed a "market order" for EGGS, which means he agrees to pay whatever the current market price is for the stock.

But as Park explains, only "schmucks"—a favorite term of his—use market orders, particularly on fast-moving Internet stocks whose prices can change drastically within a few minutes. The *Wall Street Journal* later would write about hapless investors who placed market orders for a hot new Internet stock only to find that their orders had been filled at prices several times higher than they had expected.[1]

Successful Internet stock trading, say Park and others, is partly tied to finding a fast and nimble brokerage firm. This is particularly true for anyone looking to quickly buy and sell stocks in hopes of profiting from small price movements, a practice that some call "day trading" or "scalping."

In the case of Park's EGGS order, the stock's price has moved more quickly than his order, so he is able to get only a tiny amount. "E*Trade is so popular," he complains, that sometimes it is "very slow" executing orders.

This day, Park is also trading BAMM, the symbol for Books-A-Million, Inc., a bookseller based in Birmingham, Alabama, that is selling over the Internet, like such better-known players as Amazon.com. Park, a great believer in the future of the Internet, is attracted by the company's online foray. The tip has come a few minutes earlier from another trader whom Park has met via the Internet.

He has gotten to know the electronic version of lots of people. Like him, many of them have chucked their old jobs in favor of spending their days trading on the Internet. "When you can make two hundred grand a week, why bother with other things?" asks Park.

The promise of fabulous wealth from Internet trading is one of the things that has drawn people—including reporters—to Park's door. He tells me that he started 1998 with $22,000 and currently has $540,000 in his trading account.

Not being in a position to challenge his numbers, I nod and make suitably impressed remarks in response. After all, this is America and lots of Internet traders are exercising their First Amendment rights to claim fabulous stock-trading profits. Why not a Korean-Japanese burrito maker with many names? After all, just because something sounds too good to be true doesn't necessarily mean that it is. Besides, it's not so easy to find stock traders who are losing two hundred grand a week—or at least will admit to it.

As Park sits at his computer, he receives and sends a steady stream of e-mails. He estimates that he gets about a hundred such messages a day.

Some contain stock tips. Most seem to be from other traders seeking advice. Park is rarely shy about giving it. When one e-mail asks whether to buy a certain stock, Park unhesitatingly replies:

```
"No!!!!!!!"
```

When the questioner sends another e-mail asking why, Park fires back:

```
"Scam!!!!!!"
```

He sends out a sell recommendation on another stock based partly on a recent CNBC interview of the firm's chief executive.

```
"He looked dazed,"
```

Park writes.

When another follower tries to grill him on his reasons for recommending a particular stock, he simply replies:

```
"I am Mex."
```

"My arrogance drives people crazy," he says later that day, with a laugh.

As Park and I sit together, he is in the midst of an electronic fight over a company called 800 Travel Systems, Inc. It's a Tampa, Florida-based travel agency that sells tickets mostly over the telephone, though it is starting to sell over the Internet. The company stock symbol is IFLY. A few months earlier, it soared, partly on the wings of TokyoMex.

Late one Sunday night, Park posted a message telling readers that

```
"tomorrow's buy is a baby ,,soon web travel co,, by
year 2000 web travel will be 7 billion dollar busi-
ness,,. . . .."
```

He didn't name the company.

Next morning, about half an hour after the market opened, Park revealed that the company was IFLY. In a follow-up message, he wrote that he had called the company and

> "I spoke with CEO,, board meeting on Wed,,, will go
> full web. . . imagine what it will do to the stock."

(The company's chief executive officer Mark Mastrini later acknowledged in an interview that he had discussed the firm's Internet plans with Park, but denied that he ever said anything about the company putting all its operations on the Internet. Park insists that the conversation took place as he described.)

On the Friday before Park's recommendation, IFLY had closed at a little over $2.50 a share. On that next Monday it soared to over $4 on a more than tenfold increase in trading volume. Within a few days, it reached as high as $10 a share.

By the time I am sitting with Park, IFLY has fallen to around $6.50. And Park isn't happy.

The day before I arrive, Park sent out e-mails critical of the company. As best as I can tell, Park's unhappiness stems from a convoluted tale involving the manager of his Internet stock-trading website, who is also doing some consulting work on IFLY's website and has—at least in Park's mind—given him some bum information about the travel company. Park says the man is also making what he considers unreasonable demands on him. As a result,

> "I just declared this company

[IFLY]

> a 2 dollar stock . . . and I am firing my web
> manager . . . ,"

Park wrote in an e-mail sent out at 9:06 A.M. Sunday.

Earlier in the year, Park parted ways with a previous web associate. Judging by a TokyoMex e-mail, it seemed a less-than-cordial separation:

> "You lazy bum. . . . . . you ungrateful dog. . . . . . Infidel."

Park's dumping on IFLY touched off an e-mail furor among the company's fans. Some criticized him for changing course, others simply told him to get lost. A few voiced suspicions that Park was badmouthing the company as a way to push down the price so he could buy more shares—hardly an unknown tactic in the stock market but one that Park heatedly denies engaging in. One critic even was moved to write a little limerick:[2]

```
"There once was this dude from New York,,,

who traded stocks like a dork,,,

he screams 'SELL!!!' with a grin,,

and his sheep follow him,,,

While he buys all he can,,,

God what a whore!!!"
```

If not exactly Keats, it does get across a certain suspicion that has circulated about Park and other Internet stock-trading celebrities. The suspicions involve a practice known as "pumping and dumping," or "P&D" for short. The idea is that someone with clout quietly buys a stock and then uses his influence to get others excited. As these people buy, thus pushing up the price, the party of the first part quietly sells. Financially, if not ethically, it is much better to be the pumper than the dumpee.

I ask Park about all this. He says he doesn't try to pump and dump, or otherwise manipulate trading. But sometimes events overtake him. He'll recommend a stock and others have "jumped in like greedy pigs," pushing the price up. Since he is nimbler at getting in and out of a stock than most, "I reaped most of the benefits. That wasn't fair." Rather than "ruin my reputation," Park says he is now focusing on stocks that will be held for a longer period than just a few hours or a couple of days.

However, he is in this to make money. As he later tells *Money* magazine, "Everybody knows that I'm buying before you buy, and I'm selling when you're buying. Otherwise, what am I? A charity?"

One of the attractive things about Park is a certain wacky candor concerning matters the average person might try to hide. Such as taking goodies from companies whose stock you praise.

Under federal securities law, it is generally legal to accept payments as long as you fully disclose receiving them when recommending a stock. However, many promoters tend to be reluctant to do this on the pretty logical theory that their praise might be discounted if investors know they are being paid by the company. In the late 1990s, dozens of individuals were charged by federal authorities with violating the law regarding this so-called undisclosed compensation.

Park, on the other hand, complained in one case about not receiving goodies. In an e-mail about IFLY he wrote:

```
"Free tickets,, oh yes Mastrini offered it to me,, way
back in April, when SA popped it from 1 1/2 to 10,,,,,
Mastrini says to me ,, What cane we do for you ?,,, We
love you ,, I said ,, nothing ,, but if you insist ,,
how about some airplane tickets,, Last week ,, I'd say
put up then ,, I am going to Europe,,, do it for free or
do it for bare minimum,, this was last week .. Mastrini
says ,, O.K. I will take care of it and get back to you
,, Shitty ceos offer me deals all the time......"
```

But the tickets never come, Park adds.

Park tells me he sees nothing wrong with accepting gifts as long as he discloses them. Such overtures, he quickly adds, would never affect his stock picks. "If I am influenced, I am an Internet whore," he says.

(IFLY's president Mastrini denies ever making a free-ticket offer. He says the two did discuss Park possibly buying tickets through the company, but nothing came of it. Park reiterates that the free-ticket offer was made, just never honored.)

Most of the rest of the day with Park passes quietly, punctuated by occasional curses and whoops of triumph. "Bastards, bastards," he mutters as a stock he just sold continues to rise in price. "I chickened out. Bloody hell!"

When the markets close, Park is ready to relax. He pours himself a cognac and fills my request for a beer.

As we sip, I spend some time looking around the long and narrow living room. A piano stands against one wall. Nearby is a large globe. Next to Park's desk is a small collection of books, a mixture of tomes on stock trading and classics by Kipling, Tolstoy, and Shakespeare. Photographs and paintings adorn the walls.

Park points out several paintings that he did in his younger days as a would-be Gauguin. There is a painting of a nude woman. There is a self-portrait in ink and a multicolored painting of a man being chased by a woman on a horse. "My wife chasing me," he says with a laugh.

One photograph shows Park on a horse that is jumping over a fence at a riding competition. He is wearing the red-and-white riding outfit of an English foxhunt. Park says he has been riding for years and still takes an occasional canter in Central Park. I also notice on his desk a book touting a golf resort, a sign of Park's current sporting passion.

The rest of what turns into a long evening with Park is largely spent eating, drinking, and ogling. It's my first taste of how Park loves to party almost as much he loves to play the stock market. Indeed, one of Park's more memorable e-mails, sent out about a month after our meeting, involves both subjects:

> "Just got home from a fashion show, the Elitte US ,,
> model,, Seinfeld ,,Naomi,, Vogue et ak were te
> judges,, 11 13 14 16 year old girls from Missouri..
> California,, Florida,, Yexas,, friggin awesome beauti-
> full and sknny,,, 5 ft 9 in ,,avg,, awesoem.. got
> drunk.. with a beautiful balck girl . . . met coupole
> of rCEOs,, . . . I am too drunk and abd tight., this
> black girl was like a chocolate cnady , and she liked
> me,, thank god ,, for my soul ,,I came home alone..
> mot like Clinton.. We rock .. got 2 pump and dump
> lined up ,, byt I think thewse 2 really could go ,,"[3]

That night we go first to Park's old Mexican restaurant on East Fifty-third Street. It's now owned and operated by the woman who had been Park's cook at the restaurant. Park says he gave up the restaurant business when he found he could make more money and have more fun as a full-time Internet trader. Several steps down from street level, the restaurant is small and narrow with a bar on one side and about a dozen tables on the other. The new proprietor isn't wasting any money on air-conditioning. At least the beer is cold.

We move on to dinner and more drinks at a trendy-looking restaurant of Park's choice. By the end of the meal, I'm feeling tired and a little woozy. TokyoMex is just getting revved up.

Since I—or more precisely, my newspaper—pay for dinner, Park insists that I be his guest at the next stop. I've been looking at the next stop as my hotel and bed. But Park isn't easily put off.

We grab a taxi and Park gives the driver directions. Figuring I'm at least as important as the chief executive of Tava, Park directs the cabby to Scores, which no less an authority than *Playboy* magazine has described as "the country's premiere strip club."[4]

As our cab pulls away, Park discovers that his wallet is missing. I extend sympathy and offer to call it an evening. Park won't hear of that. "I have cash," he says, pulling out a wad of cash from his pocket. But what about your wallet, I ask. "I'll deal with it later," he replies as he strides toward the club.

We enter, and from the greetings he receives, Park has been there before. Through the evening he hands out $20 bills like a man who doesn't want to be forgotten. It is quickly clear why the place gets high ratings from Park and *Playboy:* the women are beautiful and largely naked. And, oh yes, they dance. Lap dancing seems to be the specialty of the house. Park and I don't get a lot of interviewing done the rest of the evening.

In his profile of TokyoMex, TheStreet.com's reporter recounted asking Park to take him to a place in town where people know him. They ended up at Scores.

The reporter quoted one of the dancers as saying how Park is "very honest and forthright. That's so rare here." Park also has expensive tastes, as TheStreet.com reporter discovers after offering to pay for that night's festivities. When the poor scribbler howls over the $300 bar bill, which includes Park's order of strawberries and a bottle of champagne, TokyoMex responds, "Relax, loose up. Don't be so cheap. You can't work all time, invest all time. You have to have a life, you have to have good times. You have to have stories to tell."

As Park and I say our drunken good-byes—at least mine are drunken—it seems clear that TokyoMex has plans for plenty more stories from the new frontier of stock trading. But I also can't help wondering what kind of ending these tales would have. Would he find a permanent stock-trading success or a defendant's chair in some federal courthouse?

Certainly Park is piling up enemies, with more waiting in the wings. Already, Ga Bard has attacked him. Big Dog has invaded his turf. And still coming is Park's most dedicated and dangerous foe, Anthony@Pacific. Anthony doesn't merely want TokyoMex banished from cyberspace. He wants him put behind bars. Some people believe he just might have the muscle to get his wish—though he might go to prison, himself, first.

One of the things that makes Park a magnet for enemies is his great number of fans. In cyberspace, like other dimensions, your ability to generate foes tends to be directly proportional to your ability to generate followers. And Park has a whole Societe of them.

IN JANUARY 1998, Park formed Societe Anonyme. For a time, it was "Anonym," sans "e." But Park later explains that was just an early spelling error.

Societe Anonyme, SA for short, was formed at a time when the stock market was coming off another strong year. The Dow Jones Industrial Average ended 1997 over 7900, some 20 percent higher than where it began the year. While not quite in the league of the all-time one-year record rise of 81 percent in 1915—when the DJIA was still a tadpole at 99—the 1997 gain was well above the average annual increase for the Dow over its history.

Of course, investors didn't get through 1997 without a few burps along the way. At one point, the market topped 8,000. Then, on October 27, the Dow plummeted 554 points, the biggest one-day point drop in history. (On a percentage basis, however, it was still well behind several whoppingly bad days of the past when the DJIA provided a smaller denominator.) The next day, October 28, saw, what at the time was, the biggest point *gain* ever, as the Dow bounced back by over 337 points. For people who like big roller-coaster rides, the stock market in 1997 was amusement park heaven.

Possibly spent by the gyrations of 1997, some forecasters were taking a cautious view of 1998. For example, a December 28, 1997, outlook piece in the *Washington Post* carried the headline "Several Obstacles Could Slow Stocks' Torrid Pace Next Year, Analysts Say." The *Post* article listed several potential problems looming over the markets, ranging from the Asian economic crisis to questions about the continued growth in the profits of U.S. corporations.

Plus, the stock market had been going so strong for so long that at some point it had to take a breather, the *Post* suggested. The story noted that "investors with a diversified portfolio have doubled their money since the beginning of 1995. Never before in the 200-year history of U.S. stock investing has there been such a run, according to market historians."

Joe Park, for one, planned to keep the run going. At least for him.

Societe Anonyme was integral to Park's plans for a jolly 1998 and beyond. For him, its creation was a logical extension of what he had been doing. Besides his discussion-board postings, Park was already sending out e-mails with his thoughts on stock trading. Anyone who contacted him could get on his e-mail list. By the beginning of 1998, the list contained 2,000 names, he says. So he decided it was time to organize them into something more cohesive. He chose the organization's name for a simple reason: he didn't know the people who would be his members, except by their Internet identities.

Initially, membership in Societe Anonyme was free. Later, Park began charging. By the end of 1999, the fee would be as much as $200 a month.

Some early Societe Anonyme members said they viewed the organization as sort of an online investment club. If so, it was a club that Joe Park planned to swing with some oomph.

"We are here to make money and we take no hostages," he wrote in a sort of electronic mission statement that he posted on the Internet early in Societe Anonyme's life. "We only pick stocks that are sensitive to volume and momentum," he said. "It is easy to trigger momentum and we do not even have the kind of money

Soros or Buffet have." (George Soros and Warren Buffett are two of the richest and most famous investors on Wall Street.) And, he added, "regardless of the market sentiment the momentum wins on certain stocks."[1]

While there would be some longer-term stock investments, the group's primary mission would be "strictly blitzkrieg, quick in and quick out: instant gratification," he wrote. For one thing, there was the "unabomber" to worry about. Park took that name from the infamous mail bomber who wreaked havoc. For Park, a unabomber is an unexpected event that can turn around the fortunes of a stock or a stock market overnight.

He posted a long list of rules, some more like homilies, for Societe Anonyme members to follow. Never send him foolish questions. Never "bullshit" each other. Nor hype a stock. There would be a central "DD (due diligence) committee" of three people to review and research stocks that members suggest for the group to buy. But any suggestions are expected to be well researched by members, who were warned by Park not to share their suggestions widely with others.

> "Otherwise we will have every one's ideas running
> around like a chicken without a head,"

Park wrote.

Park was, in some ways, putting out a call to arms. He was certainly going beyond the traditional role of the individual investor or even investor club. He was going beyond the kind of world that the Gardners sought to create at the Motley Fool. The Gardners' aim was to encourage orderly, long-term investments in stocks. In an effort to keep things orderly, the Gardners banned discussions about the thousands of volatile—and easily manipulated—little companies known as "penny stocks," many of which were found on the Bulletin Board.

With Societe Anonyme, Park was going beyond talk and forging a mechanism for more concerted action. Instead of shying away from go-go little stocks, Societe Anonyme would seek out some of them and try to affect their price. As Park argued, given the right circumstances and with enough muscle provided by the right societe, momentum wins.

If Societe Anonyme was to be a new kind of Internet army, Park promised it would be a polyglot force, if one not necessarily blessed with perfect spelling.

> "Our society is made up of anonymousmous members from all walks of life: students, labourers, lawyers, home makers, investment bankers, Nasdaq market makers, a burrito maker, doctors, truck drivers, Asians, Afro-Americans, Anglos, Italians, Arabs, Jews, etc,"

Park wrote in his SA manifesto.

But whatever their backgrounds, Park set before his members one common, if seemingly outlandish, mission:

> "Our goal is for every member to make $5,000 per week day trading."

A quarter-million dollars a year per person could breed a lot of harmony amidst almost any diversity—if the money could be made. Park soon enough began putting his new organization to the test.

In January, Park came across a press release from BAT International. This BAT is not to be confused with BAT Industries, the huge British tobacco conglomerate. BAT International was based in the decidedly noninternational town of Burbank, California. And it was decidedly not giant. Like many small Bulletin Board companies, BAT didn't file public financial statements with the SEC. A later financial statement would show that sales for the first nine months of 1998 were a mere $131,617, which produced a loss for the period of over $925,000.

But BAT had big plans. BAT described itself as an automotive and energy technology company. Among other things, it claimed to have the know-how—in the form of the "Dolphin Pulse Charge Engine Technology"—to produce high-powered car engines that could get more than eighty miles to a gallon of gas. In its January news release, BAT said it was "prepared to offer new ideas to major auto companies . . . and we certainly believe they may listen."[2]

Up to then, not many people in the stock market seemed to be listening to BAT's story. BAT shares ended 1997 at under 8 cents apiece.

What caught Park's eye was nestled down a bit in BAT's January press release. It talked of a coming demonstration of the company's new "super-efficient engine." The demonstration, which would involve matching the BATmobile against cars with standard power plants, was scheduled to take place at the Penske California Speedway in Fontana, California, on January 15, 1998. And to believe BAT, it would be a day to remember. The affair was open to auto industry officials, the press, and the public. Invitations had already been sent out to the major auto companies. BAT was "planning to license a whole array of engine technologies to major auto manufacturers, immediately after the demonstration," according to the release. No doubt moguls from Detroit to Tokyo would be standing in line in Fontana.

Park had actually been following BAT for several months, not that he had gotten much satisfaction from the exercise. He owned a few thousand BAT shares, purchased at about 18 cents each. Needless to say, seeing the stock at half that price didn't make for a happy TokyoMex. But unlike the average investor—who would either hold his shares and curse or sell them at a loss and curse—Park saw an opportunity to recover his money and then some.

He figured this announced drive-off between a supposed supermileage vehicle and a run-of-the-mill road car would likely garner some press attention and Internet chatter—particularly if a certain Mexican food maven helped feed the conversation. Such attention just might push up the stock price. "I realized the potential of this," Park tells me later.

One of the first things he did was to call Joseph LaStella, the president of BAT, to find out more about the test. In giant companies, layers of factotums protect top executives and make them unreachable by anyone who isn't an officially anointed VIP. The top executives of many small companies, by contrast, often take calls from shareholders and would-be shareholders. Sometimes they're the only ones there to answer the phone. So, the good news is they will talk to you. The bad news is they might tell you lies.

Park doesn't recall any fibs from LaStella. But, he says, he did come away with the impression that the guy "loves hype."

LaStella remembers talking to Park. In an interview, he tells me that he is always straightforward and factual when giving out information about the company. Park did seem to be supportive of the company, which was a nice change of pace from some of the BAT followers that LaStella says he has encountered in cyberspace.

The company president says that some people on the Internet stock-discussion sites have been impersonating him and putting out "all kinds of information that is wrong. Anything you can imagine is on the chat boards." One poster, he adds, even claimed that LaStella had just been killed by a car falling on him. I don't ask if the purported killing machine was supposed to be Dolphin-powered.

In talking with Park, he didn't seem overly bothered by his impression that the BAT executive might have been a tad too enthusiastic. Indeed, for what Park had planned, a little enthusiasm could be a good thing.

He sent out an e-mail to his members telling them to start buying BAT. He estimates that 300 to 400 of them bought a total of about 500,000 shares the first day and within a few days had accumulated about 1.5 million shares. At the time there were over 70 million shares of BAT stock. (However, roughly half that total was held by company officers and other insiders. Under federal securities law those shares were considered restricted and couldn't readily be sold.)

Park also started talking up the stock on the Internet. Three days before the demonstration, he posted the following message on the BAT discussion site at Silicon Investor. He began with a reference to the company by its stock symbol, BAAT:[3]

"Just talked to BAAT..

Last Sat they ran the pre-test at the Burbank Airport..

City of Burbank gave them a red carpet . . .

```
Bloody car ran 80 miles on a friggin gallon of
gasoline . . .

Their license with Mercedes is still in effect and
they are coming as well as host of other suto manfs
from US Europe and Asia..

It will be a media blitz ,,,

15 th of January is the world demonstration . . . .

Expect news on this starting very shortly . . . "
```

And in case anyone might have failed to detect his enthusiasm for the company, Park signed off the e-mail with yet another new moniker. Now he was "Joe Bat."

Joking Joe Bat. In an e-mail discussing which media representatives might or might not be at the car demonstration, Park wrote that

```
"Al Gore will attend and report back to the White
House. Also Pope will reside over the finish."
```

Park did punctuate those points with a "<g>," which is often used as Internet shorthand to denote a "giggle" (though it also sometimes seems to be used to denote an online growl). Presumably, Park didn't want any readers to take his predictions about Al or John Paul seriously. Or at least too seriously.

As January 15 approached, Park seemed to be of two minds about the stock. On the one hand, he kept feeding the enthusiasm. In a January 13 e-mail to the BAT discussion thread at Silicon Investor, Park suggested that investors forget about the BAT car getting eighty miles per gallon because he just heard

```
"that the bloody car din close to 200 miles on a
gallon of fuel."
```

However, he also noted that the price of BAT stock had already risen dramatically. It had reached as high as 47 cents a share. While still not enough for a cup of coffee, that per-share price was nearly six times its 1997 year-end level.

"Call it hype, Mexes momentum calls, etc,"

he wrote.

Park added that he had already sold some of his BAT stock into the price run-up and was holding the rest to put into his IRA—maybe.

"But if we seen any slight on infringement against
human decency we dump this,"

Park added. He didn't elaborate on what kind of slights to the human condition might eliminate BAT from his retirement planning.

As part of his preparation for January 15, Park sent out an e-mail call to SA members looking for volunteers to attend the demonstration and report any developments back to him. "We had two members there," Park says. (During the Civil War, brokers in gold certificates had agents travel to battlefronts to wire back results that could affect prices, according to Robert Sobel in his very readable stock market history called *The Big Board.* From Bull Run to BAT Run on the carousel of history.)

On demonstration day, the "SUPERCAR," as BAT modestly called its vehicle, had some problems. The "SUPERCAR developed a mechanical mishap during initial test laps," according to a company press release. The Dolphin engine was blowing oil from its number two cylinder. While determining that further driving could damage the engine, LaStella and his staff decided to push ahead "because of the national attention that has been focused on the demonstration," the release added. However, the rest of the test was done at a relatively pedestrian speed of forty miles per hour.

Even limping along and spouting oil, the SUPERCAR averaged 92.5 miles a gallon and "and still outperformed Detroit's equivalent nearly two to one!" the company trumpeted in its press release.

Park and other Internet traders were closely following the unfolding events at the Penske speedway. Park told Silicon Investor readers:

"The start of the test was delayed by making some
adjustments. That spooked the stock price. The test is
going on now, and BAAT officials are confident of 80 mpg.
They wanted to go for 120-130 mpg, but have lessthan
ideal conditions. The test will finish around 6 pm NY
time, possibly could make it on CNN late tonight. BAAT
thinks it will get good media coverage tomorrow."

Later that night, after the demonstration was over, Park wrote
that

"BAAT has great tech but we wont go out and make millions over night.. Down the future this will be a monster.."

But within days, Park announced he had sold his remaining
BAT stock and recommended the same course to other Societe
Anonyme members as BAT stock continued to rise in price. On
February 5, the stock hit $3.25 a share on a trading volume of 24.3
million shares.

On February 8, Park anointed BAT as officially out of favor. In
a message on a Yahoo! stock-message board, he lumped the stock
in with other "shitty pennies" and contended that "their auto tech
sucks," though he did like the firm's battery technology. But bottom line: the company

"is a damaged goods,"

he wrote.

Park's turnabout prompted one Yahoo! reader to shoot back:

"I am shocked you would call BAAT a shitty stock based
on what you say on the SI

[Silicon Investor]

BAAT Board.. where you say how BAAT is for REAL and is
good enough that you putting it in your IRA!!!!!!!!!!
SO whice way is it?"

There isn't a record on the Yahoo! board of Park responding.

Park tells me his turning on BAT was partly due to reports he received back from the Societe Anonyme members who went to the demonstration. In an electronic message to SA members, he recounted what they said they had heard:

> "We had two members at the BAAT run in L.A., listening
> to the CEOs comments as the test went to pots and CEO
> was screaming on his cell phone: 'We gotta hype this
> thing!' — which gave us yellow flag. Most of us got out
> with a profit. . . . . . "

BAT's president, LaStella, says that anyone who told Park such a story "is a damn liar." He says that several individuals, who appeared to be investors, attended the January 15 demonstration. "I was telling people not to go on the phone and post stuff. Wait until we had all the results. But they were all running to the phone," LaStella recalls. "They wanted to be the hero by getting information to others first. They don't care if it is right or wrong. They just want to have something. They should be on a psychiatrist's couch instead of going into a chat room."

After reaching its $3-plus pinnacle, BAT plummeted back to under a buck by the end of February. BAT's wild stock moves attracted the attention of the SEC, which began an investigation— putting a further cloud over the company. BAT later said that the agency had called off the probe without taking any action. But the stock didn't recover. By the fall of 1999, it was back to trading in the range of 8 cents a share.

After his BAT adventure, Park quickly cast his glance toward the stock of another little company with big dreams. This one was in Denver, which had long been home to many hot stocks and go-go stockbrokers. Perhaps being in a city a mile above sea level makes it easier to launch obscure little stocks into orbit.

This time Park's pick was a company called Rentech, Inc. Rentech was in the energy business. It described itself in a press release as a "developer and marketer of a patented and proprietary process for the conversion of gases into valuable liquid hydrocarbons."⁴ Park had been following Rentech for some months. He even started a discussion thread about the company on Silicon Investor in December 1997, though few messages were posted there.

In early February 1998, TokyoMex gave a demonstration of how well Societe Anonyme ran on liquid hydrocarbons made from gas. On February 5, Mark Koenig, Rentech's head of investor relations, received a phone call from Park. The trader told Koenig that he liked Rentech and was having a meeting of his Internet followers that night to discuss the company. The next day, Park promised, he and his people would be buying a million shares of Rentech stock. It would be a noticeable purchase. At the time, Rentech's volume on the Nasdaq was averaging only about 300,000 shares a day.

The next day, February 6, Rentech's trading volume shot to nearly 2 million shares. The price jumped nearly 50 percent to $1.44 a share.

While the stock took off, Park worked the message boards. To Yahoo! readers he wrote:

> ". . . Most of you also know me as a straight shooter.. and will go the end of the world to do a DD on a company . . . I am not a paid toutist,, nor do I have vested interest,,, most of my holdings were bought at open maket . . . It is now time for RNTK."

And Park got some response. One Yahoo! poster told him,

> "You make a lot of great/astute call, including this one. Thanks a lot, I think that I am going to become richer."

But he wasn't relying on just the power of the Internet to keep Rentech rolling. That same day, February 6, he called back Rentech's Koenig. This time he had a request. Please have the company put out a press release, he asked. Park didn't much care about the topic, he just wanted a press release to "keep the stock going" and get the price higher, recalls Koenig.

Koenig turned down the request. For one thing, it smacked of being a "highly illegal" effort to "manipulate the stock market," says the Rentech official. Koenig also tried to discourage Park and his followers from continuing their buying binge. "I told Joe it wasn't healthy to do this buying," he says.

Park readily acknowledges asking for the press release and sees nothing wrong with the request. He certainly wasn't trying to manipulate the market, he says. Rather, he merely wanted Rentech to put out a release explaining why it is such a good company. When Koenig refused, "I was really pissed," says Park.

Koenig and Park continued to talk occasionally in the months ahead. Once, while in New York, Koenig even paid a courtesy call to Park, partly to offer condolences on the recent death of the trader's mother. The Rentech official says he acquired a certain fondness for Park, along with a certain wariness of him. "He is very bright. I like talking to him," says Koenig. "But he is dangerous. Here is a loaded gun without a safety on."

As 1998 rolled into its third month, Park took a new step to increase his visibility and influence on the Internet. He started his own stock-discussion thread on Silicon Investor. While Silicon Investor, like other chat threads, allows its members a wide latitude in starting discussion sites, the vast majority of threads are dedicated to talking about a specific stock or groups of stocks. Only a relative handful of individuals have the following—and ego—to start their own successful message board.

On March 3, Park opened Tokyo Joe's Café for his Societe Anonyme buddies and all others who cared to come. As he wrote to anyone visiting the Café at 11:15 that night:

> "Bars always open .. drinks on the house.. and cooks from Puebla will make your tummy warm . . .
>
> We now have close to 700 registered members with us , in this cantina called 'Societe Anonym' . . .
>
> $1.000 per person bar tab,, on our daily or weekly sojourn into cyber investing,, we can buy and sell $700,000 worth of chips.. a lot of pennies..
>
> It has an awesome implication ,, we can buy the whole

```
cabana for the night ,, or the whole town ,,, but get-
ting drunk is not allowed . . .
```

```
We play sober and we play smart,, its us Societe boys
team against Meyersons or Nite or Sniders,,
```

[references to Wall Street brokerage firms]

```
that we will be having matches with . . .
```

```
Welcome all and feel free with the amenities . . .
```

```
If this cantina gets corrupted,, we move on to our own
web site,, but thats another story . . .
```

```
See ya tomorrow,, have an exciting play in mind . . .
```

```
Joe"
```

But as soon as he opened the Café's (figurative) doors, he found that things got rowdy.

```
"Congratulations Joe on your very own thread, named by
yourself, after yourself . . . (:>) May all who come
here find themselves blessed,"
```

read the second message posted on the board. (The strange little (:>) symbol in the message was an "emoticon." See Glossary for further explanation.)

Park's response:

```
"Sarcastic sob !
```

```
ROFL,,
```

```
It was suggested by a member . . . "
```

He soon had need for a bouncer. A very big bouncer. On Friday, March 6, at 1:59 A.M., a new patron arrived at Tokyo Joe's Café. He hadn't come to imbibe from Park behind the bar. He had come to replace him. And he announced his intentions with his very first words:

```
"Move over Tokyo Mex BIG DOG is in town."⁵
```

CHAPTER FOUR

Big Dog tells me to meet him at the White Castle.

The one on 1341 Main Avenue, at the corner of Piaget. The only White Castle hamburger restaurant in Clifton, New Jersey, though there is another one in neighboring Paterson and over three hundred more scattered from Minneapolis to Nashville to New York City. More than 12 billion burgers sold.

My rendezvous with Big Dog is to come right after my rendezvous with Tokyo Joe at his Manhattan apartment in July 1998. Figuring that full disclosure isn't always the reporter's best friend; I tell neither that I plan to meet the other. As it turns out, neither asks where I have been or where I am going. I simply breakfast with the Hatfields and dine with the McCoys.

Exiting Park's apartment building, I strike out west for New Jersey. A Conestoga cab gets me as far as the Port Authority Bus Terminal on Eighth Avenue stretching between Fortieth and Forty-second Streets. The Port Authority is a decrepit-looking beehive of a building honeycombed with waiting areas where buses briefly stop and load passengers before setting out for the Jersey wilds. Buy a ticket, find the right waiting area, stand by the door, wait for the bus, get on, and you're off to Clifton. By the time I try door number four, I find the right bus. I ask the driver if he knows where the White Castle is in Clifton. He nods. Only one in town. The driver guns the bus engine and we head off toward the Lincoln Tunnel, which is a long, frequently clogged tube still used by non-Internet travelers.

In an odd way, it's fitting that Big Dog tells me to wait for him outside the White Castle. Launched in 1921 in Wichita, Kansas, it actually has similarities to the Internet stock-trading world. For one thing, White Castle has its own website, filled with fascinating facts and figures, at least some of which are undoubtedly true.[1]

The fast-food empire has its own lingo. In White Castlespeak, a hamburger isn't just a burger. It's a Slyder. (An Internet stock trader uses the same name. In response to an e-mail inquiry, he tells me that his screen name was inspired, in part, by a character in the movie *Top Gun*.) One doesn't just get hungry for a Slyder, one gets the "craves," which in 1930—according to the website— led to the creation of the new discipline of Craveology.

Craves are apparently best satisfied by a "sack." Ten Slyders to the Greenwich mean sack. That's not quite as bad as it sounds, since each Slyder consists of a mere 2.5-inch square patty of beef sandwiched between a suitably miniature bun. Still, each Slyder has 135 calories, nearly half from fat, according to the nutrition chart that follows food even into cyberspace. So enough sacks can still make your arteries look like the Lincoln Tunnel at rush hour.

Big Dog and I had our first conversation over the phone, about a month before we actually meet. He's a relative newcomer to the Internet trading world. His March e-mail message, throwing down the gauntlet to TokyoMex at the Café, was the first one he ever posted on a Silicon Investor message board. It wouldn't be his last.

He almost immediately launched an assault against Tokyo-Mex. The idea, Big Dog explains, was to make things so unpleasant that Park would be driven from his own site. That way, Big Dog adds, he could take it over. As far as he could see, Tokyo Joe's Café was on its way to becoming one of the most popular stock-discussion sites around. And Big Dog prefers to travel first class.

So electronic messages started flying. The messages contained a combination of boasts and insults mixed in with a few stock picks. Big Dog, for instance, recommended the stock of a little brewing company that produced what he described as "Hemp Beer." The stock's price rose more than 60 percent during the following week. If nothing else, the stock's price performance at least reinforced the notion that the Dog could rope in investors. Big Dog backers and TokyoMex admirers soon joined the dispute between the two men. It all turned into a nice online brawl. A sampling of the action:[2]

DOG:

"This is one dog that is amused by you Joe, but your getting stale. What this thread needs is someone that really knows what and how to play.

Well, since I just happen to have some time and I could certainly buy and sell you with pocket change, I think I'm just the guy for the job. As a matter of fact, I will re-name this thread 'Dog's Place.'

It will be the kind of place where everyone gets a fair shake because I simply don't play for the money so much as the rush I get from winning."

MEX:

"Ever see a dog make money ?

Unless of course Lassie dog..

Relax dog,, we are all here for same thing..

Don't let your ego get in the way,,, the fall of Janus was the ego..

Joe small ego."

DOG FAN:

"Big Dog,

Like your style! You tell it like it is.

Hey, if you cant run with the pack, dont get off the porch.

Man, this thread is getting worst than reruns of Ozzie and Harriet!! And I cant even get any service or a friggin glass of water in this cafe."

MEX FAN:

"Big Dog,

You can't hunt, you are barking up the wrong tree and you are chasing a penny pussy cat.

From the looks of what you left behind, it is clear you have distemper and worms. Distemper is fatal. Better get to a veterinarian fast!!"

BIG DOG NON-FAN, SPECULATING ON HOW A POOCH MIGHT RUN A STOCK SCAM (APPLICABLE TO NONCANINES, AS WELL):

"He would dub himself. . . . the Super Penny Stock Picker . . . . . . Wow, if you look at all the stocks he would tell you he purchased and the price he purchased them at, this guy must be rich, must know what he is doing and I should listen to him. So he would spread his posts across several stocks that he (somehow) would claim he got in at the very bottom. But, of course, it's because he is SOOO good at picking them. He even might adopt a catchy phrase 'Follow the money'. Sure enough, soon he would have a "following", a few lackeys that believe in this messiah and would defend him. He, in fact, would reveal his vast holdings and the price he entered them at. Not surprisingly, there would be a number of winners in there that he would claim to have scooped at the very bot-

tom. Sprinkled throughout would be a loser or two
('Hey, I take my losses too'). He even might add
'recent additions' to his portfolio that might go up.
He could defend them as 'they will come around some
time soon'. But he would always eventually focus you
on the ones he claims made him the most money. And
suddenly he would have such a large portfolio, that on
any given day he could scream 'SEE WHAT STOCK X DID
TODAY!!' and make people feel like this guy ALWAYS
picks the winners. He would dismiss a day's loss if
anyone points it out by deflecting attention to the
winners. And if you look closely, you might find that
none of his posts ever contain anything but the most
basic reference to due diligence or helpful information. Almost every post would focus exclusively on how
successful his picks are, what price he got in at and
what price he expects them to go to. . . . . . . A wolf
in sheep's clothing."

BIG DOG'S RETORT:

"I am pretty flattered that some one sees me as such a
threat to their madness . . . . Actually
none of it deserves a response."

NEWCOMER:

"Unfortunate that I wandered into this Cafe just when
the gunfight began—or should I say dogfight."

DOG TO MEX:

"Your world is caving in around you and I offer you
salvation. A few more losers and your history."

MEX BACK:

"Salvation my ass . . . .

You think you are a big dog,, more like a mutt . . .

Don't wanna play fetch with you any more . . .

Let me know when you want to join the human race . . ."

Things went on like this for about a week with the level of discourse mostly heading downhill. People complained that there was so much arguing and insulting going on that there was little space or energy being devoted to actually discussing stocks. Finally, on Friday the thirteenth of March, at 9:20 P.M., Park said "Enough!" He announced he was leaving the Café that he had opened only about a week earlier. Though hardly an eon, even in Internet time, it was long enough to inspire the following rather lengthy farewell from TokyoMex:

". . . I do not need piss poor dogs hanging around . . .

Just got home.. from a great dinner.. reminiscing all the good people here..

Societe Anonym,, people from all background,,students, labourers, Arabs, Jews, Lawyers, MDs, hair dressers, burrito makers , ,,people of all different experience,,uniting for the common good.. like how this country was envisioned eeons ago ,,through Baring Straights,, by Mayflower, by illegal steam boats,, over the Rio Grande,,, fathers carrying babies mouth gagged,,from potato famine,,from purges of Roman Catholics..,,, mothers dreaming for own bedroom . . .

I say adieu to all the folks who have patronised this humble place.. I sincerely hope you had a little pleasure of quenching your thirst,, in what ever way ,,and hope you have met people of your liking . . .

I will see you soon via,, wire, and on the web. . . . till then ,,bless you and your family ,,and may you prosper and be wealthy both in terms of money and human spirit,, so one day ,,yes we can indeed hold our hands together and sing and dance on the beach in the moon

light.. and we teach our children ,, how to play this
game early on ,, to look for the market dynamics.. the
subtle singnals of the market makers,, the world geog-
raphy ,, modern economics from industrial revolution in
England to post war baby boomers,, the Marshall Plan
..Roosevelts,, dry spell remedy ,, inviving of Japanese
economy as a stable force in Asia.. Nasser,,Suez.. Yom
Kippur.. the new Mid East,OPEC,, power shift from con-
servative constipation to 70s ,,flower children's influence,, in shaping of new order .. Dutch socio
economics..gravity of hunger.. influence of weather on
agro-economy ,,and regional economic impact..on the
rest of the world,, the IMF, . . . and much more . . .
let us teach our children ,,so that in this modern phe-
nomena,, of cyber investing,, that this indeed can be
one of the most powerful tools,, and the prievilieged
use of SI for louzy $125 for life time. . . . is a bonus
to boot.. for our children..

Let them be aware of dogs in this life,, dogs that are
ugly ,, pisses with out due manners,, dogs that walk
unpoised,, the dogs that shit shamelessly ,, the
dogs,, that mount another dog,, with out diffrentiat-
ing time and place,, and she dogs that shake the tail
like wise.. shamelessly .. with a belly button ring
,,,,ROFLMAO

Dogs of short stature.. ugly dogs ,with warts hanging
out of their lips and saliva running down from all
their crevices . . . dogs that only sniff,, cocka,,
therefor can only see other dogs with same interests,,
dogs that sway ,,dogs that sit and lay with its but-
tocks facing high towards the sky for all to see . . .
indeed dogs my friends..

A dog of sewer trying to be the top dog.. so those who
follow this dog.. becomes less than the dog ,,,little

dogs,, with expression of mistrust,, face of sad-
ness,,, face of drooping eyebrows.. dogs who always
seems to be wet and cold from the weather.. dogs who
need a warm hand and a fire place..

I say adieu to all the dogs of this world.. especially
..here in my cafe..

I am opening a new cafe in a week .. think of it as
Cafe de Paris a Monaco.. where we will meet at 5 AM ,
after a splendid night out,, we meet for champagne and
OJ and eggs Benedictine,, smoke a joint or a cigar ,,
have a cognac,, then we go bare foot to Menton ,,
where Byron stayed for 2 years,, read his poems,, then
we sit and have Boullavaise with Vin de Provence.. and
bathe ourselves,,, apre drinks in Madame Mi Mis and
drive to Genoa for some pasta,, takes only 30 minutes..

See you then . . . "

"I gave the thread to the Dog," Park tells me later. "He was coming in and was interrupting, making very provocative statements. He came in to get support for his stock picks. We said just fuck it. Make peace with him. People were getting hurt."

As my bus rumbles out of the tunnel and toward my New Jersey burger-joint rendezvous, Tokyo Joe's Café has been operating for several months as the Dog House. "We staged a hostile takeover," crows Big Dog when I first interview him. A Silicon Investor official later would describe the event as "a little coup in cyberspace."

Big Dog tells me that the Café takeover is just part of his effort to strike it rich in cyberspace. "If you get enough people behind you, you can do anything," he says. Come visit New Jersey, Big Dog adds, and "I could bring you into a world you wouldn't believe."

Would you believe that in 1949 a White Castle employee came up with the "food equivalent of Columbus' discovery of

America"? He found that putting five holes in the White Castle patty before cooking not only makes for a better Slyder but also improves productivity by eliminating "the need to turn the burgers over." Five years later, White Castle patented "its unique five hole Slyder." For those who doubt, check the Web.

By the summer of 1998, Big Dog was one of the most book-marked names on Silicon Investor. TokyoMex was still number one, but the Dog was on the rise.

The information that he supplied for his online members' profile at Silicon Investor was relatively sparse but not completely unrevealing. He listed a corporate affiliation with "Big Dog Holdings," where he was the "Head Dog." On the line for college, he put "UNC/Chapel Hill. Degree in business law." His investment style was "always a step ahead of the crowd," and his hobbies were "fishing and playing pennies." When asked for a quote, he felt three words sufficed: "Take No Prisoners."

When he first came online, he would say "he had tons of money and was just doing [stock-trading] for fun," recalls Jodi Segal-Lankry, a Philadelphia schoolteacher turned Internet stock trader. Of course, she adds, in the Internet discussion world it's hard to know what to believe.

"There is so much stress involved," Big Dog tells me over the phone. Hundreds of e-mails a day from around the world to be read and answered. "I have CEOs of companies calling me and asking me to go on the Internet and say I am buying the company's stock," he says. One company invited him to an auto race in New England. Another company offered to fly him on a private jet to a meeting to discuss how the Dog could help the company fend off "naysayers."

My bus finally starts wending its way along Main Avenue. It's a long avenue that appears to be mainly in need of new stores and fresh paint.

"There is a lot of movement to invest underground," Big Dog says in a phone interview. Online discussions are moving to private chat rooms that can be entered only with a password. "Once you tip your hand" on the more public discussion boards, such as Silicon

Investor, a stock will quickly run up 50 percent and then fall just as fast, he says.

"Next stop," the bus driver yells, and gives me a glance over his shoulder. We've reached the Castle.

It's white with blue trim. The place I'm looking at might be castle-sized if you're small enough. A certain well-placed website source has silently informed me that the "motif" is "medieval" and "was inspired by Chicago's famous Water Tower. Original White Castles sported rooftop battlements and a turret." For Saint George and the Slyder.

I head to the pay phone at the corner and punch in Big Dog's number. "Wait in the parking lot," he instructs me. I am to keep an eye out for a Jeep Grand Cherokee. Fortunately, it's a small parking lot and not overburdened by traffic.

Nearly half an hour later, a Jeep rolls in. I open the passenger door. The driver isn't a dog, but he is big. More precise dimensions, I would later learn, are about six feet four inches tall and 370 pounds with a capacity to go higher. He's wearing a blue T-shirt with the logo of the Big Dog clothing company, Santa Barbara, California. I notice that his seatback is nowhere near its full upright position. It takes a big gap between seat cover and steering wheel to accommodate a Big Dog.

His real name is Mike Nichols. He is forty-one years old but looks younger, with the kind of friendly, rounded face that big men often carry. He has curly brown hair and a mustache. I get into the Jeep, we shake hands, he steps on the gas, and the White Castle shrinks in the distance.

He parks his Jeep in front of a two-story duplex on a cul-de-sac. He lives on the top floor with his wife, Janice, and his teenage daughter, Lauren. Janice, a soft-featured woman with a friendly smile, greets me with a hello and an offer to stay for dinner. I offer to take them out to dinner. But she and Nichols both say they prefer to stay home. Besides, the roast is already cooking. Their daughter later arrives with several girlfriends. She laughingly suggests that I do a story about her. I smile and say I'll think about it.

Nichols works from a computer stuffed in the corner of a small, cluttered living room. Like TokyoMex, Big Dog invites me to pull up a chair and watch him in action. His bulk makes the computer seem small, but his fingers move quickly enough over the keyboard.

I know enough of the jargon by now to ask a few jargonaut questions. Are you using Level II? "I was, but I don't need it," he replies. "I can read between the lines." Perhaps, I think, that's Level III.

Big Dog says the drill of Internet stock trading can be pretty simple: find a few friends, find a low-priced stock, start pounding out the e-mails, and get ready for a ride.

An e-mail appears on his computer screen about WINR, a stock that Big Dog says he and a friend "are planning to run tomorrow." WINR is the stock symbol for a little St. Augustine, Florida, company called Winners Internet Network, Inc. The company's plan is to serve as the middleman handling transactions between gamblers and online casinos. WINR's website says the company is "The Missing Link for Internet Gaming."

Up to then, WINR had largely been missing in action when it came to the stock market. Its price on the Bulletin Board through the first half of 1998 never topped $1 a share. On the July day that Big Dog and I sit in front of his computer and plan his WINR play, the price is about 41 cents a share.

He says he has a group of about five traders whom he works with regularly. By picking small-company stocks with low-priced shares, even a small group can use its buying activity to start moving the price upward. "We can make it move and then call attention to the momentum," which should bring in more buyers, thus pushing the price up further, Nichols says. Such action usually lasts long enough to give him and his original colleagues plenty of opportunity to sell out at a very nice profit.

He sounds almost blasé about the money to be made. When the market for over-the-counter stocks is strong, "you get a triple every day," Nichols says. A triple is the same as a three-bagger—a threefold jump in a stock's price. Of course, Big Dog adds, none of this would be possible without the Internet and the power it gives him to send forth the word from Clifton.

Nichols has never strayed far from Clifton. Born and raised in nearby Paterson, he spent much of his childhood on Delaware Avenue, a street that was teeming with kids. Many of those kids are still Nichols's friends three decades later.

He attended Catholic grammar school and then switched over to the public high school. "I wasn't going to have nothing more to do with any nuns," he explains. "I did fine in school. Never had a problem. I wasn't a bookworm or anything. And I was pretty rebellious and the class clown and everything else like that," Nichols tells me.

His father was vice president of a local plastics company. Nichols also doesn't have a degree in business law from the University of North Carolina, Chapel Hill, or anywhere else. He never went to college.

Nichols says his Silicon Investor profile showing him with a business-law degree is just part of the persona he created for the online world. "Everybody on there has a story," he says.

However, he has been to North Carolina. Once, he and a friend from Delaware Avenue borrowed a Lincoln belonging to his friend's mother. They were supposed to drive just to the store. They finally stopped in North Carolina when they got a flat tire.

The young Nichols worked a while with his father at the plastics company. He also worked as a truck driver and lots of other jobs. "Man, you name it, I did it," he says. Mostly, he didn't do much. His father helped pay for his apartment and other bills. "I had no real interest in doing anything. Just having a good time. Partying," he says.

Partying a little too heavily, in fact. In 1984, Nichols says, he swore off alcohol.

For the past dozen years, Nichols had been working in the textile-coatings business, the kind used in such items as outdoor tablecloths. "I'm a natural at selling," he says.

But he wasn't a satisfied salesman. At the textile-coatings company, "My bosses were the ones making millions," Nichols says.

He had a stock brokerage account for years but never was an

active player in the market. In late 1997, Nichols started idly trolling the Internet and found his way into the stock-discussion world. He says he chose the moniker "Big Dog" because he planned to be the biggest player on the Internet. (It turned out that an oil-drilling consultant in Houston already had the moniker Big Dog on Silicon Investor. Normally, says a Silicon Investor official, two people aren't allowed to have the same pseudonym. But sometimes a duplication slips through.)

In September of 1997, Nichols opened an online brokerage account with E*Trade, put in $2,000, and started looking for action.

Early in his online life, Big Dog became a fan and friend of Ga Bard. As in Georgia Bard. The man behind the Ga Bard moniker is Gary Swancey, a resident of Stockbridge, Georgia. Swancey manages to stand out as an unusual figure even in a cyberspace landscape that is beginning to look like a Hieronymus Bosch painting.

Besides being an Internet trader, Swancey is a poet with five volumes of published work: *The Joyful Years; Oh, Those Youthful Years; The Angel Years; The Influential Years;* and *The Fruitful Years.* The fact that Swancey has paid to have the works published detracts not a whit from his pride of authorship. When I began interviewing Swancey in the summer of 1998, the then forty-five-year-old trader was kind enough to send me a complete set of those works. In his accompanying letter, he wrote that the books "are a teaching vessel" about "the conflicts and joys of life as seen through the eyes of a loner in this vast ominous world." It doesn't sound like a prelude to lighthearted verse.

By his own recounting, Swancey hasn't exactly had a lighthearted life. His hardscrabble story includes quitting high school after being expelled from half a dozen schools for fighting ("I won't kowtow to bullies," he explains); being expelled from his house at sixteen and surviving on the streets, partly through stealing from stores; pretending to be a blind beggar—complete with dark glasses, cup, and cane—to raise money from passersby to help pay for the birth of one of his three children. He says the kindness of strangers dropped $75 into his cup. Swancey migrated to Internet stock-trading after a heating and air-conditioning business he owned went bankrupt. It seems he greatly expanded the business in anticipation of a flood of construction work from the 1996 Summer Olympics in Atlanta. Instead, he got only a trickle.

Perhaps because he is a poet, Swancey is a great one for sayings online. Ga Bard's thousands of electronic message-board postings are sprinkled with such little ditties as "Keep your investment friends close, your day trading enemies closer," and "Character is what you stand for and Reputation is what you fall for." Swancey, who tells of once taking a computer completely apart and putting it back together just to see how it works, sometimes uses a more mathematical format for his messages. Such as:

"GREED = Buying without common sense

FEAR = Selling without common sense

RESULTS = Buying high and selling low"

In ways, Swancey resembles a Biblical prophet of stock-trading profits. Indeed, his willingness to proselytize and his certitude when doing it seems to be one of his great attractions to others on the Internet. By 1998, Ga Bard had become one of the most bookmarked names on Silicon Investor and had his own discussion thread, "Georgia Bard's Corner." There he thundered forth with brimstone and rhyme:

"SHORTER SLAMMERS, DOUBLE DUMPERS, TOUT SHOUTERS, AND DOUBT TOUTERS BEWARE!!!"[3]

Ga Bard is a fervent "DD" man, who repeatedly hammers out the message that every person needs to do his or her own due diligence (a.k.a. research) before investing. That they need to think for themselves and not be lulled by others. He reads company financial statements and composes long e-mail messages into the wee hours of the morning. He says he sleeps only about three hours a night. For fuel, he takes in four packs of cigarettes and a dozen Cokes a day.

Asked about the health effects of this regime, Swancey says he doesn't expect to have a long life and hearkens back to words from his deceased father. "Daddy told me that those who burn twice as bright live half as long," says Ga Bard.

In this caffeine and nicotine-powered universe, Swancey creates elaborate philosophies and "scenarios." There is the BTS, which stands for BARD's Trading System. In essence, trading the Bard way means that if your stock doubles in price, you should sell half of it to get back your original investment. The remaining stock is then "free" to be sold in similar increments if the stock keeps rising. If the stock drops after rising because of short sellers or "double dumpers" (people who sell all their stock after the price doubles), buy more in order to reduce your AMSC, or Average Mean Share Cost. Then wait for the stock-price elevator to rise again.

Though the idea of selling part of your holdings when the price rises is hardly revolutionary, the BTS has gained a certain fame. Other online posters have begun referring to the BTS in their e-mails. Sometimes it even gets used as a verb, as in, "I'm BTS'n & hoping for a buck." Ga Bard is, wrote another trader, an online "legend."

As a newcomer to the Net, Nichols found Swancey's pearls of wisdom sparkling. After reading Ga Bard's message-board postings, Big Dog sent him an e-mail complimenting him. Swancey sent back his phone number. The two began to converse on the phone and online. "He kind of took me under his wing. He was probably the most respected guy on the Internet when it came to doing research," recalls Nichols. Another thing that Nichols noticed about Swancey was a characteristic shared by Internet stock-chat celebrities, including a certain canine. "He was pretty vocal about what he liked and what he didn't like," says Nichols.

TokyoMex definitely fell into Swancey's "don't like" category. When Nichols made his move on Tokyo Joe's Café, a certain Bard added a few barbs to the assault.

> `"Let me tell you something right now MR>BIG MOUTH HUGE`
> `EGO TOKYO JOE>,"`

wrote Swancey in a March 10 online message, a few days after Big Dog threw down the gauntlet to Park. Swancey's rambling message contended, among other things, that Park had "slandered" him in past e-mails. While acknowledging that TokyoMex had a "massive" following, Swancey asserted that Park had made a "lot of bad calls" on stocks, partly owing to inadequate due diligence. He claimed that he had shared some of his own research with Park only to watch TokyoMex run up the price of the stock before Swancey even had a chance to invest.

> "E-mails CAN BE SUBPOENAed so keep it up Mr. Self
> Righteous Leader and KING of the Momentum Traders,"

Swancey concluded.

In an interview with me, Swancey also brags of going after Park when the opportunity arose. When he finds Park recommending a stock to buy, he makes recommendations online to sell it. "I use my influence on line to do war with him," Swancey says.

Park's online response to Swancey has been pretty low-key, certainly by TokyoMex standards.

> "Welcome to SI.. Gary Bard.. My ego will never be big
> as yours.. Have a beer while you are here."

Park wrote. In a later interview, Park dismisses Swancey as someone who is simply jealous over his success.

Like other online relationships, the friendship between Swancey and Nichols would eventually sour. The falling-out was partly tied to Ga Bard's Great Midland Meltdown. It also seemed due partly to a clash of egos. Like other cyberspace celebrities, neither wants to be a follower.

Certainly not Big Dog after he began tasting success on the Net. As I sit with Nichols that July day in 1998, he tells me that his stock-trading account has grown to about $300,000 from $2,000. Things are going so well that Janice has begun complaining, only half-jokingly, about him going to work at the textile-coatings company when he could be at home sitting on his keester in front of the computer making money in the market. By the summer of '98, Nichols is on leave from his sales job to try out life as a full-time Internet trader.

"If you ever want to do a parlor trick for your friends, give me a call. I will tell you the stock that is moving the next day," Big Dog says as we sit in front of his computer.

That would probably be more popular than charades, I reply.

"We're running WINR tomorrow,"

he types in response to a note from another trading buddy.

Nichols says he has already bought about 10,000 shares of WINR stock. He plans to start putting out e-mail messages when the market opens the next morning. He figures he'll do some reading later tonight about the company. He'll label it a long-term buy; and he actually does plan to hold on to much of his WINR stock. It's part of his new investing outlook.

In the past, "I would sell it in fifteen minutes," he admits. But things are changing on the Internet. People are tiring of all the volatility and turmoil. They are moving more toward longer-term investing and away from quick hits, he says.

He is too. The past few months have changed him, he says, made him a more cautious and wiser investor. "In my heyday of day trading, I would buy a million shares at 10 A.M. and sell them by 11," he says. "I used to say I don't care if it is a pay phone in a gas station bathroom. If it makes me money, I will buy it."

More recently, he adds, he has been focusing on a just a couple of picks a month, stocks that he and his online colleagues have researched thoroughly. "I got so popular because I'm not a pump and dump. I go out and find real stocks." Of course, he can still move a stock, if he so desires. "I can move a stock much faster than a brokerage firm can. I know that I could move a 10 cent stock to 20 cents in two hours. I won't do it. But absolutely there are others who are doing it," he says.

His intent to hold WINR shares is also partly out of deference to the online colleague who brought the stock to his attention. The man seems deeply committed to the stock. During the day, Nichols every so often receives e-mails from the person reminding him that WINR *really* is a long-term play.

```
"WINR not a mo mo stock,"
```

said one such message.

Nichols has some long-term picks of his own. He is enamored of a little company based in Houston called Cryogenic Solutions, Inc., which trades on the Bulletin Board under the stock symbol CYGS. "It's a $50 stock," Nichols proclaims. At the moment it's about $1.50 a share. Nichols is so enthused about the stock that he is planning to soon fly—at his own expense—to meet the company president and learn more about Cryogenic Solution's work in oligodeoxyribonucleotides and other outposts on the biomedical frontier. In one e-mail posting, he declared CYGS to be "the stock of a lifetime," though a little later he thought better of that and upgraded the company to "the opportunity of a thousand lifetimes."

But old habits die hard. This day, Nichols is berating himself for having sold some of his CYGS stock too quickly after starting to push it. On July 6, he posted a message on Silicon Investor that CYGS is "just about ready to rocket." Over the next ten days, the stock rose to about $1.50 a share from about $1.25. But Nichols says he put in sell orders at about $1.40, underestimating how fast and how far it would rise. He figured it would fall back to about $1.30, where he could buy in again. "I will make sure it comes down," he says with a laugh.

As we sit in front of the flickering computer screen, Big Dog says he is tiring some of the trader's life. There's the constant fighting and bickering online. There are the nasty e-mails, such as

```
"Big Dog your just talking people into getting
creamed—like your all heart, what a laugh, can't
believe people swallow your swill."
```

As we sit together, he receives a message proclaiming

```
"long live Tmex."
```

Though the Battle of the Café took place in March, an Internet age ago, hard feelings apparently also die hard in cyberspace.

Nichols tells me he has decided to expel Jodi Segal-Lankry, the Philadelphia schoolteacher turned Internet trader, from his inner circle of traders. Her transgression? Nichols believes she has given a stock pick to TokyoMex instead of his group. Even worse, the stock rose in price. "She is gone," Nichols said. (Lankry later tells me that while she has contacts with Big Dog and TokyoMex and lots of other Internet traders, she never considered herself part of any group. Therefore, she doesn't see how she could be kicked out of a club she hasn't joined.)

Like TokyoMex, Big Dog receives and sends out a steady stream of e-mails throughout the day. One from a close colleague suggests another little stock that would be worth buying.

```
"Okay, that will be the Thursday play,"
```

Nichols types back. Wednesday has already been reserved for WINR.

But as the day progresses, he expresses some second thoughts about what to do with Wednesday's pick. Rather than hold WINR stock, perhaps he will sell quickly into any price surge. Big Dog is still contemplating what to do with WINR when I leave him that night.

Nichols is thinking of expanding his Internet horizon. He says that he has received so many requests for help from small companies that he's looking at opening his own online investor-relations firm. Companies would pay him in cash or stock to get the firm's story out to the world of Internet investors.

As a rising online celebrity, he has been getting offers from all over. A recent one comes from someone merely identified as "a Swiss friend." This unknown friend has a strange offer. It reads, in part:

```
". . . we found your email address after researching
many message boards. we have been watching the infor-
mation you have been posting so far, their accuracy,
and your background when that was possible. we found
that you were a serious investor with great research
potential, good analytical skills, and (sometimes) a
contrarian mentality which we like. like you, a few
```

others were contacted via this standard email . . . who
is 'we'? that will enlighten you about this message.
this started as a 'friend' thing more than 15 years
ago. as a group of 4 friends between north america and
europe, we invested a few hundred thousand dollars
thru our personnal accounts. since then, our common
war chess has grown up to an 8 digit number in USD
. . . although we are very management friendly shareholders, very loyal, and never trade a stock for quick
profits (and we could have done it several times given
our connections on the Street and management we know),
some people could think that our investment techniques
are questionable. thats why u will never know who we
are until this thing is over, and this is also the
reason why we trade thru swiss acccounts. we need to
remain anonymous, and if u want to be part of this, it
will be your best asset and protection. secrecy is key
. . . if you are interested in us and in being part of
that very private circle, reply. you will get another
email address once we have completed our network
(which will be soon) and you have replied. in all
cases, keep it for you and dont spread the word (especially on message boards; remember, we do monitor them
even though we never post). in fact, we would appreciate if you could trash this message once you replied."[4]

Nichols says he is still mulling over how to respond to that
message. (He later tells me that he never took up the offer to go
exploring in the Alps.)

After downing the dinner roast, Nichols and I settle down in
the living room for an electronic stroll along memory lane. Nichols
pulls up e-mail picks he has made over the past few months. He
clucks over them the way some men thumb through an album of
prized vacation photos.

There is MAXX, which over two days in April jumped to $2 a
share from $1 after he recommended it on the Dog House thread.

There is CREG, which soared sevenfold, to a princely 11 cents a share, on the glorious May day when the Dog declared the stock to be "running like a freight train." It fell back by more than half within a few days.

There is TSIG and SEPC and RMGG and PDCI. So many. And so many more still out there.

He pauses. "Tomorrow," he says, "will be a good day."

ACTUALLY, THE NEXT DAY, July 15, isn't all that good for Big Dog. At least when it comes to WINR.

Around 10 A.M., not long after the markets open, he sends out his e-mails about WINR, posting essentially identical messages on three heavily trafficked Silicon Investor message boards, including the Dog House.

> "WINR, Here we go with another winner. News of rev-
> enues and contracts expected and it is upticking
> already on anticipation. BIG DOG, this one will run
> hard and I will be in taking a ride . . . "[1]

Nichols includes some basic financial information about the company in each message and says the company's chief executive is a former IRS official. He gives the phone number for WINR's public relations person, who has provided some of the information. Having done his duty, Big Dog then sits back and waits for the stock to take off.

It doesn't.

WINR's trading volume takes a decent jump that day, to over 320,000 shares, nearly double the day before. But the stock's price acts like a bird without wings. It ends the day at about 41 cents a share—exactly where it ended the day before. Indeed, for the rest of July, WINR's share price hardly moves from that lowly perch.

If nothing else, WINR points up what should be an obvious point, but doesn't always seem to be: this business of trying to move stocks through the power of the cyber-word doesn't always work. Hardly elegant enough to be called art, it isn't nearly precise enough to qualify as science. Perhaps something in between.

Big Dog's disappointing WINR results don't go unnoticed.

"Please be aware that Big Dog is pumping WINR hard today . . . I notice he is not having any effect,"

writes one poster.

"It seems as if Big Dog Mike is losing his touch,"

chimes in another.

Big Dog takes some umbrage at that last crack.

"I buy into a stock and you attack me. Man, is that a bad move,"

he writes.

The crackor fires some umbrage back:

"Don't try to intimidate me you overgrown, self-aggrandizing, pompous hound. I don't care if you have your own thread and have purportedly changed your ways and left the darkside."

The darkside apparently being the world of quick-in, quick-out stock trading.

As the weeks of 1998 pass by, Big Dog receives other reminders that Internet stock-discussion fame has its downside. Another Internet poster starts a new discussion board on Silicon Investor, dedicated to just the subject of Big Dog. He writes that he created it as a way to keep Big Dog–related messages from clogging up other discussion boards. This person names his new thread "The life and times of BIG DOG, a historical perspective." After all, Big

Dog now has an Internet history that stretches back months. The new discussion board attracts Dog lovers and loathers alike.

> "The bottom line is the DOG knows how to make money
> and I have made much money on his picks."

> "He couldn't find his own ass with a Geiger
> counter. . . . . after a Barium enema. . . . much less a
> penny stock that goes up and stays up. . . . But he
> would gladly pay you Tuesday. . . . for a few hundred
> hamburgers today. . . ."

> "I want to have lunch with BIG DOG how do I find?"

(Nobody suggests starting at the White Castle.)

> "If you place his brain on the edge of a razor blade
> . . . it would look like a Tic Tac on a 4 lane high-
> way."

In cyberspace, people often make outrageous, childish, insulting, even cruel remarks about others. The writers are, no doubt, emboldened by the cloak of anonymity that the Internet stock-chat world offers. It isn't, however, a bulletproof garment. As things get nastier and more serious, federal agents and irate company officials will prove how possible it is—with the help of subpoenas and Internet user records—to connect a moniker with a real name and real address.

Nonetheless, the ability to pick a pseudonym, create an identity, and stand firmly behind it frees many people to do and say things they probably would never otherwise consider. For some, this freedom allows them to soar. For others, it merely gives them the chance to explore the gutter.

Big Dog, in part, suffers the slings and arrows that come with success. In his case, critics sharpen their weapons on the belief that the Dog really isn't very bright. To some, that makes his rise seem particularly galling, as if God were playing a mean joke on the smarter, less successful Internet players. Nichols attributes such resentment to simple jealousy.

Nichols sometimes does things that seem to reinforce critics'
notions that he isn't Mensa material. Take his e-mail messages in
April 1998 about FBN Associates, yet another little company that
proclaimed big hopes for cashing in on the Y2K computer problem. Big Dog initially weighed in with this message on the FBN
discussion board at Silicon Investor:

> "Some of you may know me. I have been around for a
> while and many on these threads might even say, I knew
> what was up in the market.
>
> In my opinion this company FBN Associates is a down
> right sure way to lose your money. Are they selling
> shares into the float at every uptic? Are they hyping
> imaginary products? Who knows, but I would not touch
> it."

For the cognoscenti, Big Dog evidently didn't feel the need to
explain that "float" refers to the number of shares in a company
that are free to trade publicly (as opposed to total shares outstanding, which includes restricted stock). "Uptic" isn't a command to
your pet insect, but the term used when a stock's price moves up
during the trading day.

The attention from a budding Internet celebrity brought a
prompt response from the sharp-eyed investor-relations person for
FBN.

> "We are pleased by your interest in our company. How
> may we help you? If you haven't visited our website
> yet, do drop by . . . Hope to be hearing from you again
> soon."

Big Dog obliged.

> "In my opinion, this company is in for a much bigger
> fall than is already in progress. I nor anyone that
> believes in my DD would touch it,"

he wrote.

The FBN rep tried again.

"Mr. Dog—Clearly our views of the prospects of FBN
Associates differ considerably. I can disclose nothing
new of a material nature at this time, but I may say
that the analysts who follow us are by no means disappointed in our performance, and continue to be enthusiastic about what they consider to be our remarkable
potential for growth. Have you read their reports?"

Big Dog wasn't impressed.

"It just stinks to me. That's all the DD I ever need,"

he wrote.

In the midst of this debate, who should show up at the FBN
site but TokyoMex, rambling, rolling on the floor and ready to
dump on a Dog.

"ROFLMAO ,, when is the DD due ?

Lest we might find some harsh words from our crtitics,, I
humbly request to our board ,, to consider,, firing the IR
guy and string him up side down for his flippant impetuos-
ity ,,of the past,, in the fashion of Mike Irving's
enthusiasm or Scott Lialio's lack of,, and indeed to
keep our FBN and the image of share holders not tarnished
in thise wild wild west of SI frontier . . . bury his
carcasses in the dog pound,, since no normal people will
go there,,, looking for past indulgences,,, and make
sure no future IR guy has palpitating lips ,,,

I also propose that we camouflage our active, internet
, year 2,000, shopping mall in China, internet ad
agency, etc etc and concentrate on our furniture business alone ,, we are down a bit today ,, but the share
holders will understand in this sentiment
. . . .

> Until ,, one day ,,all the world will see indeed how
> diversifeied we are and what great potential we can
> offer to share holders,, with such a small market cap
> and great EPS,, and PE.. also don't forget to mention
> about our current 240 million USD new contracts.. just
> signed last night with the Minictry of Defense, Iraq
>
> Humbly ..
>
> Joe Schmall"

Add another address to the Park Avenue of names.

As this debate rumbled on, one could almost hear the snickers swelling on the FBN discussion board. As one poster told Big Dog:

> "Big Dog stop. I'm laughing too hard. I can hardly
> type. You really have been around the block a lot.
> Surely you know what's up in the market. Please, stop.
> Please, don't embarrass your self any more."[2]

As it turned out, there was a fundamental flaw in Big Dog's position on FBN: the company was most definitely *not* a bad investment. That's because it wasn't any investment at all. Nobody had ever made or lost a penny on a share of FBN stock. No shares ever traded. None existed. Neither, for that matter, did the company, except as the figment of some very active imaginations.

FBN stands for Fly By Night. FBN was a hoax.

Nichols later tells me that he attacked FBN as a favor to an online friend and in retaliation for the bashing of a real stock by FBN backers. As for FBN, itself, "I never looked into it or researched it. I didn't care," says Nichols. When he discovered it was a hoax, "I thought it was pretty funny," he adds.

FBN was the latest example of a sort of backlash that has developed in the Internet stock-trading world against the increasing amounts of wild enthusiasm and hype found there. Pranks and hoaxes are becoming ways to poke fun at all the happy-talk stock chatter. Not surprisingly, April Fool's Day is a favorite launch date for such enterprises.

An early example, and still one of the funniest, unfolded on April 1, 1994. A Fool provided it, appropriately enough.

On that date, the Motley Fool's David Gardner began sending out e-mails under the name Joey Roman, touting a stock known as Zeigletics. Roman claimed to be an investor and newsletter publisher who possessed the most useful talent of picking stocks that

"never go down"

in price. Zeigletics was supposedly a skyrocketing stock on the Halifax Stock Exchange (which also doesn't exist). Zeigletics' business claim to fame was a virtual monopoly on the portable-toilet market in central Africa. The company's products, Roman wrote, are so good that they will eliminate risks of any future

"clogulation"

crises in that part of the world. Before Gardner revealed his hoax, his Zeigletics messages attracted hundreds of responses.

"How does one go about trading on the Halifax exchange if one's broker has never heard of it,"

asked a potential buyer.[3]

The FBN hoax came off on April 1, 1998. Its founders even started a Silicon Investor discussion board dedicated to the "company," which supposedly had a Year 2000 computer product that

"could make all the other y2k companies OBSOLETE!!!"

This initial message even quoted a headline from the "Blomberg" news wire (which presumably bears absolutely no relation, besides eight letters, to the real Bloomberg news service:

"FBN ANNOUNCES TOTAL CURE FOR BILLION DOLLAR MILLENNIUM BUG."

According to messages posted on the discussion board, FBN had a chief executive, a vice president for research and development, and an official photographer who doubled as the self-appointed "Officer in Charge of the FBN Vision." While no corporate pilot stepped forward, FBN did claim to have a corporate jet, a B-52 bomber. Jerry Seinfeld, a noteworthy from a realm as strange as cyberspace, was rumored to be a nominee to the FBN board of directors. There's no evidence that the comedian was ever even given the opportunity to laugh off the offer.

Probably the most interesting guy on the FBN team was a nonguy—TokyoMex's FBN missive notwithstanding. She was the firm's investor relations, or IR, representative, who communicated with Big Dog. She did added duty as managing director of FBN's investment banker, Skruem and Leevum—an outfit just as real as the company it served.

She posts Internet messages under the name Janice Shell. Her real name is . . . Janice Shell. In an Internet stock-trading world dominated by men wearing monikers like Halloween masks, Shell stands out as a most remarkable woman.

She became a leader of an informal group that dedicates itself to exposing what they view as stock frauds, while trying to have at least a few laughs in the process. Fans laud them as sort of citizen cyber-cops, who help to clean up a very dirty landscape. Detractors lambast them as cyber-terrorists, who are trying to enrich them- selves—and shadowy foreign stock-trading allies—by destroying the market values of legitimate companies.

Whichever side one takes in that debate, Shell and others like her represent an important force that is developing in the Internet stock-trading world. Outside of cyberspace, bulls and bears have been battling since practically the first share of stock changed hands. While the Internet has given power to all kinds of new players trying to move up stock prices, it has conferred a similar power on people looking to move them down. While Shell is an early celebrity on the naysayer circuit, other, even fiercer, players will follow her.

Shell is unusual in several respects. For one thing, she is a woman in what is largely a male online world. Plus, in an environ- ment where disputes over companies often last only a few days or a few hours, Shell gets into battles that start to be measured in years.

Shell's willingness to engage in such protracted conflicts is all the more notable because she says she makes absolutely no money from her efforts. That's because she neither buys nor shorts the stocks she goes after. Shell says she does what she does to help other investors—and maybe have some fun and raise a little hell. Of course, her online critics don't believe for a nanosecond her claims of economic disinterest, though they are unable to come up with any hard evidence to the contrary.

A measure of Shell's cyberspace stature can be seen in the cavalcade of Internet discussion boards started by others and dedicated to *her*.[4]

There is, for instance, the "Janice Shell For President" thread.

> "We all know her, we all love her . . . You never know
> we just might get her elected,"

wrote the enthusiast who started this discussion site. Another writer proposed even greater responsibilities for her.

> "I think the office of President of only one country
> just isn't enough of a honor for Madam Janice. She
> already controls the U.N. How about appointing her
> 'Lord High Protector of Morons and Idiots.'"

Another fan ran down some of her political positions, which include a willingness to question why boy dolls are called "action figures" and girl dolls are called "dolls." She has also come out foursquare against electricity.

Another Shell-inspired message board is the "Janice Shell Trust Fund," started by someone for the "worthy cause" of raising funds to help finance her continued work in the Internet stock-discussion world. The tenor of the fundraising seems summed up by one message, however, which observes that Shell is probably already "set for life" since she has so many shares of FBN Associates stock.

There is the "Janice Shell Legal Defense Trust Fund" thread. While clearly done at least partly in jest, it does speak to a real problem. Shell is becoming the target of lawsuits and lawsuit threats as a result of her online work. As for the defense fund's rationale, well,

> "Clinton's got one, so should Janice,"

wrote the person who started the discussion site. He immediately offered to contribute $500. Another person offered $15 and a Japanese TV set to "throw in the kitty." Yet another poster offered to "throw in my kitty." Several have volunteered to pass along worthless shares of fraudulent companies that Shell has helped unmask—or, in one case, helped create. One budding online internationalist declined to give anything on the grounds that Shell has "wrecked the Brazilian economy" and cost him "hundreds" of dollars. The person doesn't elaborate.

Shell's literary talents were celebrated with the creation of the "Janice Should Write a Book" message board. Most of the messages here were suggestions for book titles. Among the offerings: *"River of Sleaze," "Janice in Wunderlichland," "Breakfast of Chumps," "Raging Bull Rhapsody," "Elk Hunting on Wall Street," "Catcher in the Lie," "Janice Shrugged,"* and *"Even Coolgirls Give the Woo-hoos."*

Yet another message board exists to recognize the fact that Shell has *already* written enough messages just on Silicon Investor to fill a book or two. The thread began in July 1998 as a celebration of Shell's upcoming fifteen thousandth message. When she blew past that landmark, the board modified its title to mark message number 20,000. One person called her the

```
"intrepid exposer of fraud and deceit."
```

A cynic, contemplating the time it must have taken Shell to write all those thousands of notes, wondered whether another fund should be started to

```
"buy her a life."
```

A budding poet labeled her the "Goddess of Postdom" with the added wish,

```
"Oh, to be as verbose as thou."
```

One poster actually fell back on poetry, which he credited to Rod McKuen, including this excerpt (which is about all I dare inflict):

> "You are not like anything
>
> except perhaps yourself. Even then
>
> You are never quite like You."

Weeks before the millennium ended, Shell effortlessly clicked past 25,000 messages. And that was just on Silicon Investor. She had thousands more messages on other discussion boards.

She became one of the most prolific posters on Silicon Investor, with roughly twice as many messages as TokyoMex and Big Dog combined. By that time, she had also been sued by one Bulletin Board company for libel and threatened with litigation by another. A major financial press-release service hauled her into court after she helped give it a case of acute public embarrassment.

Besides subpoenas, Shell has a stack of anonymous death threats. She was an early contributor to

> "The Death Threat Thread"

that was started on Silicon Investor in June 1998. The message board's creator asked submission of any death threats received and added that there was also room for

> "estate planning tips, possible sources of volume dis-
> count funeral arrangements, and just general small
> talk to while away the hours until you are gone."

For those who hadn't yet received a death threat,

> "you can stop by for tips on the threads and stocks
> most likely to earn you one of your very own,"

this writer added.

Shell doesn't appear to be in any need of any coaching on the threat-receiving front. She passes along one e-mail message from a "Jame Lee" warning her to

> "Please keep away from my stocks . . . you will be kill
> very sonn . . . someone will found your body at street
> very soon."

Another poster wrote Shell that this person's moniker probably had been lifted from the book and movie *Silence of the Lambs,* in which a transsexual murderer by the name of Jame Lee Gumb was killing women and making a "suit" out of their skins.

Other threats to Shell are less creepy, though more profane:

> ". . . don't even f-ck around, get the f-ck off this board you useless hag, don't you have enough legal problems already, YOU HAVE NO IDEA WHAT YOU ARE MESS-ING WITH HERE . . . STAY AWAY!!! PERIOD, don't make me come find you and act like a neanderthal, janice, when you turn out the lights tonight or tomarrow, BETTER CHECK THE LOCKS TWICE!!!!"

Some of the messages to Shell are not so much threatening as merely sick:

> "It is amazing how the people on the thread continue to respond to you and your cohorts when it is painfully obvious that you sub-human squirts of piss are paid to misinform for your own gain
> . . . . the disgust I feel from watching your performance over the past few weeks has forced me to say a silent prayer each night that you develope a malignant brain tumor and go bye-bye . . . . P.S. If the day ever comes when you are lying in a coma, I would be only too honored to pull the plug and spit upon your wretched bones."

The target of this outpouring of praise and abuse is a middle-aged art historian living alone in an airy fifth floor apartment in Milan, Italy—unless you believe her critics who have placed her in various other locales. Most of her electronic messages come out of a computer that one friend compares to a "clunky old boat anchor." Actually, Shell says, that description might be a little too kind.

The laptop computer is a hand-me-down from a friend. The device didn't arrive to her in great shape, Shell assures me. When she took it into a local Milan computer shop, the repairman asked her, perhaps innocently, if it had ever been owned by a war correspondent. She assures me the device has only gotten more battle-scarred, or at least Shell-shocked, as she describes in an e-mail:

> "By now the case is cracked all over the place; the screen's only hanging on by a thread. I have to prop it up with a pillow. It's also very very dim at the top now. And the floppy drive's totally fried. I only discovered that the other day. It has almost no available memory . . . It also makes a really annoying whining sound. And did I tell you that the AC adaptor broke two years ago? Wow. One day I turned the thing on and it started making noises like a couple of pounds of corn popping. Wild. End of adaptor . . . Anyway. It really sucks. But I don't want to be too unkind, or it may break down entirely. I'm expecting that."

(In late 1999 her old laptop died in a shower of sparks and a cloud of smoke. She replaced it with an iMAC, she says.)

Her Internet writing accomplishments, creaky computer and all, have an ironic touch given the vow that Shell made when she began her Internet voyage in 1996. Whatever else, she told herself, she was not going to become one of those cyberspace message posters. That promise survived for about twenty-four hours.

AFTER WRITING MORE THAN 25,000 messages, Shell can't remember her first one. But a fan of hers dug up this candidate, which was written only two days after she joined Silicon Investor on June 3, 1996. Like so many messages of that period, this one dealt with Iomega:

> "In my opinion the 6/3 press release was smoke and
> mirrors, obfuscation worthy of Alan Greenspan. One of
> their production managers doesn't really know what's
> going on in his sector? And did he say "Zip drives" or
> "drives" in general? Let's not forget the Jaz and the
> Ditto. My understanding is that there's great demand
> for the Jaz, and that it's still very hard to get.
> What about the "new" 200 MB Zip? Is that a "Zip" in
> the terms of the press release or not? And let's not
> forget the disks, either. Someone in an earlier post-
> ing said that he/she asked a saleswoman at a MacWare-
> house how many Zip disks they'd sold that day, and was
> told: more than 2000. Think about it. As for produc-
> tion limitations, I don't have a clue—but what was it

someone said some time ago (a couple of weeks!) about
a possible deal with CRUS to manufacture chips? True?
Hey! I'm long IOMG and hoping for the best."

The note is typical of millions of messages put on discussion sites by eager online investors. It's the kind of note that contains just enough jargon to give the writer the patina of being in the know—whether true or not. It has a touch of skepticism and a touch of the fan mail. Like much of the stock chatter online, it's about as exciting as a date with a Zip drive.

Other early Shell posts are in the same cheerleading vein:

"I'm long XICO, long IOMG—neither has any earnings
problems this quarter . . . Hey! Check out XATA."

Even when she voices concerns, she tries to put them in a positive light. Take the case of Tasty Fries, Inc., a little outfit from Blue Bell, Pennsylvania, that hopes to make its fame and fortune with a vending machine that cooks and serves french fries on demand.

"Well, let's try to be of Good Cheer. 'Tis the Season
and all. I agree that reverse splits are usually bum-
mers, but they've recently worked very well for several of the Y2K companies,"

she wrote.

A reverse stock split is, as its name implies, the opposite of the more common "forward" stock split. In a forward split, a company increases the number of shares. In a two-for-one split, for example, a shareholder who owns 100 shares before the split owns 200 afterwards.

A reverse split shrinks the number of shares outstanding. In a one-for-two reverse split, the shareholder with 100 shares ends up with 50.

Reverse splits can be a perfectly legitimate way for a company to try to raise its share price and its profile. Other things being equal, the existence of fewer shares outstanding usually translates into a higher price per share. A higher stock price has advantages.

For one thing, a stock that is $5 a share often seems more substantial and attractive to investors than the same stock at $1 a share.

However, reverse splits have also long been used by some as a way to manipulate share prices and cheat investors. The same legitimacy a higher stock price gives to a real firm, it confers on a bogus one. A higher share price also helps promoters avoid the federal "penny stock" marketing rules put into place after the stock-selling escapades of the 1980s.

Among the potential abuses of reverse splits: the company shrinks the number of shares in the hands of existing stockholders and then issues large amounts of new stock to cronies. In this way, the promoter and his allies can gain a huge ownership chunk of the company, while the other shareholders see their piece of the pie shrink to something on the order of a crumb. As the 1990s unfolded and more individual investors came to the market, the abuse of reverse splits became a growing concern to law enforcement officials.

For Shell, the more she chewed on the Tasty Fries' reverse split—which the company said was needed to help move the business forward—the less she liked the taste.

"MY GOD, a 1-for-20 goes more than a bit far!"

she wrote in one e-mail. In another, she added,

"OH GOD—20-for-1??? Disaster. Stupid. Reverse splits this dramatic never work."[1]

She might have taken solace from the fact that a 1-for-20 reverse split was hardly the biggest one ever done. Another little company did what amounted to a 1-for-20,000 reverse split. This firm then issued millions of new shares to a person who took control of the firm. One longtime shareholder, who saw his holdings drop from one million shares to fifty, says he felt like he had been sucked into some "weird sitcom from Hollywood."[2]

As Shell became more immersed in the worlds of the Internet message boards and Bulletin Board stocks, she began to exhibit traits that set her apart from the average drone of a message poster.

For one thing, she seemed at heart to be more of a cynic than a booster. Plus, she had a wicked, sometimes strange sense of humor.

Like the rest of her, Shell's funny bone has been shaped by a life that has taken her from Missouri to Milan. Born in Kansas City on March 31, 1948, she spent her childhood in and around Philadelphia and Crown Point, Indiana. Shell received her bachelor's degree from Wellesley College in 1970, only a year behind Hillary Clinton. The two haven't met—though it's often tough to be certain who is on the other end of online.

Like Hillary, Shell says she thought about being a lawyer, but unlike Mrs. Clinton, she skipped the law school admission test to spend a weekend with a boyfriend in New York. She also thought of journalism school, but ended up getting a doctorate in art history from New York University. She says she married her college advisor, who died about a year after their marriage.

Like many art historians, Shell focused on the Italian Renaissance, which led her to Italy to research her dissertation on a long-dead painter from Milan. Most people would fly from New York to Milan. Some would take an ocean liner. Shell hopped a freighter.

> "Hey, you saw all the ?30s movies I did. Ships Are
> Romance,"

she wrote me in an e-mail (among her computer's idiosyncrasies is an apparent favoritism for the question mark over the apostrophe.)

Her freighter trip sounds memorable, and if this largely stream-of-consciousness e-mail is any evidence, she has no plans to take second place to TokyoMex as a yarn spinner:

> "Grant money (not very much, naturally) in the bank, I
> went looking for transatlantic possibilities . . . . . .
> Nothing out there except for the Polish line (ugh, and
> it wouldn?t take me anywhere near Italy) and Yugolin-
> ija, the (obviously) Yugoslave line. So I opted for the
> latter. I have to say it was an incredible deal: I
> signed on for the trip from Philadelphia (weirdly, the
> port of embarkment) to Savona: total cost, board and

room, all the baggage I wanted to take along, $600
. . . . . . It was?sort of fun. Well, it really was, if
observing the follies of one?s fellow humans is your
kinda entertainment. I wouldn?t recommend it for honey-
mooners. There were 50 passengers in all, most of them
retired people. Chief sports were drinking (oh wow, so
incredibly cheap!) and bridge: gotta say most were
extremely good at it, right up till they passed out.

When I plunked down my Big Bux for this I did ask how
long the trip would take. The people I was dealing
with didn?t really have an answer, but I figured on
maybe two weeks; as you know, freighters take longer.
As things turned out, we spent all of two weeks coasting, from Philly to Fernandina Beach (note: I *think*
that?s right, but am not absolutely sure) Florida. FB
was distinguished by the penetrating sulphur fumes
generated by its only industry: paper. Even so, they
were bravely trying to recruit tourists. They had this
awfully weird muzak system embedded in the sidewalks.
And as you?ll imagine, the smell was beyond belief. We
had to go Into Town, though, because it was Halloween,
and so we needed dye and the like to turn our bed-
sheets into costumes. Shit, I?ve still got photos. We
did an excellent job. Our last night coasting, give us
credit: we entirely exhausted the supplies of booze
that had been declared. The captain contributed a Personal Case of Scotch, so it was okay, even though our
nice Canadian tablemate partook far too much of the
Cruise Cocktai

[author's note: a concoction that includes gin and apricot brandy]

. . . . . . and spent a lotta time throwing up. Merci-
fully, he didn?t remember a thing in the morning,
though he did wonder why all the gold paint on his
body itched so horribly? . . .

Heaven on earth, in a way, except for one?s companions. Within about five days everyone hated everyone
else; kindergarten all over again. I used to amuse
myself by going up on deck outside the bar, and?.wait-
ing. Within five minutes someone was sure to turn up to
complain about someone else. I know: it sounds
absolutely awful, but actually it was fun. I?d taken
along about 50 mystery novels, and never read a damned
thing. But then I?ve got a weird sense of humor.

Somewhere along the way I struck up a friendship with
the captain. I shall not be so indelicate as to
enlarger upon the nature of our relationship. Marko
was, however, a very nice guy, and we had fun.
. . . . . . We were berthed for five days in Split because
of bad weather. . . . . . . It was in Split that I had my
first exciting experience of Smuggling. Marko . . . had
a brother-in-law who was a colonel in the Yugoslav
army. Marko was smuggling stuff for him and for himself. . . . Bro-in-law and I got on like a house afire
(he later sent me a case of home-brewed absolutely
awful white wine), and we all went giggling offshore,
Bro wearing jeans, his Colonel?s jacket unbuttoned,
and his official cap, staggering under the weight of
bulging suitcases full of contraband. And then, naturally to lunch . . . . . .

After five days in Split we proceeded to Rijecka (the
former Italian Fiume); end of the journey. Forty-six
days in all; oh WOW did I get my money?s worth, in
every sense of the word.

At Riejeka I had to debark officially, get my nine
pieces of luggage through customs and then take a
train to Milan the next day. . . . . . . Unfortunately
for us, it was a Saturday afternoon, and the official
in question was a substitute: basic bureaucratic

loser, puffed out in his uniform, his head visibly
bursting his red star hat. He insisted that I open
everything. All nine pieces of luggage. The trunks
were full of photos?of ART, you know?and scholarly
journals. Little Napoleon started going on about Reli-
gious Propaganda. Back then, that was a big deal in
Yugo. . . . . . This went on for a really long time. I
just sat there and tried to look helpful. The only
thing Little N never attempted to examine was my large
shoulder bag, which I?m afraid contained quantites of
cameras and car radios that Marko?d asked me to bring
into the country for him.

After about an hour and a half of this nonsense, Marko
began to wonder why I hadn?t met him at the pre-
arranged place behind Container 320, and pitched up at
the customs shed. He made a very nice scene and got
everything sorted out in about half an hour. And then
of course I gave him the contraband and we went out to
dinner . . . . . . "[3]

After the boat ride, Shell says she settled into Milan and stayed
settled, even after she finished her dissertation. She couldn't find a
decent-paying art history job in the U.S. She couldn't really find one
in Italy either, but it's pleasanter being poor in Milan than, say, Mil-
waukee. Shell came back to the U.S. from from time to time, to
mixed greetings. She tells of the time when Pennsylvania state
motor vehicle officials decided that she was dead and briefly investigated her for impersonating herself. But that's a whole other story.

In Italy, she supplemented her income with stock investing.
In her pre-Internet '90s she was heavily invested in high-tech
issues. "If I'd done the right things, I'd be a millionaire," she says,
keenly aware that she is hardly the first person to make that statement. Needless to say, she didn't do the right things and was
largely wiped out.

By her own recounting, Shell did some of the riskier things an
investor can try. She bought stocks on margin, which means she

borrowed part of the purchase funds. Under federal stock-trading rules, an investor can borrow up to 50 percent of the price of a stock. While this leverage allows you to buy more shares and can multiply your profits when the price goes up, it can help bury you when the price falls.

She bought stock options. An option is the right to buy or sell a stock at a given price within a given period of time. One can buy an option on a stock for a lot less than the actual stock. However, if the price of the stock doesn't reach the option price, the option expires along with the money you used to buy it. Shell collected a cemetery full of expired options.

Shell made the mistake of finding a broker she liked and trusted too much. He was bright, she says, but had the "attention span of a fruit fly" and stopped paying enough attention to her portfolio. But she learned a valuable lesson, she adds: "Brokers don't necessarily know what they are doing." This is a lament that many investors would carry to the online world. The broker does, however, bequeath her the boat anchor of a computer.

When Shell began poking around the Internet stock-chat world in 1996, she found Silicon Investor. She found the "Feelings" thread.

The full name is "Let's Talk About Our Feelings!!!" The woman who started this message board laid out her aim in her opening message. It was to be a place where Silicon Investor members could

> "unwind and discuss whatever . . . . . . When you are feeling vulnerable or sad, or you've been up for two days and are having trouble holding it all together, drop by and consider this a safe place to let it all hang out, and rest assured no one will flame you—that some kind and compassionate soul will understand and commiserate, or at least listen without laughing out loud. Feel free to reveal the gentle, vulnerable parts of yourselveks here . . . "[4]

The Feelings thread represents another face of the stock-discussion world. It's the cyberspace equivalent of the after-work bar, a place to unwind from the pressures of the day. Of course, if you want to get sloshed on the Net, you have to bring your own booze and try not to spill it on the keyboard.

Officials at Silicon Investor are quite open to members setting up discussion threads that have nothing to do with stocks. They seem to realize that even hardcore Internet traders sometimes want to talk about something other than Internet trading.

Some of the Internet stock gurus also know the value of being able to talk about more than megabytes and EBITDA. TokyoMex is a master at this, though not all of his Societe Anonyme members appreciate his e-mail trips down the Nile. He occasionally even posts a criticism from one of them—often with his own tart response.

```
"Another schmuck ,, SA is not just stocks,, xxx
head,, "
```

wrote Park as his reply to one such e-mail.

When John F. Kennedy Jr.'s plane crashed in July 1999, four message boards dedicated to the tragedy popped up on Silicon Investor. There was one for the conspiracy buffs called "JFK, Jr., Is this an assasination?" Another seemed aimed at those who prefer speculating on the supernatural: JFK, Jr. Missing—Is there really a family curse?" Conspiracy attracted over 500 messages while the occult only pulled in about 70.

The Feelings thread, in the three years after its July 28, 1996, creation, attracted more than 60,000 messages. That number doesn't match the monster SI stock message boards, such as the Dell Computer board with over 140,000 messages. Still, 60K isn't bad for an avowedly touchie-feelie place in a world dedicated to the hard jingle of profit seeking. For what it's worth, the Feelings thread draws about twice as many messages as the "Ask God" thread on Silicon Investor.

Shell was an early and enthusiastic Feelings participant. She informed readers that her favorite German "tekno" rock group is Mayday, whose signature song is "Mayday," which is also the only word in the lyrics.

"WAAAAYYY COOOOOLLL,"

Shell wrote. She complained that getting into Milan's La Scala opera house has gotten much tougher in recent years since authorities cracked down on ushers taking bribes.

". . . now you have to offer 'em *REALLY* a lot."

And she bragged about "perfect Eric," her cleaning man from Sri Lanka.

"I do have to hide my pantyhose after they're washed, or he'll iron them, but that's his only fault,"

she wrote.

On the theological front, she admitted to a dalliance with animism.

"My God was a large plant I happen to own (much better to own your God) called the Great Phil. Found it largely disappointing in the end; he wasn't really very responsive, and began producing a hell of a lot of yellow leaves. But a religion built on worship of mince?"

The question of mince led Shell to food, one of her favorite topics and the grist for dozens of messages. Self-described as

"Milano's answer to Julia Child,"

Shell posted a steady diet of completely inedible, but frequently hilarious recipes. She tells me that the meat and potatoes of the recipes were mostly lifted, either from the writings of the ancient Roman Apicius or the 1992 book *Unmentionable Cuisine* by Calvin W. Schwabe.

Suggestions *a la* Shell included: raw marinated jellyfish; dried locusts and milk (don't forget to grind the locusts into a powder in the blender); red ant chutney; roasted palmworms with orange juice (palmworms, she informed the uniformed, are the grub of *Rhynchophorus palmarum*); earthworms, which taste like shredded wheat and are particularly good in oatmeal cookies; grilled rat, Bordeaux style (Bordeaux was apparently chosen because of the recipe's need for;

> *"alcoholic rats inhabiting wine cellars"*)

and, for those without wine cellars, mice in cream.

Naturally, after a time, such online chewing chatter turned to the matter of cannibalism. Here, Shell admitted to being a bit stumped.

> "Trouble with cannabalism is that even the best lit on
> the subject doesn't offer much in the way of actual
> recipes. Favorite cuts, yes, age and sex preferences,
> yes, but no real instruction. Except for what I've
> already noted about the origins of the barbecue, and
> the suggestion that the Aztecs liked theirs with toma-
> toes and hot peppers. But then they liked *everything*
> with tomatoes and hot peppers."

She added, perhaps with a glance forward at the Internet bulls she would roast,

> "As do I."

She did offer a recipe for "obnoxious neighbors": cook the neighbor very slowly over a wood fire, adding a spicy sauce for flavor. And speaking of man-sized appetites, there was Taniwha, to whom Shell fed

> "a healthy diet of plump succulent bond merchant."

Shell seemed to view such sacrifices as a plus for the credit markets. Taniwha, Shell later explained to me in an e-mail, is a dragon from New Zealand who visits Silicon Investor. However, Shell added proudly, Taniwha

> "got his bond merchant habit from me."

> "Your sick,"

observed another Feelings poster.

> "However, I like that."

Others also have liked what they were reading. Indeed, as Shell meandered around cyberspace she began connecting with like-minded people. They share a sense of humor and a sense of outrage about some of the things happening in the stock market generally and in the raucous market for small-company stocks in particular. Together, Shell and her friends would become cyberspace's equivalent of merry pranksters, pulling off online jokes and tormenting companies that they believe deserve it.

One of Shell's online cohorts is Jeffrey Mitchell, a computer software writer from Westport, Connecticut. Like Shell, he travels online under his real name.

The two met online and were soon communicating daily, often many times in a day. They have never met in person, and have talked only once on the phone. After Mitchell saw the cost of a phone call from Westport to Milan, he decided that e-mail was really a wonderful way to stay in touch. Shell says that, living on an art historian's income, free communications is about what she can afford. (In keeping with the spirit of cyberspace communications— and my book project's limited travel budget—Shell and I also haven't met. However, phone calls increasingly supplement e-mails between us ever since a helpful MCI representative told me about a calling plan to Italy that costs about 20 cents a minute instead of $1.60.)

Mitchell started exploring the Internet stock-discussion world in 1996. In November of that year, he joined Silicon Investor. Mitchell signed up under his real name because, as he puts it, "I was totally naïve." It's a naivete that the father of two young children would later sometimes regret.

To Mitchell, Silicon Investor initially seemed like "the Wild, Wild West." Mitchell and others believe that some individuals have multiple memberships and multiple pseudonyms. One person posting messages under a dozen different monikers can create the aura of enthusiasm for a given stock all by himself.

Mitchell quickly encountered some of the early gurus of the Internet discussion world, ones before TokyoMex or Big Dog. He came to believe that some were frauds. Indeed, he came to believe that there was lots of fraud and manipulation occurring in the Internet stock-trading world. And he was entranced by it.

Mitchell began to wonder what it would be like to have an alias and hype a stock with false information and then sell it for a huge profit. He knew that there were lots of good reasons—moral and legal—to keep him from *really* doing it. But he could pretend. "I was really fascinated by playing a scam artist," he says.

So on April Fool's Day 1997, Mitchell created his first fake company. He called it TechniClone Inc. and started a Silicon Investor discussion thread for it. Mitchell wrote that TechniClone had been granted a patent on the first "neural network" computer chip that uses "blastamere separation." He labeled the company "the next Intel."

Despite the lofty rhetoric, TechniClone was a modest prank. For one thing, Mitchell posted messages on other SI threads early on April Fool's morning revealing his joke and inviting others to take part. Plus, it turned out that the name he picked for his creation actually belonged to a real company—though Mitchell at least managed to pick a different stock symbol for his fictitious entity. This gaffe prompted one poster to create a fake press release about how the real TechniClone was suing Mitchell—an example of where art in the not-too-distant future would be imitated by life.

Even with its limitations, the TechniClone hoax attracted over 200 e-mail messages on the first day and dozens more over the next few days. Among those lending a hand to pump the nonexistent stock was Shell. In the spirit of the prank, Shell abandoned all inclinations toward cynicism and urged everyone to ignore the "evil machinations" of naysayers and

"BUY BUY BUY ! ! ! ! ! "

From working together on an absurdly fake stock, it didn't seem like such a large leap for Shell and Mitchell to start working together on stocks that they viewed as simply absurd. One was a Big Dog favorite, Houston-based Cryogenic Solutions, also known by its trading symbol of CYGS.

In the jaundiced eyes of Shell and Mitchell, the company was a tempting target. According to a 1996 *Wall Street Journal* article,

Howard Turney, who helped start Cryogenic Solutions and served for a time as its chairman, did his interview for the story wearing nothing but a red Speedo bathing suit. He reportedly wanted to demonstrate the effect on his sixty-four-year-old body of an anti-aging medicine being offered by another of his ventures, the El Dorado Rejuvenation & Longevity Institute.

An initial Cryogenic Solutions business was to preserve aborted fetuses for up to several decades by deep-freezing them. The idea was that the fetuses could be later reimplanted in the womb. The *Journal* quoted Turney as saying that the company already had one "baby in the can."

However, Cryogenic Solutions later acknowledged in a press release that the world wasn't quite ready yet for its "pregnancy suspension technology." So, the firm moved into the business of manipulating DNA to fight aging and treat cancer, among other things.

This new endeavor had one capitalistic twist that caught Shell's eye. In a press release announcing a licensing deal for its technology with a Costa Rican clinic, Cryogenic Solutions said the clinic had agreed to give "preferential access" for anyone owning 5,000 or more shares of the company's stock.

This sort of shares-for-treatment program was

```
"truly shocking. Should be all anybody needs to know
about the company and the people who run it,"
```

wrote Shell in a Silicon Investor e-mail.[5]

Dell Gibson, Cryogenic Solutions' executive vice president, defended the Costa Rican clinic stock arrangement. "Some people may say that it isn't gloriously altruistic. But we have an obligation to try to increase share value," and the preferential access offer is potentially "a way to make people buy more stock," said Gibson in a November 1999 interview. However, he added, the plan hasn't been put into practice because the company is still in its research and development phase and doesn't yet have any marketable products. Gibson added that the company has, unfairly, been a "favorite target of the bashers," with Shell as the "leader of the pack."

Big Dog's enthusiasm for Cryogenic Solutions helped solidify Shell's low opinion of the Internet guru. Shell took digs at Big Dog online. When he wrote of spending $3,000 to fly to Miami to meet with Cryogenic Solutions' president to discuss the company, Shell and another poster speculated on how he spent the money.

"My guess is he got ripped off by the Escort Service,"

wrote Shell.

Big Dog didn't think that crack was funny.

"I consider your post libelous. . . . . I am a married man and you have insulted my wife. You have crossed the line and your all mine now,"

he barked back. As for the $3,000 tab, he added,

"I don't know about you, but I only fly first class and stay at 5 star hotels. Don't forget about the limo service to and from the airports."

Once the online battle was joined, Big Dog took a few shots at Shell. On a day when Cryogenic Solutions' stock rose despite Shell's criticisms of the company, he told her to

"keep it coming baby. You are doing wonders for our price. Just look at what you have done here today. I think I'm in love."

It was Shell's turn to be unamused.

"Hype and scam really do WORK. In the short term. But hey! Go ahead! Give specious hope to cancer victims. Anything to make a buck, right?"

she wrote.[6]

Cryogenic Solutions served as a warm-up for bigger online battles, which would take Shell from the Amazon rain forest to the Las Vegas strip and down the dark pathways of one mind that tried to give her a case of cancer online.

On the CYGS message board, Shell and her compatriots jousted with others, as well. One went by the online moniker Cavalry. In real life, he is Jesse Cohen, who ran a New York sign-making business before moving to Southern California to enjoy the Pacific surf and to surf the Internet. Cavalry and Big Dog became online allies and later business partners in cyberspace.

On the Cryogenic Solutions message board, Cavalry praised Big Dog, criticized Shell, and dreamed of possible new uses for the company's technology.

> "After cygs helps rid the world of disease, they will
> develop a way to erase all the dna of bashers, they will
> turn into what they really are nothing but hot air,"

he wrote.

"Bashers" is a label that adversaries would increasingly try to stick on Shell, Mitchell, and others like them. It's a term that fans of a company use to describe people who criticize the firm. One CYGS fan even posted a

> "***BASHERS ALERT***"

to warn of the arrival of Shell and others. Another SI member referred to Shell as the "ringleader."

As time went on, the posts on various message boards increasingly reflected a belief that there was some dark cabal going on to knock down the price of small-company stocks. Shell was viewed as being part of this network that by some versions originated with anonymous but "evil" short sellers out of Canada. Cavalry wrote that the short sellers even had a song: "HOORAY FOR CANADA."

Shell's critics refuse to believe that anyone would spend as much time as Shell does at a pursuit that brings her no financial return.

> "ARE THEY BEING PAID TO INVADE THREADS?"

asked one message-board critic about Shell and some of her online colleagues. Spending so much time attacking stocks "fits the profile" of someone paid to do it, wrote this poster.[7]

Shell says speculation about foreign cabals don't concern her because she doesn't trade in the stocks that she criticizes. Any speculation to the contrary, she says, is "nonsense." As for the time she spends online, Shell says critics should realize that before migrating to the Internet she'd spend several hours a day playing solitaire on her computer.

Also, the debate about amateur sleuths such as Shell begs a larger question. If the Internet is the new Wild West, where are the real lawmen?

LIKE SHELL, ATTORNEY John Reed Stark has vowed to help clean up the cyberspace stock-trading world. However, he surveys the Internet from a rather more imposing perch. Stark sits in Washington, D.C., at the headquarters of the U.S. Securities and Exchange Commission.[1]

And in the online world, Stark is much more than just another smart, hard-charging SEC attorney. When the agency created its first office of Internet enforcement, the thirty-four-year-old Stark was named to head it.

While this promotion was no doubt a cause for pride among Stark's family and friends, there are a couple of aspects to his ascension that might give investors pause. First, Stark's new office wasn't created until July 1998, several years after alarm bells began ringing in the press and elsewhere about a rising tide of stock fraud on the Internet. Second, the SEC's new office of Internet enforcement has a full-time staff of two, Stark and an assistant.

And for Stark, getting that far was the culmination of a four-year campaign to raise the visibility of the Internet-enforcement cause at the top levels of the SEC.

Stark joined the commission in 1991 on something of a reverse commute. After graduating from Duke law school, he spent a couple of years at a private law firm. But he concluded that the firm world of currying and representing well-heeled clients wasn't for him. He decided what he really wanted to be was a government lawyer, a prosecutor. Stark is out of the ordinary in this sense. Over the years, a more familiar script has seen smart and ambitious law school graduates go to work for a few years at the SEC before moving on to the higher-paying world of private securities law, often on Wall Street.

Stark went to work in the enforcement division, the arm of the SEC that is charged with combating fraud and manipulation in the nation's securities markets. For three years, he worked on cases, but thirsted for more action. The enforcement division isn't renowned for speed and sometimes takes years to put together a case. In some instances, no case is ever brought after all the work.

In 1994, Stark wangled a temporary transfer over to the U.S. Attorney's office for the District of Columbia. Since the district is a federal entity, federal prosecutors handle the kind of street crimes that normally would fall to the local district attorney's office. Stark got to handle a stream of violent crime and drug cases. It's the daily stuff of big-city life, but they were the kinds of cases he never saw in the cloistered halls of securities law. In his several months at the federal prosecutor's office, Stark was involved in some twenty trials, more than the average private or SEC attorney would see in years. "I was in front of a judge every day," he recalls. Stark wanted courtroom experience and he got it.

So when the attorney returned to the SEC in the fall of 1994, he was reluctant to just fall back into the slower-moving routine of enforcement division cases. He was looking for something different, something calling for a little more adrenaline. "I wanted to do big cases," says Stark.

He discovered a big new place, the Internet.

Stark stumbled into his new calling in the same way as millions of other Americans. He bought a personal computer and began exploring the online world. The SEC lawyer quickly saw that when it came to investment opportunities, lots of wild and crazy things were already happening in cyberspace. The same glittering—and suspect—promotions that were drawing investors to the Internet drew a cop looking to nab the promoters.

For Stark, the first challenge was to convince his superiors to extend the SEC's reach into the online fraud world. If the past was any guide, he wouldn't have an easy road.

Things don't exactly speed along when it comes to policing the securities markets. It took Congress nearly 150 years to create the SEC as the first federal agency responsible for regulating stock trading. During those decades, the nation's legislators managed to ignore the blatant frauds, monstrous manipulations, and disastrous crashes that periodically hit the markets.

Not surprisingly, the very powerful men who run the nation's financial markets have applauded this hands-off policy. Richard Whitney, a prominent Wall Street broker and president of the New York Stock Exchange during the early 1930s, even went so far as to describe the NYSE as a "perfect institution," according to Sobel's stock-market history. (Perfect for whom is another question. In 1937, Whitney provided at least one pimple on that flawless face when he was convicted of larceny for stealing money to cover his stock-trading losses. He went from the Big Board to the Big House.)

Finally, the Crash of '29 and the subsequent Great Depression stirred the federal government to act. Investigators sorting through the rubble of the 1929 debacle found evidence of widespread manipulation and corruption in the markets during the prior decade. For instance, major brokerage firms, in an apparent effort to curry favor, gave prominent citizens the opportunity to buy low-priced stock that could be quickly sold at a profit. According to a 1986 *New York Law Journal* article on the subject, recipients of such favors included former president Calvin Coolidge, World War I hero General John Pershing, aviator Charles Lindbergh, a member of the Supreme Court, and a Treasury secretary.[2]

Even with all this, the SEC wasn't created until 1934—five years after the bottom fell out of the market and much of the country. If the race truly does go to the tortoise, Uncle Sam has the potential to be a Triple Crown champ on the securities circuit.

And from the beginning of the SEC, the government seemed of two minds about regulating the markets. While officials clearly saw a need to rein in the excesses, there seemed to be a fear of doing it excessively. As a result, the exchanges, and later Nasdaq, were given a large measure of autonomy to police themselves with oversight from the SEC. Thus, still today, a client's complaints about a broker's conduct go to the exchange's self-regulatory arm for action. So do many disciplinary actions against brokers and firms. In some instances, the SEC acts as a sort of appeals board to review decisions by the self-regulatory bodies.

Though the SEC has direct responsibility to root out stock fraud, it doesn't have the power to criminally prosecute swindlers. The SEC only has the authority to file civil cases against alleged wrongdoers. Federal criminal actions remain the sole purview of the U.S. Justice Dept. And as the decades roll on, it becomes clear that federal prosecutors often don't put stock fraud at the top of their crime-fighting to-do list.

In the mid-1990s, as Stark began getting excited about policing the Internet, the SEC's to-do list often seemed much larger than its resources or powers. The SEC is responsible for overseeing the activities of thousands of public companies and stock brokerage firms as well as tens of thousands of brokers and other financial professionals. The issues facing the agency range from the proper way for a company to report earnings to such basic definitional questions as when is an investment a security and when isn't it.

To further complicate matters, with Republican control of the Congress, the SEC has run into lots of resistance to requests for budget increases. Amidst the greatest surge in stock trading—and stock fraud—in history, the agency found itself fighting at times to keep its budget from being cut. In 1998 congressional testimony, SEC chairman Arthur Levitt said that between 1980 and 1994 the number of authorized positions at the agency had increased by 35 percent but had been flat since then. "Additional resources are urgently needed," Levitt said.[3]

The SEC also found itself fighting a frustrating and often losing battle with its most persistent foe: the career swindler. While an

SEC suit might scare the pants off the average investor, broker, or corporate executive, it hardly causes a crease in the trousers of a professional fraudster. If nabbed, he simply accepts the SEC's injunction, hangs it on the wall with its cousins, and keeps on stealing.

Perhaps no story better exemplifies the limits of the SEC's powers to curb stock fraud than the tale of Ramon D'Onofrio. D'Onofrio has built a storied swindling career that spans four decades. He has stolen tens of millions of dollars from the public. The SEC has "permanently" enjoined D'Onofrio from future violations of securities laws—half a dozen times. He has also been criminally convicted a like number of times. A federal appeals court once referred to D'Onofrio as "ubiquitously criminal," and that was relatively early in his career.

Yet, this master swindler has spent only about one year behind bars. The recipient of a heart transplant, D'Onofrio has probably seen more time inside of a hospital than a prison.

What's the secret behind D'Onofrio's ability to do the crime but not the time? He refuses to discuss that question or any other. As one of D'Onofrio's attorneys Ira Sorkin, former head of the SEC's New York office, once told me, some of his clients talk to the press and some don't. Ray D'Onofrio is a definite don't.

But there isn't anything too esoteric about D'Onofrio's ability to stay free, say law enforcement officials who have studied his career. He knows when to cooperate with federal investigators and whom to rat on. He apparently also knows whom not to rat on. For instance, while a government witness in a 1971 trial, D'Onofrio actually chose to spend a few weeks in prison for contempt rather than reveal information about a Swiss bank account.

But D'Onofrio and others like him have also long been helped in their efforts to stay free by the very system that's supposed to stop them. The sad reality is that the criminal justice system often doesn't seem to take white collar crime all that seriously.

Federal criminal justice statistics, gathered in the mid-1990s by the Transactional Records Access Clearinghouse, or TRAC, at Syracuse University in New York, show that people convicted of fraud receive a median jail term of twelve months. By comparison, violators of pornography and prostitution laws receive thirty-three months behind bars, while drug traffickers are sent away for sixty months.

Prosecutors also generally have to work harder and longer to put together fraud cases, which often involve sifting through piles of complex financial records. On average, it takes more than ten months for a white collar criminal case to be filed in court from the time it's referred to a federal prosecutor's office, according to the TRAC data. That's nearly three times as long as for the average drug case. Given this dismal arithmetic, it isn't hard to see why many prosecutors prefer chasing crack dealers or porn peddlers to stock swindlers.

Sometimes, though, the failure to punish stock swindlers almost defies belief. In 1990, a young SEC attorney named Jacob Frenkel managed to dust off a potentially potent but little-used tool in an effort to put away D'Onofrio. He wanted to charge the swindler with criminal contempt for violating one of his several SEC civil injunctions.

The criminal-contempt weapon has been around a long time. It's little used partly because it isn't easy to find a prosecutor willing to file the case. Like all white collar cases, a contempt charge can take time to assemble. Plus, criminal contempt cases usually don't result in long prison sentences. While Frenkel realized this, he argued that even one year or one month less of D'Onofrio running around free would definitely qualify as a public service.

Frenkel finally convinced a prosecutor in Salt Lake City to bring the case. D'Onofrio, perhaps knowing the justice system better than Frenkel, pled guilty to the charge. The judge in the case gave him probation. D'Onofrio remained free.[4]

Such outcomes contribute to another problem plaguing the SEC as it faces the burgeoning challenge of policing the Internet: a steady exodus of some of its best and most veteran people. Some of this migration can be attributed to the prosperity of the bull market. As the 1990s roar along, SEC lawyers and other agency officials are increasing their incomes several-fold by going to work for Wall Street.

Frenkel, for one, left for another government assignment and then to private practice. Another damaging loss was SEC senior investigator Stuart Allen. In nearly thirty years with the agency, Allen became something of a walking encyclopedia on stock swindlers and organized crime's role in the securities markets. But Allen has said he increasingly feels that the SEC isn't giving enough attention to nabbing career swindlers, particularly those operating in the small-company stock world. So in 1992 at the age of fifty-five, Allen retires from the SEC and goes to work as a private investigator specializing in securities and banking.[5]

It isn't that the people left behind at the agency are bad or incompetent. Most are actually dedicated public servants. But the defections hollow out important parts of the SEC's institutional memory.

Thomas Quinn, who had allegedy been a major stock manipulator over the years, was safely behind bars in a European jail. In fact, Quinn—who regulators say is responsible for stealing perhaps several hundred million dollars—had been out of the European prison for months and was living on Long Island. And even Long Island's biggest critics probably wouldn't argue that living there qualifies as incarceration. (Mr. Quinn, in a brief telephone interview at the time with me, insisted that he was no longer involved in the securities business and that he was merely trying to get on with his life. He declined to discuss in what direction that effort was taking him.)

Besides confronting a full plate at the SEC, Stark in 1994 also had to deal with something of an empty Net. Lots of bogus investment schemes, some of which qualified as securities under federal securities law, were proliferating on the Internet. But actual online trading of listed securities—the bread and butter of the SEC's regulatory mission—was still in its infancy. Hardly any stock trades were done over the Internet and many of the major online stock-discussion and brokerage operations didn't even exist yet. (By 1998, about 22 percent of all securities transactions were done over the Internet, according to a report by the General Accounting Office, the investigative arm of Congress.)

Stark did have a couple of things working in his favor. The Internet—and its possible implications—was increasingly being talked about and worried about in lots of quarters, including government cubicles. State regulators in California, New Jersey, and elsewhere were getting concerned about Internet stock-selling abuses. But states, even more than the SEC, are hampered in fighting securities fraud by limited resources and powers. State jurisdiction stops at the state line. This is a particularly troublesome fact of life when trying to chase a cyber-crook who, with the reach of the Internet, can pull off his scam from Sao Paulo or Senegal almost as easily as from San Francisco.

By 1994, worries about the Internet as a new arena for investment fraud were also percolating into the press. In June of that year, for instance, one of the *Wall Street Journal*'s best personal-finance writers, Earl Gottschalk, did a story about the growing menace from online crooks. "Con artists can have a field day on electronic systems because they can tout their scams anonymously, and it's difficult for either regulators or the services themselves to police the information," Gottschalk wrote.

Having a sense of how the SEC works, Stark began his Internet campaign with a memo. He planned to give it to his boss, who like other top SEC officials wasn't yet very familiar with the Internet. Stark decided he needed to write something more than just a few paragraphs.

By the time he was finished, Stark's memo had become a fifty-page behemoth with a hundred pages of attachments. To give his opus a little more heft, Stark had thirty copies of the document printed and bound. At the end of 1994, he began circulating it around the top echelons of the SEC staff. "Our equipment and technological support barely even allowed us to obtain access to the Internet," recalled Richard Walker, head of the SEC's enforcement division, in a 1999 speech.[6]

Stark's bosses were impressed. They agreed that something needed to be done. Initially, that something was pretty modest. Stark began writing internal agency guidelines for Internet surveillance activities. He also began to train people in the enforcement branch on surfing the Net. Stark also got the go-ahead to recruit volunteers from the agency. The volunteers agreed to spend an hour or two a week online to look for suspicious securities offerings. About sixty people signed up for what became known as the "Cyberforce."

As soon as SEC officials started looking online, "we immediately witnessed some of the most outrageous frauds we had ever seen," SEC enforcement chief Walker said in that 1999 speech. One of Walker's early favorites involved an advertisement for the "Online Scam Guide," which claimed to contain 1,001 ways to defraud people online. When SEC officials called the number in the ad, they discovered that the perpetrator wouldn't be home for a few hours. He was still at school. The scofflaw turned out to be a teenager, who burst into tears when confronted by the law and pleaded with the SEC not to tell his mother.

More real, though perhaps no less strange, frauds were also being found. Stark says that an early SEC's case against online fraud was brought by the New York office involving an allegedly bogus investment opportunity in eel farms.

SEC cases against online operators began slowly accumulating in 1995 and 1996 as the online operators became more numerous and active. The cases ranged from an alleged $3 million lottery scam to supposedly "riskless" investments in a Costa Rican coconut-chip business.

In May 1996, regulators and the public were given a dramatic display of the power of the Internet to move a stock's price. The stock belonged to Comparator Systems Corp.

Based in Irvine, California, Comparator was a tiny and largely ignored company trying to market a fingerprint-identification technology. The stock sold on the Nasdaq stock market for a few cents a share.

Then in early May, trading in Comparator stock went crazy, fueled by "tens of thousands of Internet bulletin board postings where . . . misleading information was discussed," according to later testimony by the SEC's Walker before a Senate committee. During the May frenzy, the price of Comparator's stock price rocketed to nearly $2 a share, briefly giving the fingerprint outfit a market value of over $1 billion. The company's trading volume over one four-day period totaled over 530 million shares, a record for any stock on the Nasdaq stock market, which is home to such heavily traded securities as Microsoft and Intel.

The SEC later sued Comparator and some of its officials for alleged securities fraud, claiming the defendants put out false information to pump up the value of the stock. The defendants eventually settled the charges without admitting or denying wrongdoing, though parts of the case are under appeal.[7]

In June 1996, a month after Comparator, Stark received approval from his superiors at the SEC to open an online complaint center. This move, Stark hoped, would encourage the public to e-mail information to the agency about suspicious investment pitches or stock trading.

Stark counts the complaint center as a potentially major step forward in the battle against Internet stock fraud. He and others firmly believe that there is a remarkably strong and active self-policing element to the Internet. Many regular Internet users hate the idea of crooks and hype artists polluting their electronic world. And like the vigilantes of the Old West, they aren't willing to just sit around and watch it happen. Stark wants to give "cyber-sleuths" a place to send their suspicions. Now he can only hope they will take advantage of it.

Slowly, things seem to be coming together for Stark's Internet crusade at the SEC. He is teaching a course on the Internet and securities law at Georgetown University law school. He is winning kudos from his bosses. They've even given him a new title as "special counsel" for Internet projects. Of course, he is still a special counsel with no subordinates.

Though Internet enforcement is moving up the priority ladder, it still has a ways to go to reach the top. One measure of this is the speeches that have been given by top SEC officials. A list of such talks by the SEC's five commissioners—the presidential appointees who make up the agency's ruling body—can be found on the commission's website. The talks cover topics ranging from corporate governance to insider trading to the role of accountants.

However, the words "Internet" or "online" don't appear in the captions or titles of any of these speeches until January 1999.

But as the 1990s roll along, evidence of securities-law violations on the Internet is mounting. Stock-picking newsletters and services are popping up all over the Web. Nobody knows how many of these are being secretly paid by companies to tout their stocks in violation of federal securities law. Regulators clearly believe that some are.

In early 1997, for example, George Chelekis, publisher of Internet and print newsletters, was sued by the SEC in Washington, D.C., federal court for allegedly taking over $1.1. million from companies he had written about without telling his readers about the payments. Without admitting or denying wrongdoing, Chelekis agreed to an injunction against any misdeeds of that type in the future. He also agreed to pay over $162,000 in fines and other penalties.

So while the SEC's new office of Internet enforcement was still a modest operation in 1998, Stark has reason to look to the future with optimism. His bosses have been talking more and more publicly about the Internet problem. "The technology has made it easier for the bad guys, and this is a logical response," the SEC's enforcement division chief Walker told the Dow Jones News Service in announcing the new unit headed by Stark. Another hopeful sign for Stark's budding empire: the SEC's Internet complaint center is already averaging about 120 messages a day. And the number is growing.[8]

Ironically, the SEC's Internet enforcement office was created the same month that online traders were confronted by a challenge far bigger than anything regulators had thrown at them. In July 1998, stock prices began to fall and fall, as if someone had taken away the floor.

JULY 17, 1998, WAS A very pleasant day for most stock investors.

The Dow Jones Industrial Average reached a new closing high of 9337.97, some 17 percent above where it began the year. Other major stock indices, such as the Nasdaq Composite and the Standard & Poors 500, were also up substantially through the first six months of 1998. While some of the smaller-stock measures weren't doing nearly so well, the bull market was still purring along in its eighth year.

In the Internet stock-discussion world, things were also moving along nicely and generally quietly on that July 17. Big Dog put in an appearance at the Dog House and other Silicon Investor sites late in the afternoon, still singing the song of CYGS. He wrote that he had heard of coming major news releases within the next week from Cryogenic Solutions, the frozen-fetus-turned-DNA-research company. The announcements, Big Dog predicted, "will set the medical world on fire." He was so enthused that he continued sending out e-mails until nearly midnight about "the biggest opportunity I have ever had since trading." In another message, Nichols says "Man, after CYGS there is no more reason to play the market. Well, maybe one reason. ADDICTION."[1]

Across the Atlantic in Italy, Janice Shell had spent a good chunk of the previous few weeks pointing out what she felt were the numerous defects of a company called Mountain Energy. (Later in July, the SEC would suspend trading in the stock because of its concerns over the company.)

Shell used part of her evening of July 17 to defend her favorite company, FBN Associates, against enemies, real or imaginary.

> "Hah, evil summer shorts! We will squeeze you like
> toothpaste. The kind that has three different colors.
> I like that best,"

she wrote. She added that she might even turn one suspected short seller over to

> "the SEC, the NASD, and the House Committee on Un-Amer-
> ican Activities. You will be stripped of your shorts."

Happily, she noted that naysayers had been unable to hurt the price of FBN stock, which was up 347 percent. Of course, it could have just as easily been up 3470 percent. That's one of the advantages of a stock that doesn't really trade.[2]

In New York, the man who is arguably king of the cyber-guru hill spent July 17 as he does almost every day: busily sending e-mails and following the market. TokyoMex was still the most book-marked name on Silicon Investor. Park's Societe Anonyme was up to about 400 members, each paying him $300 a year for electronic access to his trading wit and wisdom.

On that halcyon July day, Park's mind, as reflected in his electronic messages, was on many things and lots of stocks.

> "CYT has bottomed and has been consolidating with pos-
> itive BOP and TSV ,, if I am not wrong,, it will start
> to move,, up soon ,, an will see a recovery towards 40
> dma of 54 .. I would settle for ,, 48 level .. in 3 -
> 4 weeks or less,,"

Translation: Various technical market indicators suggest that the share price of Cytec Industries, a chemicals and materials-technology company, has bottomed out and should be rising soon from around $40 a share to over $50. TokyoMex, not being overly greedy, would happily exit at $48 a share.

> "SVSR Weird shitty little penny stock ,, that no body
> follows on SI ,,. . . . . popped 100% yesterday on
> 10 times nirmal volume, I am not saying buy it,, let's
> look at it,, it has a very small float,, do not buy it
> ,, just watch it ,, OTCs are pain in the butt,,"

Translation: Park doesn't think much of Silver Star International, a little company that markets toys and other consumer products. However, it did double in price in a day and with a small number of shares outstanding, it could jump again. But these little stocks are a pain in the butt.

> "BDE Last time we played this it was a mo mo ,,, as
> usual we are always early with our picks,, too early
> .. recent news and yesterday's gap ,, can this be sus-
> tained ?"

Translation: Societe Anonyme previously traded in Brilliant Digital Entertainment, an e-commerce outfit. The previous attraction came perhaps less from the company's long-term business prospects than from the upward price momentum its stock was experiencing. It now seems SA got in and out too early. Recent news and yesterday's price jump suggest that the stock is worth at least one mo-mo look.

Park congratulated himself on seeing drug giant Pfizer reach $120 a share, the target he set for it about a month earlier when he recommended the stock. He berated himself for missing a short-selling opportunity on another stock that had run up in price the previous week and already run back down. TokyoMex urged members to be patient with another stock he had recommended, even though

> "it moves like a slug,,"

In another message, he seemed to be urging himself to show the same kind of forbearance on another stock.

"I am getting an itch finger,, but will hold a bit
longer,"

he wrote.

Park spent part of this day trying to impart broader messages
to the SA members, such as how basketball great Michael Jordan
could help them be successful stock traders:

"70% ,, stocks open ,, gap up ,, where MMs get out
while amateurs buy as soon as market opens ,, depending on the news,, volume ,, etc by 9:50 EST ,, the
direction of the stock becomes clear,, and about this
time profit takers get out ,, here you have to use your
savvy ,, intelligence,, level II ,, and your judgment
,, to buy on the dips,, or get out with them and re-
enter,, etc,, But then every stock behaves diffrently
,, they have individual personalities ,,like people ,,
watch particular stocks that you follow ..like a
trainer in a stable,,or a manager for a boxer,, or if
you are a basketball fan ,, you know whether Jordan is
feeling slow,, whether he is off sync etc,, does he go
full out in first quarter ? Or does he pull surprise
moves,,, etc ,, you watch and learn ,, And if you
become proficient in following a particular stock ,,
you don't have to run around the SI ,,like a chicken
with no head,, and go see what others are buying ,,
Almost 90 % of the stocks that have heavy volume has
1/4 to 1/2 intra day swings,, unless of course there
is a major sell off or gap ,, by trading let say 1,000
shares at a time for 25 cents,, you can make 250 a day
,, and if you do it 5 days a week ,, and say ,, you
screwed it on two days but made it on 3 days ,, you
still make 750 a week ,, thats 3,000 a month ,, you
can do this probably with stocks trading over 5 dollars with large volume every day ,, then you select 2
or 3 of them ,,and just watch that like a painter

studying nature,, you do it for 3 months or so ,, and
you will be on your way ,, once you become consistant
,, you will become confident,, you can live off same
stocks rest of your life ,, LOL .. You only risk 5 to
10K ,,, and the bottom side is 10% ,, as long as you
don't play silly mo mo plays and get stuck at top as
every one sells.. Once a stock has passed 10 - 15 %
from open ,, no matter ,, who or how many people
breaths heavy ,, just look away ,, and wait for
another day ,, do not get greedy ,,and say,, well ,,,
so and so says ,,it's going through the roof ,, etc ,,
and blindly jump in ,, Just stay out ,, for another
day ,, your time will come ,,"

Translation: MMs aren't melt-in-your-mouth candies, but they are brokerage firms that "make markets" in certain stocks. One should be careful of market makers at all times, since they have great power to affect the price of a company's stock. But one should be particularly careful during the first hour of trading, when many a novice trader rushes in to buy and ends up watching the price fall in the second hour. Also, if you focus on trading a small handful of stocks, you can ride them to retirement. And stay away from stock pickers who pant.

Park on that July day was also tying up a few unpleasant loose ends. He was taking shots at IFLY, the publicly traded travel agency that won and lost his favor. He had a few more harsh words for his former website manager, whom he threatened to sue for libel and slander. In an interview and Internet messages, the man defended his own actions and integrity.

Park reminded Societe Anonyme members that the membership price was going up to $499 per year, though he wrote that he was making a few exceptions for cases of financial hardship. There was, for example, a free membership to

"the scarsley employed actor"

who

```
"was recently on a Fox show as a chicken farmer,,"
```

—presumably being paid chicken feed. However, Park turned down an appeal from a member in Indonesia, who he decided had made enough profits to start paying full fare. Besides, TokyoMex added, the Indonesian member

```
"sent me a cheeky e-mail."
```

With summer in full blast, Park's thoughts also turned to his upcoming vacation in Europe.

```
"I will be leaving for Europe next Sunday ,to go to
golf school in Scotland,, go see old friends in Dus-
seldorf , Paris ,, and see about living in Monaco
. . . . . . . . . , swing by Mykonos for old time's sake,,,
and will be gone for 4 weeks,,"[3]
```

Park had been talking about possibly moving to Monaco. He was attracted, among other things, by the prospect of being in a time zone where he could play golf in the morning, trade stocks in New York in the afternoon and evening, and then do his e-mail and research after that. Given the hours he was already logging in New York, it wasn't clear that he would have time to both play golf and sleep.

Of course, who needed sleep? The market was booming, membership dollars were flowing in, and Park was an Internet star. On a day like that, anything might seem possible.

Then came the next trading day, July 20.

Stock prices began falling. They continued falling through the rest of July and into August. Stocks dropped across the board, from blue chips to cow chips. By August 31, the Dow had plunged more than 19 percent from its July 17 high. A 20 percent drop is generally viewed as a marker of a bear market.

Some of the big technology and Internet stocks were hit even harder. Yahoo! was down some 22 percent. America Online fell 35 percent. Little companies were also caught in the downdraft. Big Dog's beloved Cryogenic Solutions tanked by over 70 percent.

Market pundits had plenty of theories on the causes of the skid. There was the Russian economic crisis, the Asian economic crisis, the Latin American economic crisis, as well as the Bill Clinton caught-with-his-zipper-down crisis. There was also the not-illogical thought that stocks had risen so much, so fast, they were finally experiencing what professional market observers like to call a "correction." Of course, a correction to an observer can look like a train wreck to an investor. One of the odd things about the downswing was that the traditional reason for a sour stock market, a troubled domestic economy, was nowhere in sight. The nation was purring along with steady growth, low inflation, and low unemployment.

Whatever the reasons, the drop hit hard at Internet stock traders—many of whom had never before noticed the down button on the stock market elevator. Cyberspace celebrities weren't immune to the pain of the falling prices.

"It's not as easy to make money as it was," lamented Big Dog during an interview early that August. Nichols said he invested heavily in Cryogenics Solutions stock at prices up to $2.37 a share. It's now under $1.

He complained about the "bashers" who had come onto the Internet discussion boards and "destroyed" CYGS stock with their unrelenting attacks. But Nichols was also beginning to wonder whether he had been misled during his long conversations with company management. CYGS had "the most unbelievable story you ever heard" and it could still be "the greatest thing since sliced bread," said Nichols. "But I don't know what to believe anymore." (Cryogenic Solutions officials say they don't think they misled Nichols or anyone else about the company's prospects.)

Probably the hardest fall, though, belonged to Big Dog's early mentor, the poet of the air-conditioning ducts, Ga Bard, a.k.a. Gary Swancey. Ironically, Swancey's woes had little to do with the broader market's problems, though they were coming at the same time.

On the other hand, Ga Bard's downfall in ways holds broader lessons than those that come from the periodic mass retreat of stock prices. His is a tale that points to the rising hubris on the Net, where a trader's easy access to mountains of information and lots of like-minded individuals can breed a dangerous sense of control, even invincibility. Not to mention downright stupidity. Such was the case of Gary Swancey and his Midland debacle.

Swancey first ran across Dallas-based Midland Inc. in late 1997. He thought he had unearthed one of those neglected gems sometimes found in the small-stock mines. He was particularly attracted to the company's capital structure. Besides common stock, Midland had publicly traded preferred stock. Each preferred share, over time, would be convertible into 35 shares of common at an extremely attractive price, says Swancey. He started loading up on Midland shares, preferred and common.

Ga Bard naturally began to talk up Midland and even started a Silicon Investor discussion thread about the company. He labeled Midland a

"sleeper"

and a

"meat and potatoes diversified holding company that acquires successful meat and potatoes profitable companies in deverse industries."

He added that as part of his DD, he had called the company and

"talked to Mr. King who was extremely energetic and my kind of no nonsense guy."[4]

Well, yes, there was Mr. King and Midland's meat and potatoes.

In early September 1997, Steven A. King was named Mid-land's chairman. King was a "highly regarded financial consultant and entrepreneur" who would "utilize experience, vision and strong capital market relationships" to build Midland, promised a company press release. All that, and the man wasn't yet thirty.

King left the throne after a month. In announcing his resignation as chairman, Midland said he would continue as a company consultant. (A year later, King was sued in a Tampa federal court by the SEC. He was charged with having "fraudulently touted" Midland and four other stocks through an Internet stock-information website he operated. King eventually agreed to an injunction without admitting wrongdoing.)

Other members of the management team also came to the attention of law enforcement authorities. In December 1997, the SEC filed suit in New York federal court against Midland's chief financial officer, Robert Marsik, and the corporate secretary, Mark Pierce. The two men were charged with hiring a convicted felon to manipulate the price of the company's stock in 1995 and 1996 when the firm was known as America's Coffee Cup. Marsik and Pierce denied wrongdoing but resigned their Midland positions.

Then there was the matter of Midland's business lines. Up to February 1997, Midland was perking along as a coffee company. It shed that, and over the next several months announced plans for a bewildering array of business deals including tourist hydrofoils in the Greek islands, cold-storage facilities in the Russian port of Taganrog, and a "restaurant/bar" business in Las Vegas with fifteen slot machines and deals to manage "several up and coming" (though not named) Las Vegas entertainers.

In early 1998, Midland announced that it had acquired the rights to an ethanol-based fuel additive called DF-144. The "DF" stood for Dynamic Fuel, and Midland's enthusiasm for the product was dynamic, to say the least. "Industry experts have cautioned us that we may be underestimating and possibly undervaluing DF-144," declared a company press release. Midland also got a new chief executive along with the fuel additive.

The new CEO was gone a few months later, however, along with the DF-144 deal. In a press release, Midland asserted that the outgoing executive had gone to the Bahamas after committing "fraud" against the company—a charge that the gentleman vehemently denied via postings on Silicon Investor. Midland's new president was Mark Pierce, the official who had been accused of attempted stock manipulation by the SEC.[5]

At the same time, Midland announced a new investor-relations representative: Gary Swancey, who the company said had graciously offered his services "free of charge." Swancey says he volunteered for the investor-relations job because he felt responsible to his Internet followers who had also put money into Midland. His move, initially, won some cyberspace kudos.

"You are the right man for the job,"

said one Internet posting.

"The best thing that could happen right now,"

added another.

Swancey had stuck with Midland through all the preceding months of thin and thinner. He acknowledged that the failed business deals and management turmoil had given him moments of pause. But almost every little company has blemishes, he believed. That's the nature of the market.

Besides, the Bard just *knew* that Midland had a future. Early on, he says he flew at his own expense to company headquarters and grilled their officials. He felt he understood the company inside and out. He read Midland's financial documents so intently that he could quote specific pages from filings with the SEC. By the summer of 1998, he says he had most of his wealth tied up in Midland stock. Swancey was like a man who had sweated to learn every nook and board of a building. He just hadn't noticed that the building was burning like a five-alarm barbecue.

On August 18, with the broader market still diving, the roof caved in on Midland. The SEC suspended trading in the company's stock, citing concern over the "accuracy and adequacy" of information disseminated about the firm. In announcing the suspension, the SEC said it had questions about the company's assets and liabilities, its announced acquisitions, its current operations, its "purported" management, and "the possible misappropriation of assets by Midland officers." Other than that, everything was presumably okay.[6]

Things definitely weren't peachy for the Georgia Bard. He had ignored his own online advice and the BARD's Trading System and put most of his money into Midland stock, whose value had just been torched. Then Swancey received a subpoena from the SEC ordering him to appear for questioning along with all his Midland-related records. Now *he* was under investigation.

Plus, the online kudos previously tossed to Swancey had turned to bricks. One unhappy trader using Midland's stock symbol, MIDL (with a slight misordering of the letters), proposed a new equation for the BTS:

```
"DO THE MATH . . . BTS . . . Here's some math for you
. . . GaBard + MILD = SCAM."⁷
```

Swancey was feeling broke, downtrodden, and none too bright. He found himself sitting on plastic-covered furniture in an apartment above a garage in Kilgore, Texas. He had gone there to try to make some money by setting up an Internet website for a small company he got to know as a trader. Ga Bard had lots of time to think about what he had done. And lots of the thoughts weren't too complimentary to a certain sage of cyberspace. He had been, he says, "a moron."

While GaBard was going down in flames, TokyoMex was fighting to survive the summer stock market conflagration. The fall in stock prices ripped into his net worth. His trading account, which he says had risen to $540,000, dropped to $180,000. By the fall of 1998, membership in Societe Anonyme fell by some 50 percent to about 200. Some remaining members seemed to be having second thoughts. Park passed along to his online readers one such missive from a Societe Anonyme member in Sweden:

```
"Joe I dont even know your real name and I am sending
you money ,, such is the craziness that we have come
to."
```

Park had his own moments of despair about the falling market. He wrote that the "massacre" and "blood bath" have finally arrived and that if stock prices keep falling "we are all dead."

But TokyoMex isn't a man easily beaten down for long. All through that dismal summer drop, he worked to rally his remaining troops and himself, to map out new trading strategies—and to enjoy his monthlong vacation in Europe. After all, there is more to life than just trading stocks.

```
"I am down 40%,"
```

he wrote in one early August e-mail from Nice on the way to Venice.

```
"But i am not selling. not daytrading. this is my 40-
day vacation. i have been very conservative. when
travel don't daytrade. We live off our fat a little
until things settle down."
```

And remember, he added, no matter how bleak the present looks, the

```
"internet is the future."
```

Park wrote about many stocks during this period, including one of his longtime favorite stocks, CMGI Inc. This Nasdaq-listed company is, in some ways, the ultimate Internet play. Its business involves investing in promising Internet companies. So investing in CMGI is similar to buying a basket of online issues. Park is a fervent CMGI fan. Even as it fell that summer from above $70 a share to below $40 a share, he was predicting that by the end of 1999 it would be above $200 a share. (As it turned out, Park was too cautious in his enthusiasm. CMGI shares surpassed the $200 level in January 1999.)

Being a CMGI admirer didn't stop Park from frequently buying, selling, and shorting the shares. When he profitably caught an upswing or downswing in the price, he got kudos from the Net.

```
"He is a genius,"
```

gushed one e-mail posted on a Silicon Investor message board when CMGI stock popped up following a TokyoMex buy recommendation.

But there was also CMGI angst.

```
"What a heart burn,, where is the bottom on this one,"
```

lamented Park in one e-mail. In another message, he complained that CMGI is "is driving me nuts."

While Park was certainly willing to trumpet his successful stock picks, he also admitted to some bum ones. On one stock he declared that he had his "butt whipped."

Even worries about a declining market weren't enough to keep Park's mind fully occupied. He managed to mix a little of his travelogue in with his market log:

> "Ah,,, buck nacked ,,sitting at the Super Paradise
> Beach , Mikonos,, watching all the browned bodoies,,
> . . . . All my 10,000 little brown CMGIs
> screaming ,, il pa pa ,,I come to you now . . . "

He also had time to contemplate death and good-byes. His own mother had died a few months earlier. Park admits to being wracked by concerns over whether she received all the medical care she needed. Finally he asked a Societe Anonyme member who is a doctor to read over her medical records. When the doctor wrote back that nothing more could have been done, Park shared his relief with SA members:

> "Mumsie haunted me every day for past 4 mos,, I had an
> autopsy done and the report finally came and I asked
> our resident MD look st the report . . . He kindly
> spent many hours,, and had this to report ,, Thanks to
> Scott,, I was finaly able to let mumsie go last night,,
> got drunk in process but I feel relived,, and glad for
> mumsie,,"

When a Societe Anonyme member died, Park wrote that the deceased member

> "always had a laugh for humanity ,, a laugh I used to
> hear,,, with constant encouragement for good over ,,
> evil,, passed away ,, suffering from Lou Gehrrig's
> disease,,, it was a long battle .. . . . . He passed
> away peacefully in his sleep ,, ...I am sure he
> went smiling . . . I offer him a bon voyage . . . "

He sent out other messages of hope. He noted that while "our equity dwindles," stock prices were also falling, which meant it didn't take as much money as it had to buy that next 100 shares of CMGI. The logic was true enough, though it might not have been much solace to someone who was watching money bleed from his or her trading account.

Mostly, though, Park's optimism was based on a simple belief in a happy ending.

> "Market will come back ever more stronger,, with ven-
> gence,when the bottom has reached,,,"

he wrote in an August 29 message.

While he was wrong in a number of his predictions, he was right on this one. Two days later, on August 31, he informed members,

> "We die at open,, but that is the bottom,, IMHO."[8]

His humble opinion turned out to be dead-on. The last day of August marked the nadir of the market plunge. Beginning in September 1998, stock prices started rising again—with a vengeance.

As the stock market began soaring back up toward new records, it perversely enough opened the door ever wider for a group of people who make their money from falling stock prices. And on the last day of November 1998, the man who was to become probably the best known, most popular, and most reviled such player in cyberspace made his official online debut.

ON NOVEMBER 30, 1998, at 8:46 P.M. Eastern standard time, a new message board was born on Silicon Investor. Given the fireworks that would follow there, the opening message by the founder was relatively low-key. It read, in part:

> "This thread is dedicated to helping investors maxi-
> mize the profits and minimizing their losses, I deal
> primarily with overhyped, overvalued, fraudulent, pro-
> moted, spammed, or suspect equities. I will almost
> always carry a personal position that is consistent
> with my postings. My positions may be considerable and
> may change and often times do change without notice..
> A simple request will always result in the most truth-
> ful answer possible. Those who tout and or hype can
> find other threads to satisfy their needs."

The message board's title managed to be bland, personal, and vaguely official all at the same time. It was called Anthony@Equity Investigations, Dear Anthony.

The new board's founder went by the online moniker Anthony @Pacific. In real life, his name is Amr Ibrahim Elgindy, though he prefers to be called Tony.

Tony Elgindy is what's known in the securities business as a "short seller." Unlike the average "long" investor, who buys shares of a company in hopes the price will rise, a short seller looks to profit when stock prices fall. Though there are variations, the traditional method of short selling goes like this: find a stock you think is overvalued; find an investor who will lend you some shares of that company; sell the borrowed shares; hope the price then falls so you can buy back shares at a lower price to replace the borrowed ones and pocket as profit the difference between your selling and buying prices.

Of course, if the price of the stock goes up after you sell and you have to replace the borrowed shares at a higher price, short selling can produce fast and large losses. That's one reason short selling is generally considered a riskier investing strategy than going long, where the investor often has months or years to realize a profit.

Yet short selling has been a fixture in the stock market since the beginning. Sometimes the role of short sellers is honored. In the middle of the nineteenth century, according to one stock market history, short seller Jacob Little was so well known that his portrait hung at the offices of the New York Stock Exchange.[1]

More often, though, people simply want to hang short sellers. After all, stock markets tend to be filled with optimists, who believe that, gravity notwithstanding, the natural direction of stocks is up. Such sunny dispositions tend not to appreciate pessimists peeing on their parade.

Plus, short selling doesn't generally attract passive investors. Besides looking for overinflated stocks, many short sellers carry their own arsenal of pins designed for bubble bursting. There is a long history of shorts attacking stocks, by fair means and foul. Sometimes they dig up real dirt on a company; sometimes they just make up the dirt. Some put out press releases attacking their targets. More often their attacks move as whispers through the market, frequently planted first in the ear of a reporter in return for a promise of anonymity. Given their line of work, short sellers have traditionally preferred the shadows—sometimes out of legitimate concerns for their own safety, financial and otherwise, and sometimes out of the knowledge that they are doing some pretty slimy things.

At the same time, short sellers can provide an important, even essential, service to the investing public. The natural optimism of the markets often gives way to hyperbole, a.k.a. hype. And hype is the kissing cousin of fraud. While regulators are supposed to help guard the public against fraud, they tend to be too few and too slow to do much good in many cases.

That's where the short seller comes in. He or she has an immediate, often substantial, economic interest in uncovering any seamy seams of a company. And some are quite good at doing it. As a species, short sellers tend to be smarter and quicker than their counterparts on the long side. Short sellers quickly discover that there are no companies anxious to give them access and feed them mounds of information. Like predators, they don't get dinner invitations from their prey.

Perhaps no stock market in history needed a short dose of pessimism more than the Internet-driven bull stampede of the late 1990s. The entry of a figure such as Elgindy marks, in a sense, a new phase of the craze. Cynics such as Shell and Mitchell may be bright, but they are still relative amateurs. They even disdain any economic interest in the stocks they attack. By contrast, players such as Elgindy have very real economic interests—and act accordingly.

Elgindy is a professional short seller, and had been for several years at the time he made his Silicon Investor debut. He knows much about the scummy side of Wall Street because he has lived there and wallowed in it. He has done business with swindlers, taken part in and profited from their swindles—and then fingered them to the cops. (Elgindy says that he didn't knowingly do anything wrong and didn't break any laws.) He came to the Internet loaded for bear, so to speak, and looking to build a short-selling machine that would suck in companies and spit out profits. There is nothing amateur or laid-back about Tony Elgindy.

He also happens to be a smart, some say brilliant, trader with a keen eye for baloney in the meat market of stocks. He shows an eagerness to wrap himself in the mantle of public servant. (He doesn't shy away from talking about his accomplishments. One day, for example, he sent an e-mail to some fellow traders with a link to an online IQ test. Elgindy wrote that he had just taken the test and scored 169, which an accompanying chart showed to be well above the "definitely genius" level and in a range reached by less than half of 1 percent of all IQ test takers. "I was having an off morning," he added.)

To online critics who assert that his trashing of stocks actually hurts investors, Elgindy responds that they are looking at it from the wrong perspective. Going after a bad company

```
"has to be done quickly and harshly ..because I cant
usually sdave trhe momops and pops that refuse to take
my advice and who want tio hold on.. But I can prevent
hundreds of future investors [from being hurt],"
```

he wrote in one e-mail.

```
"But the key is TIMING and Strategy and PSYCHOLOGY,"
```

he explained in another message.

```
"By figuring out how the criminals and hypsters make
their money ..you can figure out how to take it away
from them."
```

Elgindy recognized that the communicating power of the Internet added a potentially huge new weapon to his short-selling arsenal. It allowed him, from the comfort of his computer terminal, to play Paul Revere and warn the investing countryside about suspect companies. In the frenzied market of the '90s, there seemed to be no shortage of candidates.[2]

Sometimes they were as close as the next press release. One day, for instance, Elgindy was scrolling through various online news and discussion sites when he came across an announcement from Firstwave Technologies Inc. The press release from the small Internet software company announced a business deal with Microsoft—a name almost any small company would love to ally itself with. Fueled by this news, Firstwave shares more than quadrupled in price to over $8.50 a share on a volume of 16 million shares, an eye-popping 5,000 times its trading volume of the day before.

The release didn't smell right to Elgindy. For one thing, it didn't give details about the size of the Microsoft deal. So Elgindy started working the phones, reaching officials at both Firstwave and Microsoft. Though they declined to give him dollar figures, he wheedled out enough information to conclude that the Microsoft order was worth only about $100,000, a relative pittance compared with Firstwave's annual revenue of $14.5 million.

In his low-key way, Elgindy started launching online bombs. He described Firstwave's press release as a[3]

"DECEPTION OF MASSIVE PROPORTION"

and pronounced it

"A Criminal Shame"

that the announcement had moved the stock price so much. Though a Firstwave spokesman defended the release as fair and accurate, he acknowledged in an interview with me that Elgindy's dollar estimate of the contract was "in the ballpark." From its frenzied high, Firstwave's stock fell some 40 percent in price over the next two days.

Like other short sellers, Elgindy is always on the lookout for any evidence tying a company to individuals who have a history of legal problems, particularly in the area of securities law. Legal problems of a civil nature are okay, especially if it's a lawsuit by the SEC. Of course, criminal problems are better, with criminal securities fraud being the short seller's equivalent of blackjack. While a corporation's connection to an alleged scofflaw doesn't necessarily speak to the firm's products, services, or business prospects, it does cast a nice pall—from a short seller's perspective, that is—over the enterprise. And in the world of shorting, pall can just be another way to spell profit.

Which is why a little company called FindEx.com blipped into Elgindy's field of interest screen one day.

By the time FindEx found its way to Elgindy, the stock was

well on its way to rocketing to over $18 a share from about $1 a share. That kind of rush up, alone, would have attracted the attention of any self-respecting short seller.

Based in Omaha, Nebraska, FindEx.com planned to become "the premier financial content provider on the Internet," according to a company press release. That same release announced that a software industry executive named Joe Szczepaniak had just been named the company's president and chief executive officer.[4]

What interested Elgindy about that FindEx.com press release wasn't so much what it said but where it led. The contact phone for Szczepaniak was in Florida, not Nebraska. Dialing that number connected the caller to the telephone extensions of two men, Lionel Reifler and Yanni Koutsoubos.

Reifler had been the target of civil injunctive action by the SEC for alleged violations of federal securities laws, according to agency records. SEC records also showed that in August 1989, Reifler had pled guilty to criminal securities fraud.[5]

In a 1999 phone interview with me, Reifler acknowledged his past legal problems but said he had nothing to do with FindEx.com and doesn't know how the phone number made its way to the company's release.

Koutsoubos, whom I interviewed that same day, just an extension away, said that he personally wasn't connected to FindEx.com. However, a company for which he worked was an investor. He acknowledged knowing Szczepaniak. But, like Reifler, Koutsoubos said he doesn't know why his office phone number is on the FindEx.com release.

In 1995, a Texas-based retailer called 50-Off Stores, Inc. filed suit against Koutsoubos and others in San Antonio federal court for allegedly obtaining shares in the company but never paying for them. In that litigation, 50-Off, which later changed its name to LOT$OFF Corp., described Koutsoubos as also being Ioannis Koutsoubos, who was sued by the SEC in a 1991 case involving the allegedly illegal trading of shares in an Arizona company. LOT$OFF Corp. obtained a $30 million default judgment against Koutsoubos when he didn't respond to the charges.[6]

JOHN R. EMSHWILLER

In my phone interview with Koutsoubos, he acknowledged being sued by 50-Off but didn't comment beyond that about the case. He denied being the Ioannis Koutsoubos who was sued by the SEC. He said Koutsoubos is a common name in Greece. He added that out of curiosity he even once tried to contact Ioannis Koutsoubos but got no reply. When I asked how he tried to make that contact, Koutsoubos paused and then said that he put a message out over the Internet.

FindEx.com's Szczepaniak, during a mid-1999 phone interview, said he knows Koutsoubos and through him once met Reifler. Szczepaniak said that the pair's phone number shows up on the press release because he met the previous FindEx.com chief executive at their offices in connection with getting his new job. He said that as far as he knows neither of the two had any role at FindEx.com.

Szczepaniak admitted, however, that there were some gaps in his knowledge about his new company. For instance, he didn't yet have a list of the firm's shareholders. He said he was working on one. Also, the company didn't yet have a board of directors. He was working on assembling one. Where was his predecessor, who gave him the chief executive's job? Don't know, said Szczepaniak. (Szczepaniak didn't respond to later interview requests or e-mailed questions.)

With the names of not just one but two suspect figures to bandy about, Elgindy began his e-mail offensive against FindEx.com. At the time, the stock was dancing around $17 a share.

"Pure shit . . . . . . very strong smell,"

wrote Elgindy, evidently not wanting to have his feelings about the company lost in subtlety.

"Everyone should already be short FIND,"

he counseled in another message. He also started passing the word to reporters, including myself.[7]

The names Yanni and Lionel begin popping up in the messages of other Internet posters. On the Raging Bull message board for FindEx, someone using the moniker "cantFINDme" posts the Florida phone number and says this

> "is where the real info on this non-company is. When you get a hold of Lionel ,ext 107, ask him his last name and then search the SEC enforcement archives to FIND out who is really behind FIND."

Another Raging Bull poster using the moniker "k.yanni" writes that

> "FINdex is a real company with a real ecommerce business and fantastic prospects."

This person adds that

> "you should buy some stock at this price and hold until it gets to $35."

To which a message writer using the name FUKuREIFLER responds:

> "Dear Rotten #######. You and Lionel are going back to jail shortly. Make sure you bring soap with you."

(This poster is inaccurate on at least one point. There isn't any evidence that Koutsoubos ever had a criminal violation.)[8]

Within two weeks of this battling breaking out, FindEx stock has fallen as low as $6 a share, though it then rebounds to about $10 a share.

From the time of his entry into cyberspace, Elgindy knew he needed allies to accomplish his goals. And with the communicating power of the Internet, he found them. Or they found him. Indeed, within a few months of starting his Anthony message board at Silicon Investor, Elgindy was able to join the ranks of the Democrats and Republicans and Elks. He held a convention. Of short sellers.

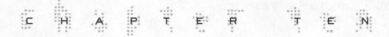

OVER TWO HUNDRED MEN AND WOMEN fill the meeting room of the Hyatt Islandia Hotel on San Diego's Mission Bay. Outside, the air is pleasantly warm. The waters of the bay and the Pacific beyond sparkle.

As I sit there with these people, I can't help thinking that given the reputation of short sellers as bloodthirsty predators, this gathering should be taking place in the shark tanks of nearby Sea World. But on the whole, this group seems mild and friendly. One couple are wearing Hawaiian shirts. Perhaps in honor of the occasion, they also wear shorts. The gathering is overwhelmingly male and white, but there don't appear to be any Great Whites prowling around.

They come from all over the country, hauling their laptops and their Internet monikers. Flodyie is in from New Jersey, carrying the message of the Truthseeker. Bear Down comes from South Carolina with his adored five-year-old daughter and an eye for fun. Pluvia of Nevada, however, cancels at the last minute. Word is that he doesn't want to risk running into any process servers after just being slapped with a $90 million lawsuit by an irate company.

However, uninvited guests won't find it easy to get into this gathering. The fee for the two-day meeting is at least $1,500—plus hotel, airfare, and whatever extra fun one buys in and around San Diego. Before attendees arrive, they receive an e-mail, which lays out some of the security rules while ignoring a couple on spelling and grammar:

> "Everyone will need to have a Govt or state Picture ID
> .. upon checking in .. and in response to some ques-
> tions there will be no body cavity searches .. But
> expect to go through metal detectors and X-ray so leave
> your weapons at home .. there will be Police Personal
> on hand to lead away those who forget, to our luxury
> rooms especially reserved for the weapon yielders."

The badges and metal detectors are there. So are the off-duty cops, wearing guns and looking beefy. However, no weapons rooms, luxurious or spare, are evident.

While many come to meet in the flesh names that they have only known online, all come to see and listen to the man who organized this get-together, the man of the hour: Tony Elgindy.

Elgindy stands at the podium in the front of the room. He's about five feet ten inches tall, broad in a muscular way that comes from weight lifting. Swarthy, with closely clipped black hair, he wears a tight black T-shirt and dark slacks. He looks no older than his thirty-one years.

The people here this day are only some of Elgindy's fans. He is already one of the most bookmarked names on Silicon Investor, with over 1,000 people signed up to follow his postings. His Anthony message board has attracted tens of thousands of messages. Many of those attending are already paying Elgindy several hundred dollars a month for access to his online stock service, where he gives tips on what stocks to short and when.

Elgindy has named this gathering "Autopsy of Wall Street." At the very least, it's a brash choice, since Wall Street seems to be one very lively corpse. But Elgindy is nothing if not brash.

For a good chunk of the two-day gathering, he stands at the front of that room and partakes of one of his favorite activities. He talks. He talks about his trading techniques, his trading philosophy, his trading tricks as well as the tricks that other traders play. He talks about his life.

Flanking Elgindy at the front of the room are two huge screens hooked to an array of computers. Using a cordless keyboard, Elgindy projects tables and charts and news stories as he speaks and walks about.

He shares the spotlight at times. At one point, a two-foot-eight man, bald but wearing the same garb as Elgindy, strides purposefully into the room and straight toward the front. He is carrying a wrapped package that looks large compared to the courier.

"I just ran into Tokyo Joe," the small man says. "We had security take him out, but he had something to give you."

"Maybe I should have security check it," says Elgindy in a dubious tone. He opens the package and, in mock surprise, says "Oh my, a six-pack of Diet Coke."

It's an inside joke, and judging from the laughter that erupts in the audience, most of the people get it. Elgindy and Joe Park are by now bitter rivals. Recently they clashed over a stock that Park insisted was a good buy and Elgindy insisted was, in his words, a "pig." They made an online bet. If Park wins, Elgindy pays him $5,000. If the short seller wins, Park pays him a six-pack of Diet Coke. Needless to say, the two have a bit more to say to each other than just the basics of the bet. In proposing the terms of the bet, Elgindy refers to Park as

`"Loser boy"`

and

"Oh smelly one."

In accepting the bet, Park writes

`"Wow ,, I want my 5k from that bog Buxx Sxxiter,, aka A anus ,,, I will send my boys in LA to collect,, R O F L M A O."`

It is an incident that illustrates the differences between the two men beyond the fact that one says buy, the other sell. Five grand versus six soda cans? Elgindy seems to revel in grand, some-times grandiose gestures, while Park is looking to minimize his downside. Besides, Elgindy tells me later, he was sure he was going to win the bet.[1]

Shortly after the wager, regulators suspended trading in the disputed stock Elgindy claimed victory. He says he is still waiting for his Coke. Park says he doesn't believe he owes Elgindy any-thing.

The delivery man in this skit is actor Verne Troyer. He has recently rocketed to fame as Mini-Me, the adorably evil bite-sized clone of Dr. Evil in the latest Austin Powers movie epic, *The Spy Who Shagged Me*. A very short man hired to entertain a gathering of shorts. Troyer's next scheduled stop is an event at Hugh Hefner's Playboy mansion in west Los Angeles. From abreast of the market to the market of breasts. Such is the actor's life.

The morning of the first day of this announced evisceration of Wall Street starts before 6:30 A.M., Pacific time, when the stock markets open in New York. Elgindy gives his audience a "live" demonstration of his online stock-trading techniques. The perfor-mance consists mostly of Elgindy talking, punching computer keys, and flashing charts on the big screens. It goes smoothly enough, but tends to demonstrate that as a spectator sport Internet stock trading is only slightly more exciting than watching grass grow. And with grass you at least can enjoy sunshine and breezes.

A potentially more interesting autopsy session is closed to reporters. It has to do with offshore trading accounts. Though off-shore accounts have been part of the financial landscape since long before the first computer geek had even a web dream, they've become popular with Internet traders, particularly short sellers. Canada and the Caribbean seem to be especially hot destinations for U.S. short sellers.

Foreign brokerage firms often allow short sellers a lot more latitude than their U.S. brokerage counterparts. For one thing, for-eign firms will allow traders to short stock without first borrowing it, a practice called "naked shorting." While this leeway makes it easier to short a stock, critics of naked shorting argue that the practice also makes it easier to unfairly beat down the price of a stock. One Canadian brokerage firm known to be popular with American short sellers has already garnered news coverage because a few of its brokers supposedly had dealings with alleged American Mafia figures.

In some ways, though, the most interesting part of the Elgindy show comes on the morning of the second day of the gathering. Elgindy gives a one-hour, nonstop monologue about his life and career. It is quite a story.

By the time of the short sellers gathering, I've known Elgindy for three years, mostly by telephone. I already know enough about him to have concluded he is one of the more extraordinary figures in the securities industry and certainly one of the more resilient.

I first crossed Elgindy's path in the summer of 1996 while reporting a *Journal* story about bribes to stockbrokers. At the time, federal investigators in cities around the country were looking into whether stock promoters were illegally paying brokers to convince their clients to buy certain stocks. Law enforcement officials were telling me that they suspected possibly hundreds of stockbrokers around the country had taken millions of dollars in illegal payoffs, in the form of either cash or stock. Ironically, prosperity seemed to be fueling the problem.

By that summer of 1996, stock prices had been rising for nearly six years. The Dow Jones Industrial Average, a bellwether indicator that includes the stock prices of thirty of the nation's biggest companies, had risen from under 2,400 to over 5,000 and was showing no signs of abating. Individual investors, carrying their wallets, were flocking into the burgeoning bull market, looking for things to buy.

Along with the well-known titans of industry—the Disneys, the General Motors, the Microsofts—there are thousands of obscure little public companies vying for attention. Most are legitimate, though not necessarily possessors of bright futures. Many are and always will be vessels filled with more hope than accomplishment. Some will turn out to be complete frauds. Whatever category a particular firm falls into, its stock price—and the wealth of its owners—can increase tremendously if it can just catch the fancy of investors even for a little while.

In the stock marketplace, there are many ways for a company to gain attention. Unfortunately, one relatively cheap and efficient method is to bribe brokers. A few hundred thousand dollars—sometimes much less—in well-placed cash can produce customer orders that raise the value of a company's stock by millions of dollars or more.

Again, under federal securities law, a broker can accept such a payment—if he discloses it to his customers when recommending the stock. However, such honesty seems rarely to leap to the lips of a bribed broker. And not speaking up is a federal offense.

In the course of my reporting, I was told about a broker who supposedly knew a lot about bribes being paid and the federal investigations into the practice. His name was Elgindy. He worked at a firm called Key West Securities in Hurst, Texas. I'd never heard of the man, the firm, or the town. But I dialed him up.

As it turned out, Elgindy knew quite a bit about broker bribes, along with a few other things on the crooked side of Wall Street. It was clear from our first conversation that Elgindy was unusual in at least one respect. People intimately familiar with securities fraud, be they lawmen or lawbreakers or something in-between, tend to be a closed-mouth lot. Many of them consider "no comment" a tad on the talkative side.

Elgindy, on the other hand, loves to talk. There were big broker-bribe investigations going on, he informed me. He was regularly talking to federal investigators and helping them out. In one investigation, he had secretly tape-recorded conversations with suspected lawbreakers. He was in a position to help because he had been right in the middle of a major broker-bribe scandal. He even received tens of thousands of dollars personally. Of course, Elgindy added quickly, *he* had done nothing wrong.

As we talked more, he told me about his past. It is a tale that he repeats—in shorter form, with some additions—in his San Diego speech. It began a long way from Mission Bay.

Elgindy was born in Cairo, Egypt, on November 28, 1967, but grew up in the Chicago area, where his family moved when he was three. He eventually headed off to college in Southern California, but soon dropped out and went to work in the San Diego area. In what would be useful training for his securities career, Elgindy became a car salesman, specializing in Chevrolets.

The young Amr found he had a knack for selling Chevys. A customer "would be looking for a red Camaro and he would leave in a brown Nova," he tells his San Diego audience. "And his girl-friend would come back the next day crying and say, 'We need a red Camaro.' But that brown Nova's what he bought and for some reason I took pride in this. I thought that that was great—I could sell people things that I had on the lot or I had in inventory even though it wasn't for them." The teenager was soon pulling in $4,000 to $5,000 a month and thought he may have found his career.

Then an older man, all of twenty-four, walked into the dealer-ship with a beautiful woman. The man was a stockbroker, the woman was his wife. He wanted to buy a Corvette. He said he was pulling down $20,000 a month as a broker. The "a month" part particularly caught Elgindy's attention. Moving paper began to sound a lot more attractive than moving metal.

He soon was knocking on the doors of local brokerage firms looking for a job. "I knew nothing about the market—I didn't even know what the Dow Jones was," he tells his San Diego audience. He contacted about ten firms and got a matching number of rejec-tions. Many told him he was too young to be a broker.

Finally he found a firm that gave him a chance, called Blinder, Robinson & Co.

For a man who later would seek fame and fortune by uncover-ing stock frauds, starting at Blinder provided an embarrassing beginning. By the time Elgindy arrived at the Englewood, Colorado-based brokerage firm, it was already the biggest—and in some eyes the baddest—player in a wild and woolly world known as the "penny stock market."

Penny stocks get their name from their price, which is gener-ally below $1 a share—at least when the shares start trading. Dur-ing the 1980s, hundreds of new penny stock issues were peddled to the public. Nobody was peddling faster or with more gusto than Blinder. By the fall of 1986, the firm had 1,000 brokers in seventeen states and was hiring dozens more each month, according to an October 9, 1986, story in the *Wall Street Journal*. At the same time, the SEC was trying to close Blinder, Robinson because of alleged violations of the securities laws, the *Journal* story said. Thirty states had also taken some sort of regulatory action against the firm.

Elgindy insists that he was unaware of all the controversy surrounding Blinder. He just wanted to learn how to make $20,000 a month. He was sent to Blinder's Denver-area headquarters for training. "So (they) teach you all these different skills which you have to use, cold-calling a complete stranger and asking them for money and they trust you. And I found it incredibly distasteful. However, I did excel at it," he tells his fellow short sellers.

Back in San Diego, Elgindy joined Blinder's office, where successful brokers were making tens of thousands of dollars a month and managers as much $75,000. Soon Elgindy was doing well enough that he bought himself a Corvette. The license plate read "Stok God."

But for Elgindy, the Blinder party lasted only about eight months. In November 1988, Elgindy saw an extremely negative piece about the firm on *60 Minutes*. He says it was his first inkling of something amiss. About a week later, he got a second inkle when federal agents raided Blinder's Colorado headquarters and seized thousands of documents. Not needing a third, Elgindy quit the firm. (Later Blinder, Robinson went out of business and its founder, Meyer Blinder, was convicted of securities fraud—all the while protesting his innocence.)[2]

After Blinder, Elgindy worked the next couple of years at two small brokerage firms in the San Diego area. In November 1989, he married Mary Faith Lumpkin. The raven-haired daughter of a Tennessee minister was working as a receptionist at one of the Chevy dealers where Elgindy worked. They met when he came back to the dealership to show off his Corvette to his former co-workers.

At the 1999 San Diego seminar, Mary Elgindy, known to her friends by her middle name of Faith, is the perfectly supportive wife. She works the front desk, helping to register people and hand out identification badges. At Elgindy's insistence, she circulates around the audience with a cordless microphone for participants who have questions for her husband. She is beautiful and poised, with a dazzling smile. She and Elgindy appear devoted to each other. But like Elgindy's professional life, his marriage has had some strange twists and turns.

By the early 1990s, Elgindy was doing fine and falling apart. As he later would tell Silicon Investor readers in an e-mail:

```
"I used to be one of the biggest OTC
```

[a reference to the over-the-counter stock market]

```
brokers in the US.. I earned 1.6 million in commis-
sions my last year as a retail broker.. persuading
people to buy and trying to keep them from selling..
that was in 1991 I was 23 and thought I was the
hottest thing around. I didn't sleep well. I drank too
much and partied way too much and the worst part of it
was that I felt like a scum bag when a client lost
money because I had to hype a recommendation to induce
them to get excited so I could earn a commission. . . I
was a broker who made people broker."[3]
```

In 1991, Elgindy leapt at what seemed like a great opportunity. He became a partner in a new San Diego brokerage firm called Armstrong, McKinley. Here, he says, was a chance to run his own firm as he saw fit.

He says he met many interesting people at his new firm. One was Melvin Lloyd Richards. Richards had helped found a company called Alco International Group, Inc. San Diego-based Alco marketed a device to alert surgeons to tears in their gloves so they could avoid possible infections from AIDS and other diseases.

Richards wanted Armstrong, McKinley to sell Alco stock to its customers. He was willing to pay for the service, Elgindy says and made a special offer to the brokerage firm's new part owner: if Elgindy could sell 150,000 shares of Alco stock, Richards would pay him at least $200,000. "I think, 'This is a great deal. This is awesome,'" Elgindy tells his San Diego audience. "How do I do it, where do I sign?" In later interviews, Elgindy insists that he was blissfully ignorant at the time of the federal requirement to tell his clients about such payment arrangements when peddling the stock, though he says he did tell his clients about his compensation deal.

Elgindy says he and the other Armstrong, McKinley brokers began working the phones, singing the song of Alco to their clients. Investors seemed to like the tune. Alco stock rose to $14 a share from $3. Alco's AIDS-prevention product was getting some favorable press attention. Elgindy says he met his Alco stock-sales target and got his payment from Richards, which he plowed into Armstrong, McKinley to increase his equity position. After all, it was like investing in himself.

Elgindy was feeling as flush as someone holding a fistful of diamonds in five-card draw. There was just one problem. "The problem is the whole thing was a fraud," he tells his San Diego audience. Elgindy says he was slow to pick up on this little item. He did notice that each week, brokers at the firm were getting envelopes with cash and taking them across the street to the local Bank of America branch to deposit. But everybody, himself included, seemed to be getting money.

By the middle of 1992, Elgindy's world started to crumble. In May, the *San Diego Union-Tribune* newspaper reported that in 1987 Alco's Melvin Lloyd Richards had gone to prison for a uranium tax-shelter scheme. It also turned out that the SEC banned Richards in 1973 from associating with any broker dealer because of alleged securities-law violations. There were similar stories in other publications. Elgindy says that he knew nothing of these past problems when he started dealing with Richards.[4]

Elgindy also received a phone call from a man in New York named John Fiero.

Fiero is a professional short seller, one of the best and certainly one of the most durable practitioners of this peculiar art. His firm is called Fiero Brothers. Fiero started shorting Alco stock. Alco responded by filing a $900 million slander suit against Fiero and other short sellers. Fiero says he settled his part of the suit without paying anything to Alco.

The boyish-looking Fiero is a low-key but friendly sort. He often calls brokers who are promoting a stock he is shorting. Partly, he hopes to glean useful information, partly he likes to banter. He also doesn't mind giving the other side a little grief.

Fiero remembers calling Elgindy about Alco. He's hazy on the details, though he recalls Elgindy as something of a "trading-room novice." Fiero, whose stock-trading career dates back to 1983, dismissed Armstrong, McKinley as one more "bucket shop" in a bucket brigade of sleazy brokerage firms. He figured Elgindy, as part owner, had to be part of the sleaze.

Elgindy, on the other hand, remembers Fiero's phone call as something of an epiphany. He recalls Fiero telling him of how crooked promoters pay cash to crooked brokers to push worthless stocks. Elgindy says this started him thinking about those envelopes of cash that Armstrong, McKinley brokers were hauling across the street to the Bank of America. He started thinking about his own lucrative deal with Richards.

A "light went on for the very first time in my life" and "a bead of sweat came down my forehead. (For) the very first time it dawned on me that something was wrong," Elgindy says in his San Diego speech.

Though the two later became friendly, Fiero never really bought Elgindy's claim about being in the dark about Alco. It was all so obvious, he says. How, then, does he explain Elgindy never being charged by authorities with wrongdoing? Fiero has a one-word answer: "cooperation."[5]

Elgindy did become an active helper in the federal government's investigation of Armstrong, McKinley and Alco. He photocopied records at the firm and turned the copies over to the government. He says he even rifled through his partner's office for evidence.

Some of Elgindy's work for the government is detailed in a 1997 letter from the U.S. Attorney's office in San Diego, which handled the investigation. Elgindy supplied me a copy of the letter. He was clearly very proud of it, though the copy he supplied has its odd aspects. The name of the recipient has been whited out, as has a section of the letter. Elgindy says this was done to protect the identity of certain individuals. I later would learn that at least part of the reason for the secrecy is that the letter was written in connection with a separate matter that could early in the twenty-first century send Tony Elgindy to federal prison.

(While Elgindy is clearly proud of this letter, he has a hard time keeping track of it. After faxing it to me, he asks me on three separate occasions to fax back a copy because he has misplaced his. I gladly comply. How often does a reporter get to slip a source the source's own documents?)

The letter he sent me also has a handwritten change, done by Elgindy. The letter, as typed, says that Elgindy has entered into "a cooperation agreement" with the U.S. Attorney's office. That language usually means that an individual has reached a deal to lessen or avoid a criminal penalty by helping the government nab others. Elgindy has written in "volunteered to enter" a cooperation agreement. He says he did this to emphasize that he didn't have any criminal exposure and was just offering to help—as any good citizen would.

The rest of the letter certainly indicates that Elgindy did help, as these excerpts show: "He was debriefed numerous times. . . . He made numerous monitored telephone calls at our direction. . . . He met our major target two different times for extended conversations while wearing a body wire. . . . He met another target in a hotel room in San Diego where the meeting was video taped by Government Agents. . . . He provided boxes of records." The letter says that three targets had already pled guilty and two others were negotiating deals. "The government could not have made its cases without the assistance of Mr. Elgindy," the letter concludes.

Yesmin Saide, the assistant U.S. Attorney whose name is on the letter, declines to comment on the document. She also won't talk about Elgindy.

Among those pleading guilty to tax-fraud charges as a result of the probe was Melvin Lloyd Richards. Government court filings in that case and related ones say that Richards partially controlled Armstrong, McKinley. He also arranged for "cash kickbacks" to be paid to brokers there to peddle Alco and other stocks Richards was promoting, the filings say. Richards was sentenced to twenty-seven months in prison.[6]

Though he avoided criminal sanctions, Elgindy felt the ripples of the Armstrong, McKinley debacle for years afterwards. In 1997, for instance, Ohio regulators rejected his application for a securities broker license in that state. According to the report by the state hearing examiner, Elgindy was "not of 'good business repute.' "

Among other things, the hearing examiner found that the broker had altered a letter from a former Armstrong, McKinley client and then submitted it in the Ohio licensing case. The client, a Dr. Laila Gomaa, won $30,000 in an arbitration complaint against the brokerage firm and its principals, including Elgindy. To bolster his argument that others at the firm were responsible for her losses, Elgindy obtained a letter from Dr. Gomaa absolving him of any misdeeds.

Elgindy submitted the letter. But then the hearing examiner called the doctor. According to his report, she said she recognized only part of the letter and that a large chunk of it was different from what she had sent Elgindy. The hearing examiner found that Elgindy had "altered" the letter before submitting it.[7]

Like other parts of Elgindy's life, this incident has an unusual twist. The unhappy client, Laila Gomaa, was also Elgindy's mother. When Elgindy joined the brokerage firm, she opened an account, which, Elgindy says, was handled by others. And handled badly, he adds.

He says he supported her decision to file an arbitration case against Armstrong, McKinley, even though it meant that she was filing charges against him as a part owner. (In the securities business, clients who feel wronged by their brokers are generally required to go through an arbitration proceeding at the National Association of Securities Dealers, or NASD, rather than file a lawsuit.)

When the Ohio licensing case came up, Elgindy says that he called his mother. She asked him to write the letter and she would sign it, Elgindy says, and that may explain why she wasn't familiar with the contents of the letter. When the Ohio decision came out, he angrily called his mother and accused her of "having destroyed" his career. "I was very upset with her. We didn't talk for a month," he says.

Gomaa, in a telephone interview, essentially supported her son's version of events. While she admitted that she was for a time "very mad at my son" for what happened at the brokerage firm, she emphatically added, "I am always very proud of Amr."

But to hear Elgindy, he was hardly proud of himself in the wake of the Armstrong, McKinley mess. The firm closed amidst scandal and investigations. The broker fell into what he describes as a "deep depression," and went on disability.

The change in the normally outgoing and self-assured Elgindy—who is usually so charged up that he sleeps only about five hours a night—was enormous and frightening to his wife. "He would shut himself away and not want to talk to anyone," says Mary Elgindy.

Indeed, the next few years would be very rocky ones for their marriage. At one point, Mary Elgindy filed for divorce in Texas, where the couple had moved. In her divorce petition, she said they had "ceased to live together as husband and wife." She also claimed that Elgindy was guilty of "cruel treatment" and "adultery." She obtained a restraining order against her husband. Elgindy acknowledges "cheating" on his wife and "abusing" alcohol and drugs. "I was for a time a raving lunatic," he says. "But I was able to change my ways." The Elgindys eventually reconciled and the divorce action was dismissed.[8]

In early 1994, Elgindy was back in the brokerage business, going to work in the Dallas-Fort Worth area for Bear Stearns & Co. But he lasted there only a few months and the relationship ended badly. Elgindy filed an arbitration claim with the NASD against Bear, alleging that the brokerage firm had reneged on a pledge to pay him over $100,000 in promised compensation. He also asked for $1 million in punitive damages.

Filings in that case show that Bear contended Elgindy overstated his capacity to bring in new business. While at the brokerage firm, "his performance and production were poor," said one filing. The arbitrator sided with Bear and ordered Elgindy to pay $60,000 to the brokerage firm.

That ruling outraged Elgindy and helped nurture his growing animosity toward the securities-industry establishment in general and the NASD in particular. To him, the idea was ludicrous that a self-regulatory organization whose board includes representatives of big brokerage firms could somehow police those same big brokerage firms. (Elgindy vowed he would never pay the Bear Stearns judgment and as of February 2000, he hadn't.)

> "The NASD needs to be dissolved ..Whoever thought that
> an industry could regulate itself obviously works on
> Wall Street.. we should just allow Criminals decide
> their own punishment and rely on them to turn them-
> selves in when they break a law.. Thats what we have
> on Wall Street,"

he wrote in a 1999 message posted on Silicon Investor.[9]

In 1995, Elgindy started his own brokerage firm, Key West Securities, in the Dallas-Fort Worth area suburb of Hurst. From the beginning, he says he intended Key West to be very different from Armstrong, McKinley. Key West would handle few individual brokerage accounts. And the firm, led by its head trader Elgindy, would focus on shorting stocks. Elgindy says he had decided that he would rather expose cruddy stocks than peddle them.

At Key West, he performed with a whole new cast of suspect characters. One of them was a federal prosecutor who was eventually criminally convicted himself. The case of this prosecutor highlights the murky nature of Elgindy's world—where it is sometimes difficult to tell the good guys from the bad guys amidst the madness that increasingly engulfed the stock market on its rocket ride of the 1990s.

The prosecutor's name is Andrew Sturgis Pitt, though almost everyone calls him Drew. He worked in the Los Angeles office of the Justice Department's Organized-Crime Strike Force. By 1995, Pitt's mob hunting had taken him deep into the bowels of Wall Street.

As part of this work, Pitt had assembled a rather astonishing rogue's gallery of informants. Several were veteran swindlers who were working with Pitt in hopes of reducing future jail time. Included in this motley crew were the venerable Ramon D'Onofrio and his son Mark. Like so many fathers before him, he was passing the family business on to his son.

Pitt assembled this informant group to combat what he and other officials saw as a rising tide of stock fraud and Mafia incursion into the markets. By early 1996, stockbrokers and traders were telling reporters—usually only after a promise that their names wouldn't be used—of a rising level of threats and violence.

One of the people talking about the problem of criminals in the stock market was Elgindy. However, unlike others, he was talking on the record. Way on the record.

In May 1997, ABC's news show 20/20 did a segment called "Shakedown on Wall Street," featuring Elgindy as a crusading stockbroker working to clean up the securities markets—at considerable risk to himself. In it, Elgindy tells of receiving a bullet in the mail with his name on it. He tells of seeing three-hundred-pound thugs walking into brokerage offices and beating people up.

For 20/20 viewers, Elgindy plays some of the many secret tape recordings he has made. There is the voice of a guy who tells Elgindy, "You're a family man. You've got more to lose." Another taped voice warns Elgindy about how other brokers who took the wrong position in a stock are "looking up at the ceiling. You understand what I mean?" Elgindy also shows off his pistol and his Ferrari.

Barbara Walters, 20/20's co-host, is certainly impressed. "Why is Tony doing this?" she asks ABC correspondent Brian Ross, who reports the story. "He's endangering himself."

"He's one of those people, Barbara, who just won't be pushed around by anyone, including the mob," Ross responds.

Elgindy met Pitt, the federal prosecutor, at a barbecue in an upscale section of Los Angeles. The party was at the home of Michael Zaman, who owned a local stock brokerage firm. Elgindy and Zaman had gotten to know each through stock-trading activities.

How Zaman knew Pitt is a more complicated story.

For much of his federal career, which began in 1988, Pitt was admired by colleagues as an honest and aggressive prosecutor, albeit an unconventional one. Unlike the average hard-eyed federal attorney off the Brooks Brothers assembly line, Pitt rarely wears a suit. He prefers jeans and cowboy boots. He often gets around Southern California on a motorcycle. He loves dogs, especially black ones, and keeps half a dozen or more at his home in the hill country outside of Los Angeles. He calls his home the Black Dog Ranch.

Zaman, a small and intense man, had been under investigation by federal authorities and the NASD for possible securities-law violations. He began helping Pitt in the prosecutor's stock fraud investigations. Pitt helped Zaman. At one point, he wrote a letter to the NASD vouching for Zaman's honesty and telling of his help chasing down stock swindlers. The letter suggested that the NASD hold up on its investigation of Zaman.

For a prosecutor, few things are trickier than long-term relationships with informants. After all, many such individuals are deeply dishonest and untrustworthy figures who will try to manipulate the prosecutor like they manipulate everyone else.

In working with his panoply of snitches, Drew Pitt lost his way. He crossed lines that prosecutors should never cross.

Pitt was involved in a business in the Denver area with one of his swindler-informants. He made a special trip to Dallas and intervened in a court case to keep another informant out of prison on a bank-fraud conviction. That same informant used his reprieve from jail to pull off a multimillion-dollar stock fraud that eventually did send him to prison.

Zaman helped Pitt and his wife take control of a small public company. The company's name was BDR Industries, as in Black Dog Ranch. Later it changed its name to Conectisys Corp. It was involved in various businesses. For a time, its stock price soared.

Finally government investigators caught up with the prosecutor and his friends. In June 1997, Pitt pled guilty to criminal charges of fraud and conflict of interest for taking about $1 million from convicted felons and others involved in federal investigations. He was sentenced to two years in prison. Pitt's lawyer, Charles Wehner, says that his client's transgressions arose from a "failure to keep his private business relationships separate from his involvement with obtaining information on behalf of the government."

The SEC also sued Pitt and Zaman in Los Angeles federal court for engaging in a "fraudulent scheme" to manipulate the price of Conectisys stock. The SEC's star witness in the case: Tony Elgindy.[10]

According to a declaration from Elgindy that the SEC filed in the case, he had traded in Conectisys shares at the direction of Zaman. Elgindy said his brokerage firm posted buy and sell quotes "at prices dictated by Zaman," with Zaman promising to cover any losses that might result from such trades. The SEC argued that such rigged trading is illegal under federal securities laws.

Elgindy also claimed that Zaman threatened him after the SEC filed its suit. "Zaman called my home and told my wife . . . who had answered the phone, that her husband 'was a dead man,' " said Elgindy in his declaration. He added that he also personally received a phone call at his office from a Zaman business associate "who told me I 'was a f***ing dead man.' " Zaman denies trying to threaten Elgindy.

At the 1997 trial of Pitt and Zaman, Elgindy was the "killer witness" who enabled the SEC to win injunctions and monetary sanctions in the case, said Irving Einhorn, Zaman's attorney. Both Pitt and Zaman deny wrongdoing in the case.

Einhorn, the former head of the SEC's Los Angeles office, argued in an interview that if his client was guilty of stock manipulation, so was Elgindy. "He was a co-conspirator with my client," said Einhorn, who added that regulators should at the very least revoke Elgindy's brokerage license.

Several other former senior SEC officials, who read Elgindy's declaration at my request, drew the same conclusion. Like Einhorn, they expressed puzzlement, astonishment, and outrage at the SEC's lack of action.

The SEC won't comment on Elgindy, other than to say that he

hasn't been given any promises of protection. Elgindy says anyone who thinks he broke the law doesn't understand his role in the transactions with Zaman.

The Conectisys case, like the Armstrong, McKinley case, marked another instance where Elgindy survived a potentially sticky legal situation. Such occurrences, along with his ongoing relationships with SEC and other law-enforcement officials, would later feed into Elgindy's aura on the Internet. Here, it seems, is a man who can bring down others without toppling himself.

But Elgindy's roller-coaster ride was hardly over as new problems cropped up on the professional front. On September 22, 1997, the NASD's market regulation committee censured Elgindy and barred him from certain brokerage activities for up to a year. It also fined him $30,000. The committee found that in 1993 Elgindy had violated certain stock-trading rules, including improperly using a stock-trading system that had been created to handle small orders from individual investors.

Though ammunition for his critics, the NASD sanctions did little to restrain Elgindy's ability to be an active trader. The committee pointed to mitigating circumstances in determining his penalty. At the time of the violations, "Elgindy was suffering from severe mental illness and commenced full disability shortly after these events occurred," says the committee's report. The document also notes Elgindy's help in pointing out "potential securities law violations" by others.[11]

Elgindy freely admits to committing some of the alleged violations. But he says they were inadvertent and came at a time when he was deeply depressed and distracted by the troubles at Armstrong, McKinley. While he accepted the sanctions and agreed to a payment schedule of $500 a month for the fine, the case only added to his belief that the NASD is hostile territory.

As Elgindy moved into and through 1998, he began to think more and more about making some major changes in his life. He had already begun seeing the power of the Internet, how certain online "gurus" could move and, he believed, manipulate stock prices. "It's a whole new frontier," Elgindy told me in a June 1998 interview.

He began posting e-mails on various Internet stock-message boards, mostly critical of companies he was shorting. He put messages up under a number of different monikers, including "Freshcash," "Zerobid," and "Dntwstmytm"—the last one being shorthand for "don't waste my time."

In 1998, Elgindy took three major steps. He moved his family back to the San Diego area. He closed down Key West Securities, and he stopped making payments on his $30,000 NASD fine. This prompted the NASD to revoke his membership, meaning he could no longer be a stockbroker. (Also blocking any return to the brokerage business was his failure to pay the $60,000 Bear Stearns judgment.)

Which was perfectly fine with Elgindy. He had other plans.

CHAPTER
ELEVEN

"...OVERINFLATED PIG.....RED FLAG central!!!!"

"...one of the stinkiest stocks......What a scam."

"This thing needs to be halted ..."

"RUMOR ... Im hearing a possible wise-guy connection."

"Look for very bad news soon."[1]

IT'S JANUARY 1999. As the stock market, revived from its summer swoon, roars toward new records, Tony Elgindy is having fun with his new toy.

Of course, Elgindy will tell anyone who asks (and perhaps a few who don't) that he is engaged in serious work. He has dedicated his new Silicon Investor stock-discussion site, now two months old, to scam busting. And there are so many frauds to be exposed, investors protected—and, of course, money to be made doing it. In its first two months, the Anthony@Equity Investigations site has attracted 6,000 messages and uncounted numbers of readers. Its become one of the new hot spots in the cyberspace stock-chat world.

Despite all this weighty work, it is also clear from Elgindy's postings that the short seller is having a blast. He is like a kid with a sack full of cherry bombs and a china shop full of targets. Consequently, Elgindy is busy firing out e-mails and playing Sam Spade, sans trenchcoat.

> "I Will be in Anaheim with a handful of fake business
> cards and wired for sound tomorrow in Anaheim checking
> out a few of the latest losers,"

he writes of a planned trip to an investor presentation by several companies.[2]

> "Will send a message if I see something that is
> notable.. I expect to be completely awe-inspired by
> these Companies so they better not disappoint me."

Elgindy uses the Internet to visit, and dump on, a variety of stocks. In February 1999, for example, he dips his toe in the trading frenzy around the JB Oxford brokerage firm, long enough to take a few swipes, such as

> "JBOH<—SELL/SHORT!!! @ 11 3/4!!! Do it now,"

and then move on.[3]

One early Elgindy target (and the subject of the messages at the chapter's beginning) is USA Talks.com, Inc. The firm is based in La Jolla, California, just a short drive from Elgindy's home. But a larger divide separates the company and the trader.

In January 1999, USA Talks.com is in the process of building what a company press release calls "the first national and international Internet-based long distance telephone service to offer unlimited use for a monthly flat fee" of between $20 and $60 a month. However, the company is still very much a work in progress. It's just testing its system in a limited area. It doesn't yet have any revenues but does have over a $6 million loss in 1998 from the costs of the start-up effort.[4]

Nonetheless, USA Talks.com has been riding the Internet rocket ship, which after the previous summer's crash has been refueled, seemingly more powerfully than ever. Trading under the symbol USAT, USA Talks.com's stock has risen from $3 a share in November to over $50 a share in January. Though the USA Talks.com can't yet speak of any sales, it does boast a stock market value of $1.5 billion.

No revenues, a billion-dollar market cap (short for capitalization). This sort of combination is music to the ears of a short seller. Elgindy is soon playing his USAT symphony at full blast in the silence of cyberspace.

The stock trader tells of signing up to try out the USA Talk.com's phone network, which is being set up and tested in the California market.

```
"California network does not work well and SUCKS!!!"
```

he contends.

```
"Your comments smell of a canadian short,"
```

shoots back a message poster.

```
"If I were you I would get a good lawyer."
```

```
"I have lots of lawyers and they all think it sucks
also,"
```

Elgindy responds.

Elgindy also contends that the company has failed to disclose enough about the past of its chairman and chief executive, Allen Portnoy.

```
"PORTNOY is hypester behind failed DIGITECH!!!"
```

he writes.[5]

In the 1980s, Portnoy headed a small St. Louis–based company called Digitech that was developing what it portrayed as a major breakthrough in computer voice-recognition technology. To all those still punching keyboards in 1999, it is apparent that computers with ears haven't yet arrived.

The corporate biography of the USA Talks.com chief executive on the company website doesn't mention Digitech, though it does name a number of other Portnoy-related ventures dating back to 1946. Company officials say the firm has made all necessary disclosures about the past activities of its officers. Portnoy also denies ever hyping any company.

Elgindy and others attack USA Talks.com's use of a Memphis, Tennessee, telemarketing firm called TrendMark to sell its Internet phone service to consumers. In 1998, TrendMark was charged by the Federal Trade Commission with making "a host of unsubstantiated" claims about weight-loss products it was selling, according to an FTC press release. TrendMark settled that case without admitting wrongdoing. USA Talks.com later stopped using Trend-Mark.[6]

While Elgindy raises the specter of the Mob in connection with USA Talks.com, he doesn't provide any basis for that claim. When asked about it months later, he says he can't recall why he suspected "wise-guy" ties to the firm. The company strongly denies any such ties.

Besides dumping on the company online, Elgindy says he is shoveling dirt over to the SEC. He isn't bashful about reminding people of his past roles on this stage.

> "I am a nationally recognized expert witness in Securities Fraud . . . catch a rerun of my interview on 20/20,"

he writes.

Whatever one thinks of the quality of his criticisms, Elgindy turns out to be a seer on USA Talks.com. On January 26, he writes that for the company

> "very BAD NEWS LOOMING OVERHEAD!!!!"

The next day, he reiterates that prediction.

> "It will be crystal clear soon,"

he writes.[7]

On January 29, the news is bad—unless you happen to be shorting USA Talks.com. The SEC suspends trading in the stock. In a release, the agency says that questions have been raised "about the accuracy and adequacy of publicly disseminated information concerning, among other things, the status and extent of USA Talks' business operations." The release doesn't elaborate and an SEC spokesman declines to comment.

The company defends its disclosure practices and vows to push ahead with building its phone business. But in the stock market, great damage is done. When USA Talks.com's shares resume trading, the price eventually falls to a few dollars a share from over $50. A billion dollars in market value evaporates faster than a teardrop on the revved-up engine of Elgindy's Ferrari. But anyone who has shorted the stock near its peak stands to make a handsome profit.

For Elgindy, his success on USA Talks.com extends beyond just the $300,000 he says he made trading the stock. The episode helps establish his reputation online as a man who can pick 'em and drop 'em. And for anyone interested in shorting stock, that's the kind of guy to know.

Elgindy revels in his success.

> "Well.. it just proves that we know what we are doing
> . . . Nice ONE!!! Sweeeet!!!"

he writes in one message. In another missive, he invites other Internet traders to

> "come over and join our thread."

Adding to the mystique is an unanswered question that hangs over Elgindy like a charge of static electricity. Just what is this aggressive short seller's relationship with law enforcement officials?

He obviously has worked with federal officials in the past. He claims that he routinely feeds information to the government about individuals and companies. But is Uncle Sam feeding anything back to Elgindy? Is his prediction of bad news for USA Talks.com, quickly followed by an SEC trading halt, merely a lucky guess? Or is it something more tangible, and darker?

It doesn't take Level II software to figure out the enormous profit-making potential of receiving advance information from government regulators. Of course, any SEC official passing such information would be violating fundamental secrecy rules of the commission. That person would be subject to firing and perhaps worse.

An SEC spokesman says the agency doesn't have any reason to believe that any official leaked any information to Elgindy. He also declines to discuss his agency's dealings with Elgindy. When the man himself is asked, Elgindy says, with a sly laugh, that the SEC "did . . . not" give him any advance word about the coming USAT trading halt.

Of course, perception can be as important as reality. And the idea that the SEC *might* be feeding Elgindy information begins to infect the Internet stock-talk world. One Internet poster worries that if Elgindy has a pipeline to regulators, he would have "absolute power" over other investors. And, if so, would Elgindy "choose the dark or the light," this investor wonders.

TokyoMex does more than just wonder. "He is using his government connections to terrorize people on the Internet!" Park shouts during a 1999 interview. "This is very dangerous thing and it has to stop."

Park has a very personal interest in Elgindy's relations with Uncle Sam. In March 1999, the SEC sends out subpoenas as part of its investigation of one Yun Soo Oh Park. The subpoena notes that the gentleman in question is also known as Joe Park, Joe Matsudaira, Tokyo Joe, and TokyoMex. The name list could have been longer.

The SEC wants any documents involving Park or Societe Anonyme, including printouts of e-mails, going back to January 1, 1998. The subpoena also asks for records of any payments sent to Park or Societe Anonyme.[8]

Park insists that he has done nothing wrong. He is equally emphatic concerning who is fomenting trouble for him at the SEC.

It's Elgindy. Park says that in a conversation with Kellie Blattner, an SEC attorney on his case, he mentions Elgindy. There is silence from the other end of the line, he says. "She knows him," Park says, who talks of suing Elgindy.

Park notes that Elgindy is in the process of starting his own private e-mail service/website, similar to Societe Anonyme, but dedicated to short selling. Being the man who brings down Tokyo-Mex would be a big boost to Elgindy's reputation and his new enterprise, says Park.

As usual, the SEC declines to comment on the Park investigation or even acknowledge that it exists.

For his part, Elgindy brags about going after Park. He says he mailed the SEC a thirty-five-pound package with 1,885 pages of TokyoMex e-mails and other documents—a pile that Elgindy argues shows a widespread pattern of securities-law violations. The trader insists, however, that his motives have nothing to do with economics or rivalries. Elgindy simply wants to rid the markets of a man he considers to be a major stock crook.

Elgindy gleefully spreads word of the SEC's Park investigation around the Internet, along with a few editorial comments of his own.

> "Wake up people . . . This guy is in my opinion the
> worst the Internet produces. He doesn't have a shred
> of credibility or experience in the Industry,"

writes Elgindy. He likens taking stock-trading advice from Tokyo-Mex to

> "gettin marital tips from OJ Simpson."

Elgindy also publicly hopes that the SEC probe will lead to

> "Criminal action next."[9]

To Park, he warns,

> "don't try to intimidate any witnesses . . . It's a
> Felony . . . "

Elgindy is so eager to tar Park that he even passes along bum information. He posts a list passed along from another online message writer that purports to show the most subpoenaed names on Silicon Investor—a sort of Who's Who of the suspected scofflaw set.

"The MOST WANTED Scammer around—Guess who??? Over
300,000 subpoenas!!!"

Anthony@Pacific roars. No points for guessing the name at the top of that list, though it does take a certain feat of imagination to conceive how anyone could be the target of so many subpoenas. When Elgindy later learns that the list headed by TokyoMex is just someone's joke, he backtracks, but not completely.

"Want to bet he has a number closer to 300,000 that
anyone else on SI, or anywhere in the world . . . hee
hee,"

Elgindy writes.[10]

TokyoMex's e-mail responses to Elgindy's assault are a bit more cryptic but hardly friendly.

"And we will see A dog.. seems, your closet is full of
dead bodies,, we will see my friend,"

Park writes. Park also starts doing a little investigating of his own.

"Any one here feel bullied, manipulated,,suffered any
emotional, psychological duress or financial loss
because of intimidating posts by certain individuals?"

Of course, Park has moments when he lets his feelings about Elgindy hang out a bit more.

"I think this bazzar tea boy from Alexandria is a sxxx
bag extraordinaire..,"

he writes in one e-mail.[11]

Being in the online stock-discussion world, others feel obliged to get in their two bytes.

> "Good luck in prison and good luck when you drop the
> soap. . . ,"

writes one poster to Park. Lest Elgindy feel left out, another person
tells him that

> "you rank right down there with the sludge on the bot-
> tom of a septic tank!"

Besides Park, the SEC is looking at other hot online stock-
picking services, according to an April 1999 story in the *Wall Street
Journal.* In a certain perverse way, these investigations are a measure of how far Park and other Internet gurus have come in a very
short time.[12]

These new Internet players have gained enough influence that
they can no longer be ignored. The question confronting regulators
is what to do with them. Should they be subject to licensing, as are
stockbrokers and other market professionals? Is a burrito-maker-
cum-stock-picker free to share his trading opinions? How does
charging for those opinions change that picture? Where does the
First Amendment end and the securities rule book begin?

To further complicate matters, regulators are having to come
up with rules in a rapidly evolving medium where any Tom, Dick,
or Dog with a computer, a modem, and at least a modicum of talent has the opportunity to become a stock-trading star.

While not happy about being investigated, Park seems
resigned to the scrutiny, and at moments, almost to welcome it. He
hires Sorkin, the former head of the SEC's New York office, to represent him in the investigation. He exudes confidence that he will
get a clean bill of health. In an e-mail message to Societe Anonyme
members, he writes that the

> "SEC as well as market makers are wondering,, what is
> going on witin SA,, they can move stocks ,, individual
> investors and traders can create more forceful and
> dynamic changes in the market,, a new boundary and
> questions are arising,,."

Park counsels members who are contacted by the SEC to

"cooperate fully and tell the truth !!!!"

He also provides SEC attorney Blattner's phone number and address at the agency for those who haven't been contacted but want to pass along their opinions.

Besides attention from the SEC, there are other signs of TokyoMex's growing stature. He starts getting treated as something of an icon of the Internet '90s. Not necessarily a good icon, but you can't have everything.

"With the Dow Jones industrial average on the verge of closing over 10,000, I can't get my mind off a strange stock picker known as Tokyo Joe," writes financial journalist Joseph Nocera in March 1999. This is the same Nocera whose 1996 *Fortune* magazine cover story on Motley Fool and Iomega proclaimed the rising power of the Internet stock-discussion world.

While Nocera praises the Internet for giving investors faster and cheaper ways to trade and to learn, he also worries. "But along with this empowerment has come an extraordinary bullishness that borders on arrogance," writes Nocera. "In the view of many Internet investors, stocks move up because, well—who cares why they move up? That's what they've always done."

The rise of Park—whom Nocera describes as "without question, one of the most influential stock pickers on the Internet"—shows how far this new go-go mentality has gone, the journalist argues. "When a character like Tokyo Joe arrives on the scene, it's a sure signal that the end of the bull market is near," writes Nocera. "But I'm not sure I have the nerve to say that out loud anymore. I've been burned too many times these past few years."[13]

By the end of the first quarter of 1999, Societe Anonyme has over 1,700 members, according to the quarterly report that Park e-mails to members. They hail from

"from Australia,, Indonesia,. Hong Kong, Korea, Japan
, Peru, Argentina, Venezuela, all across USA fro American Samoa to Vurging Islands,, many in Canada,, UK,,

```
Scotland .. 2 in Ireland,, Norway, Sweden ,, Germanu,
Italy, Greece Russia, Pakistan, Saudi Arabia,,,"
```

the report says.

Just over six months earlier, membership was down below 200. The membership rise came despite higher dues, which are now $100 a month. At 1,700-plus members, the new rate translates into some $2 million a year coming into Societe Anonyme's coffers. And that doesn't count any money Park makes actually trading stocks. He says his personal trading profits since December have been $600,000.

And when the SEC inquiry is completed and that shadow is gone,

```
"as promised, we will go mainstream America,,"
```

Park writes to members. Details to follow.

As Park is laying plans to expand his empire, Elgindy is building one of his own out of a cluttered office in his home near the Southern California seaside resort of Del Mar. I arrive at the house one morning around 6:30 A.M., when the markets open in New York, to interview Elgindy and watch him in action.

The two-story house is large and is the target of lots of construction work. The front door is, at the moment, short its lock. I knock and do it quietly, since I'm not completely sure who might be asleep or awake. I wait, knock again, this time a little louder. A voice inside says something. I can't quite make out the words but take them as an invitation.

I step into a large foyer occupied by a large German shepherd. The foyer seems to pay me no mind. But the hound is looking straight at me and is either having a very tense morning or appears ready to pounce. I freeze. Being a veteran reporter, I do notice that the dog has very fine teeth, though I can't help thinking they would look much nicer if he'd lose the snarl.

"Steef!" yells Elgindy from another room. The snarl disappears, the leg springs unwind, and the pooch trots meekly off in the direction of the voice. I follow him. First, I start breathing again.

Elgindy is sitting at a desk surrounded by four large computer screens. We shake hands and say hello. He is wearing a black sleeveless T-shirt and blue jeans. A small earring shines in his left lobe.

His office also contains cartons, children's toys (presumably belonging to his three young sons), a safe, a large globe on a stand, and a hat rack with caps. A copying machine stands against one wall with its paper trays piled on top. Behind him, on a windowsill near a table filled with knickknacks, is his California license plate "Stok God." There is also one from Texas, clearly issued after Elgindy had gone over to the short side. It reads "O Bid"—a reference to a stock whose price has fallen to zero, something closer to heaven than Fort Worth for a short seller. Next to the desk is a paper shredder.

Steef has settled himself comfortably near Elgindy. The Egyptian native explains that the dog worked for a time at the Frankfurt, Germany, police department. Elgindy bought him for $15,000 from a trainer in Los Angeles who specializes in guard dogs for the rich and famous. Steef is trained to kill, Elgindy says. In response to a question, he adds that the dog is perfectly friendly as long as he doesn't think his master is in danger. I assure Elgindy that I left my brass interviewing knuckles back in the car.

Later, while I'm sitting next to Elgindy at his computers, Steef ambles over and rests his head in my lap. Nice doggie. I pet him. I smile at him. I regret that Gap doesn't sell trousers with titanium inseams.

Of course, Steef isn't Elgindy's only protection against a hostile world. Resting near his license plates is an open case that holds a pistol, a reasonably large one. It's a .40 caliber Smith & Wesson, Elgindy tells me. He used to have a .38 caliber Colt, he explains, but people in Texas made fun of his pea shooter.

As I spend the day watching him trade and puff on Marlboro Ultra Lite 100's, Elgindy tells me a bit about the fine art of shorting. For instance, he doesn't short New York Stock Exchange stocks. That's because of the trading system used on the Big Board that uses specialists. The specialist has too much power to move the stock's price to the detriment of a short seller, says Elgindy.

He prefers the market maker system used on the Nasdaq and

Bulletin Board, where for any given stock usually a number of brokerage firms post buy and sell prices. Elgindy's old firm, Key West, was a market maker. While the market maker system can be a snake pit in its own ways, says Elgindy, he is at least familiar with the slither marks. And it's a place where he believes he can catch a meal rather than be one.

During our day together, he also talks of the trust others feel for him online. He tells of receiving $20,000 and an e-mail request from a man he has never met. The man wants to short a certain stock but can't find any shares to borrow. Would Elgindy, with his better connections, short the stock on his behalf? Elgindy would and did. The man making the request later confirms this story to me and adds that Elgindy made a profit for him on the transaction.

One of things that strikes me about Elgindy as I watch him in action during the day is the similarities to his mortal enemy Park. Both clearly love being plugged into the Internet and revel in the high-stakes version of stock market Pac Man that each is playing. Anthony, like Joe, cheers and groans and curses as the day's battles unfold on his computer screens—which Elgindy assures me are the largest and best available, and cost $3,000 each. Elgindy says he sometimes gets so excited that he flings his phone across the room, often breaking it. He keeps a stock of replacement sets on hand for such moments. Both Park and Elgindy send out e-mails and work the phones with gusto. Each man wishes the other would fry in Internet hell.

"I heard it will be suspended. It's got fraud connections, convicted felons, that kind of stuff," Elgindy tells someone on the phone about some company. It hardly seems to matter which one. There are so many.

Perhaps because of his days as a broker cold-calling suck—er—customers, Elgindy clearly feels at home on the phone. He tells me he places all his stock orders by phone and never uses any of the online brokerage firms that are all the rage with many investors. Elgindy says he wants another human being taking his orders. At the very least, he adds, he will have someone to yell at if things go wrong.

"Bro, call me. Don't PM (private e-mail) me. I don't read that shit. Call me, even if you have to call collect," Elgindy tells Bear Down during a phone conversation.

Bear Down is part of Elgindy's informal network of fellow short sellers around the country. It takes a certain temperament to be a short seller. You need to be part detective, part troublemaker. A few dashes of pushiness, obnoxiousness, and flame retardant don't hurt.

Bear Down works with Elgindy and others on FindEx.com, the Nebraska firm with the interesting Florida phone number. Acting on a tip that Reifler, the scofflaw, might be found at FindeE.com, Bear Down and others go online and begin doing some basic online digging. Among other things, they pull up company press releases and begin calling the contact phone numbers. Often, those calls are made late at night when no person is likely to answer. Automated phone directories, says Bear Down, often prove to be a much better source than a human being for learning who can be found at the phone number.

When the nocturnal call is made to the Florida FindEx phone number, the automated answering device gives two extensions to choose from. One is for "Yanni," the other for "Lionel." As far as Bear Down is concerned, there could be a third line for Eureka.

Bear Down says he calls back during business hours and reaches Lionel. Posing as a FindEx.com shareholder, Bear Down asks about the company. "He seemed to know all about" FindEx.com and claimed to be a major shareholder, recalls the short seller. The trader is so excited by the conversation that he forgets to ask Lionel his last name. (When I called later, Lionel acknowledged that he was Reifler, but vehemently denied telling anyone that he was connected to FindEx.)

Bear Down, of course, has a real name. He even has a real life, some of which he tells me about when we meet at Elgindy's San Diego seminar. Slim, with a goatee, Bear Down is full of laughs and full of stories about his life, his five-year-old daughter whom he adores, and blondes, whom he adores to a lesser degree. He asks that his real name not be used because of concerns about personal security. He says one company that he has criticized on the Internet has already made a surreptitious effort to find his home address. Because of safety worries, Bear Down sometimes bears up with the help of a 9mm pistol on his nightstand.

Like almost all investors, Bear Down started out buying stocks. Back around 1995, he ventured onto the Internet and found gurus who led him into Canadian mining stocks. "I got my ass handed to me," he says.

His personal mine shaft got him longing to be a short. He started experimenting with shorting Canadian mining stocks and found that he not only liked that side of the street better but seemed to have a certain talent for it. The rewards can be faster and bigger, especially in a bull market where buyers are pushing up the prices of "a lot of junk," he says.

However, short sellers face correspondingly big risks in such a market, he acknowledges. One day, Bear Down took a nap only to awaken to a big surge in the market that reduced the value of his trading account by some 90 percent. Since then, he says with a laugh, there is no dozing during market hours.

Though shy about publicity, Bear Down is at least willing to reveal his real name in private. By contrast, another sometimes Elgindy short-selling colleague is mum on that subject even though his supposed real name has appeared in newspaper stories and court documents.

His online name is Pluvia. During a telephone interview, Pluvia explains that he wanted a distinctive name and since he hails from a desert area—the number I first reach him at is in Nevada—he chose the Latin word for "rain." On his Silicon Investor profile, he lists his company as Pluvia Capital Research and his title there as Head Rain Master. He also answers to "Steve," and tells of having been a professional in the brokerage business since the 1980s.

But asking him whether he is Steve Keyser brings only a terse "no comment." A story in the April 4, 1999, edition of the *Los Angeles Times* identifies Pluvia as Keyser. The story says that in 1987, the SEC obtained a permanent injunction against Keyser for allegedly diverting proceeds from a stock offering to his personal use. In the *Times* story, Pluvia denies involvement in the SEC case but won't say whether his name is Keyser.

In August 1999, a little company called Sabratek Corp. filed a $90 million fraud and defamation suit against Pluvia, whom it also identified as Keyser. "It's hard to fight wraiths over the Internet," says a Sabratek official in a Dow Jones News Service story about the suit. "People believe anonymity over the Net allows them to behave in what I believe to be an illegal and unconscionable fashion." (During our interviews, Pluvia denies any wrongdoing in connection with Sabratek).[14]

Another company created a stir when it posted an online offer of $5,000 "to anyone who provides the most complete dossier on 'Steve Pluvia.'" Information sought included name, addresses, and identities of "co-consipirators." The bounty offer prompted one online traveler to start a discussion site about the matter. The site's creator called the "bounty" offer a "slanderous attack [that] is aimed directly at the investor's ability to get or give their views on stocks." The site attracted over 1,000 messages.

Though bashful about his real name, Pluvia isn't at all shy when it comes to expressing his opinions online. He called one company

```
"pure garbaaage."
```

About another firm, he wrote,

```
"police to spend the weekend."
```

Regarding a third, he said,

```
"if you believe the prostitutes, I suggest you buy."
```

Like Elgindy, Pluvia is also willing to tangle with other big-name Internet players. He publicly challenged Jenna, an online trader who is the second most bookmarked name on Silicon Investor after TokyoMex, to a stock-trading contest.

Pluvia wrote that Jenna had intimated she is a better trader than he, and he won't let that matter go unchallenged.

```
"I would bet good money you are not. . . . We can start
with whatever amount you want 10k 100k, 1 million, 2
million whatever sweetie. As they say—this is where
```

the rubber meets the road, put up or shut up."

His rival chose neither of those options.

"I'm not 11 and into 'dares' by such as you,"

Jenna wrote back.

"By the way, I never came across your name in the list
of billionaires or in Who's Who in the financial
world.. Now in the Most Wanted List I admit I never
searched. So put a lid on it little boy, I'm not
impressed."

Pluvia even went after his fellow short seller and ally, Elgindy.
When Elgindy announced plans for a private website where members would pay up to $600 a month for his short-selling picks, Pluvia dumped all over the idea and the guy who brung it.

In a note to Elgindy that he posted on Silicon Investor, Pluvia wrote that

"I cannot sit idly by while you IMO

[in my opinion]

take advantage of many of these followers by herding
them towards a pay web site."

For one thing, he said, most of Elgindy's short picks came from others. For another, Elgindy isn't completely trustworthy, Pluvia argued. He wrote that he had analyzed Elgindy's online trading claims and matched them against the actual trading activities of the particular stocks. Pluvia said he concluded that Elgindy couldn't have done some transactions at the prices claimed.

"It is my opinion that Anthony has used what appear to
be false entry/exits to make his trading record look
much better than it is,"

asserted Pluvia. He described Elgindy as

"an ego that's out of control."

Elgindy's feelings were hurt.

"Good luck Steve.. you've turned out to be a quality
guy.. and to think I stuck with you when the *LA Times*
article hit,"

Elgindy wrote. A few minutes later, he added,

"Im a nice guy but Ill eat your lunch trading."

Elgindy said that it's never been a secret that he gets many short-selling suggestions from others, but he still has to pick the ones that will work. As for Pluvia's claim that he inflated his trading claims, that's

"a lie and false and damaging.. you don't want to go
there.. back off.. and do it soon."

His newest critic wasn't yet ready to shift into reverse.

"Feel free to take your weak ass threats elsewhere,"

Pluvia wrote.[15]

The war between these shorts turned out to be short-lived—about twenty-four hours. The two publicly agreed to iron out any differences in private and to again work together as "crim-seekers and floggers," to borrow a phrase from Elgindy's online peace offering. Just to show politics has nothing over online trading when it comes to bedfellowing, Pluvia became a featured stock picker on Elgindy's new private website. Call that what you will, but just don't call him Keyser.

Flodyie, on the other hand, has no problem if you call him Schneider. After all, that's his name: Floyd D. Schneider, mortgage banker, Rochelle Park, New Jersey.

If some of those in Elgindy's stable of fellow shorts might be compared to racehorses—fast but temperamental—Schneider seems something closer to a workhorse. He is a tall man with a large appetite for online research. At Elgindy's seminar, he wears a baseball cap and carries a satchel of files. He will happily talk for hours about his personal rogue's gallery of crooks and companies, pulling files from the satchel to supplement the conversation. He does much of the USA Talks.com research and gets the initial FindEx.com tip. The hours he logs on the Net are already the stuff of stories.

Bear Down recalls sitting at his home one morning at 3 A.M. and seeing Schneider still sending out messages from his New Jersey office. "I'd send him e-mails telling him 'Get out! Go home!'" says Bear Down. Flodyie would reply that he just had a little more research to finish. Anyway, Schneider adds, he's sometimes online more than twenty hours a day.

Schneider loves looking into the crannies of companies and then looking into the crannies of the crannies. He has assembled a long list of favorite online information sites, from Edgar to KnowX. The former is the SEC's free archive of company filings. The latter is a website that charges for information such as court judgments and bankruptcy records. Flodyie has a favorite Internet search engine for names and another for phone numbers and e-mail addresses. He is particularly fond of the Arizona Republic's online library as a guide to the Southwest, where crooks traditionally have helped fill some of the wide-open spaces.

Within days of Elgindy starting his Silicon Investor thread, Flodyie was posting on it, clearly an Anthony acolyte.

> "The pumpsters , scam artists and hooligans on the
> message board spreading their lies throughout the
> financial world need education Anthony. Please give us
> the reasons Anthony so that we may punish them for
> their sins 'for they not know what they do,'"

Schneider wrote.

Perhaps more than anyone in Elgindy's informal inner circle, Schneider seemed to be transformed by his online experiences. He started a website called TheTruthseeker.com. According to the

> "grand opening announcement"

on the site,

"The Truthseeker is on a mission from God to expose
the Underbelly of Wall Street. The Truthseeker and
his Truth Police conduct extensive research and

investigation into companies and individuals who may
be pulling the wool over the eyes of the investing
public . . . .. TheTruthseeker.com is here to lead you
to the light, and to teach you how to research like a
champion Internet cybersleuth. Remember, The Truthseeker does not lie, and The Truthseeker only tells
the truth."

Schneider began posting Truthseeker Reports about companies. He labeled one a "litany of lies and a dossier of deceit." Another firm's principals "have been in serious trouble with the IRS." A third company's list of sins includes being on the buy list of one TokyoMex.

He initially charged a monthly membership fee of $9.95, but later made it free.

"As a member of the Truth Police, you can receive
research and investigation leads from The Truthseeker.
You will know what companies and individuals have
caught the attention of The Truthseeker, and you will
have the opportunity to contribute to actual Reports,"

Schneider wrote. In Internet messages, Schneider began referring to himself as The Truthseeker.

As others have discovered, Truthseeking can be a contentious business. In June 1999, an Internet company called ZiaSun Technologies Inc. filed suit in Seattle federal court against Schneider and seven other Internet posters for allegedly carrying on a "cybersmear campaign" to spread "false and defamatory information" about the company. Schneider denied wrongdoing.

As 1999 progressed, Elgindy was attracting an increasing amount of attention and flak. He estimates that he was getting 1,000 e-mails a week from friend and foe. He battled online with a series of

Internet posters. One critic called Elgindy a "pompous stock market hen." Elgindy at least gave his attacker credit for being limber:

> "Thank you so much for putting both of your smelly
> feet in your own mouth.."

In a sure sign of making it online, a Silicon Investor discussion thread was created to discuss Elgindy. It was called "A&P, Can we trust him." In his opening message, the site's creator insisted he wasn't aiming to impugn Elgindy.

> "We just want to know if he is telling the truth or
> not,"

this person wrote. Nothing too sensitive.

Elgindy quickly offered his own guidelines for this discussion.

> "BEFORE ANYONE GETS CARRIED AWAY, ..let me warn
> them. . . I will protect my treputation and my record
> against any damaging or libelous statements. . . . . . so
> get a good lawyer,"

he wrote.

However, Elgindy soon had to confront a new threat to his rising cyberspace status that had nothing to do with lawyers or traditional law enforcement officials: banishment to Jill Jail and its annex, Fort Bob.

C H A P T E R

T W E L V E

BEING AN ONLINE SHORT SELLER, Elgindy gets into more fights than most message posters. After all, he focuses on companies that he thinks are overvalued or worse. Expressing such views tends to produce disagreements with fans of the firm. And Elgindy, being Elgindy, seems to have a particular knack for controversy. He even managed to get into an online brawl over a mercy mission that he made to the refugee camps of Kosovo in April 1999.

Elgindy got quite a bit of favorable response from the trip, which he says he took to help bring relief supplies to the refugees and help some of the refugees emigrate to the U.S. On his way home, he stopped in Washington and met with members of Congress about his trip. There were newspaper and television pieces, such as the one in the *Chicago Sun-Times* that started, "Wall Street analyst Anthony Elgindy was on vacation in Hawaii, sitting on the beach at Maui, watching his three children play in the surf, when he realized he had to do something about the tragedy unfolding in Kosovo."[1]

While overseas, Elgindy kept up a running online dialogue with his Silicon Investor mates, even hitting them up for donations and other help to the cause. Sometimes he hit hard.

> "ATTENTION!!!!!<---I have asked nicely and I have begged now Im telling you all to please get of your cans and please stop what ever you are doing and help me out.. I have helped all of you for the last 5 months for free.. I have helped some of you for the last 5 yeras and I have saved the investing public millions if not billions in potential losses. . . But if you can send 5 bucks you are my best friend. . . . . A pissed off A@P."[2]

Elgindy's friends sent in thousands of dollars to a charity he designated, and provided other help in trying to aid refugees. A@P was appeased.

> "I wanted to thank everyone on this site that pitched in,"

Elgindy wrote.

Well, maybe not everybody. There was the matter of Scanshift, the man who accompanied him to the camps. Scanshift's real name is Fane Lozman. Lozman is a Chicago-based trader and creator of a computer quote-display system. While Elgindy and Lozman went together on a self-proclaimed mission of peace and mercy, they came home fighting like mad with each other.

Lozman cast an early e-mail stone with a long message that he posted on Elgindy's Silicon Investor thread on April 29, 1999, at 3:23 A.M., Chicago time. He contended that Elgindy had a "personality breakdown" in the camps. Lozman wrote that Elgindy was "playing some weird control game" where he had to be the center of attention—to the point of allegedly trying to stop Lozman from using his own laptop to communicate with SI members. "I also am out a nice piece of change in expenses for this trip that Anthony" had agreed to cover, Scanshift added. In later e-mails, Lozman challenged Elgindy's claims about his Kosovo accomplishments and raised questions about where the donations from online followers had gone, since they don't go to the originally designated recipient.

Needless to say, Elgindy had something to say in response. But first, his attorney, Matthew Tyson, posted a message that

"Anthony would like everyone to know that he will respond to Mr. Lozman's comments when his mission is complete. At this time he is too busy with the media and Congress to deal with personal egos."

Elgindy finally got a free moment. Besides defending his own actions, he called his travelmate "pathetic," though he did give him a certain credit for "jealousy and paranoia, and arrogance." Elgindy also claimed that Lozman "never helped anyone" in the refugee camps and "became a burden to travel with." In a later interview, he said that all the donations had gone to help Kosovo refugees, though he acknowledged that the money didn't all go to the originally designated charity.

Lozman returned serve with a lengthy response to Elgindy's "despicable compilation of outright lies." (In a later interview, Lozman said he felt he did important and good work on the Kosovo mission.) The debate on Silicon Investor continued, with others joining in. One Lozman critic began referring to Scanshift as "Scumshift" and called him "a major fool toying with Tony. He can destroy you."

Then, suddenly, Lozman was posting no more. He had been put into the Silicon Investor stockade, his posting privileges suspended. Elgindy didn't get suspended as a result of his fight with Scanshift, though Silicon Investor management removed one of his Kosovo-related posts that called for the assassination of Yugoslav president Slobodan Milosevic.

Elgindy did get suspended for other things. By SI's count, Elgindy says, he has been suspended seven times, though he thinks it is really only four. He may hold the record for the shortest message to produce a suspension, he says with a hint of pride in his voice. It consisted of just two letters: "F" and "U." Evidently, SI didn't think he was referring to Florida University.

Of course, all that was just a warm-up for Elgindy's starring role in probably the biggest—and certainly the strangest—donnybrook yet in the brief history of the online stock-discussion world's efforts to police itself.

Though it's sometimes hard to tell from reading the insults and abuse that pour forth on Internet message boards, there are rules of conduct for those who write there and consequences for those who cross the line. At Silicon Investor, violations of the rules can lead to loss of membership privileges that can last from a day or so to forever and some.

For most of Silicon Investor's brief history, the main keeper of these rules has been a slim, attractive, twentysomething redhead named Jill Munden. She has been SI's webmistress since 1996, when the Dryer brothers hired her as the company's first—and for a long time only—employee. She worked with the Dryer brothers at a San Jose, California, office littered with papers and Jack in the Box wrappers. Silicon Investor's early operating budgets didn't include space for a cleaning service. From these humble quarters, complete with futons for overnight stays by the Dryers, the trio oversaw a burgeoning online empire that soon included thousands of stock-message boards and tens of thousands of members.[3]

Eventually, Munden got an assistant, Bob Zumbrunnen, to help her police the operation. Thus, those who get into trouble are sent to either Jill Jail or Fort Bob. Indeed, these electronic hoosegows have become such a part of SI culture that there is even a discussion site called "SI Jail Mail ExpressÖ." The site has a strictly humanitarian purpose, according to its opening message:

> "Your favourite guy or gal in Jill Jail or Fort Bob,
> and you can't reach them? No problem! Post your mes-
> sage here for your favourite suspended guy or gal and
> we will soon have morons to deliver these messages to
> your jailed loved ones."

Almost since its inception in 1995, Silicon Investor has had a ticklish balancing act. Unlike the Gardner brothers, who emerged as the stars of the Motley Fool, the Dryer brothers aimed to stay more in the background of their operation. The idea was "to make stars out of regular people who would not normally be celebrities," says Jeff Dryer. He admits that he never envisioned how far some members would take this chance at fame.

As Silicon Investor grew in popularity and influence over stock prices, the job of keeping some semblance of order amidst the competing egos and ambitions became an ever tougher job. While "we love the inmates," says Dryer with a laugh, "we can't have the inmates running the show."

One step to keep the inmates in line came in 1997 when the Silicon Investor began charging for membership. Up to then, joining had been free. Like many Internet entrepreneurs, the Dryers firmly believe that the online race goes to those sites that can attract the most visitors—"eyeballs" is the term of art. Bring in enough eyeballs, and advertisers and revenues and riches will follow. (The formula ended up working pretty well for the Dryers. In 1998, they sold Silicon Investor for stock in a Seattle-based Internet company called Go2Net, Inc. By late 1999, the stock received by the Dryers and other SI shareholders, including Munden, had a market value of about $400 million.)

While the new membership fee, initially $45 for a lifetime pass, produced revenue, it also helped the brothers get more control of their creation, says Jeff Dryer. When memberships were free, individuals were signing up multiple times under multiple monikers. This allowed one person to post under many names, which could be a big help for anyone trying to create the illusion of widespread enthusiasm for a particular stock.

By charging, Silicon Investor got a name and credit card number. So anyone wanting to cage the system would at least have to get another credit card under another name at a different computer location. It's not a foolproof protection, admits Dryer, but it helps.

The code by which SI tries to keep order is known as the "terms of use." Of course, Internet posters, in their seemingly relentless drive to turn the English language into one very long string of acronyms, often simply refer to these rules as "TOU."[4]

What puts a trader in the SI stockade? Well, some surprising things *don't*. Calling a company or a company official a low-down, lying loser and fraud is generally permissible. While the writer might be sued—or worse—by the object of such insults, SI deems such remarks a matter of free speech. Maybe the company is pond scum, maybe it's not. But SI, like other stock-discussion operations, doesn't want to get involved in trying to separate the crud from the cream. With tens of thousands of messages being posted each day on its thousands of active message boards, it's easy to understand SI's reluctance to take on the badge of truth police. Better to leave that to truthseekers.

Nonetheless, Silicon Investor members still have plenty of ways to get into trouble with their host. And they seem to exercise all of them. "Spamming"—the practice of putting the same message on many different discussion boards in hopes of multiplying its impact—is a definite no-no. Members posting messages advertising products or businesses on the message boards also isn't tolerated. Posting more than twenty messages in six hours—another sort of spamming—also can bring down the bars of Jill Jail. So does posting personal information about another member, such as his or her real name, address, phone number, or Social Security number. In his Kosovo battle with Elgindy, Lozman was suspended after posting Elgindy's full name and passport number.

Then there is a sort of catch-all section of the SI TOU that forbids any message that is "harassing, libelous, invasive of another's privacy, abusive, threatening, harmful, vulgar, obscene, tortuous or otherwise objectionable."

At SI, suspensions occur daily and usually last for a few days. The SI death sentence, membership termination, is invoked about once or twice a week, though by the end of 1999 that frequency is down to once or twice a month. Almost all the leads, says Munden, come from members who e-mail in complaints about others' conduct. Some call these reports good citizenship. Others call it tattling—or worse.

Being a sort of cyber-cop for an Internet community of tens of thousands of people, Munden sees a wide variety of reactions when she has to invoke the TOU. Some suffer in silence. Others are abjectly apologetic, while still others are apoplectic and send her private e-mails that would get their memberships terminated—if they weren't already.

A few just can't accept being severed from the motherboard. For some, being able to share their insights or vent their spleen or just make themselves heard on Silicon Investor becomes like an addiction. "These guys get so into it," says Munden with a certain astonishment in her voice.

Guys such as the man that Munden came to call "Bob Monster." She encountered him early in her SI career. He was a flagrant and repeated violator of the TOU, and Munden finally terminated his membership. But he kept reapplying under different names—some seventy-five times. Fortunately, Silicon Investor was able to identify him through his Internet address each time. "He started threatening me," Munden recalls. Among other things, he found out her hometown is in his area. He wrote that he would be waiting for her at the airport when she came to visit her family. Thankfully, she adds, she never met Bob Monster among the skycaps. He eventually faded away. But like any good monster, he was scary.

Nonetheless, Munden wasn't scared off. She and her assistant Bob (the SI version, not the Monster) ended up disciplining the biggest names in the Silicon Investor community. They suspended Janice Shell and Ga Bard. In August 1998, Silicon Investor terminated the membership of Mike "Big Dog" Nichols. He says they caught him having multiple accounts under different names. Big Dog took it well, even joking that it took SI officials long enough to discover his multiple identities. For him, his six-month run at Silicon Investor had been fun and opened all kinds of profitable new horizons.

Per its privacy policy, Silicon Investor officials say they don't comment on the status of a person's membership or any disciplinary actions taken against him or her.

TokyoMex says he was kicked off SI in June 1999. He says he doesn't know why and doesn't care. Like his old nemesis Big Dog, Park has other cyber-fish to fry.

In some of his final SI messages, Park wished some well, one not. To Jenna, who stood to take over from him at the top of the Silicon Investor most-bookmarked heap, TokyoMex wrote:

> "You will see massive number of people book marking you
> ,, next 30 days ,,You will also surpass me ,, in a few
> days . . . As I leave ,, you will bury that dog ,, some
> where in the bottom ,, that dog will never get what he
> wants ,, so desperately ,, R O F L M A O ,, ;-)"

Though the message never mentioned Elgindy, he clearly seemed to be referring to his West Coast rival. Elgindy certainly thought so. Anthony@Pacfic was the only person to reply to that message. He actually sent two, though one would have been sufficient to get his gist:

> "Oh you mean the same masses that are unbookmarking you
> because they dont want to lose more money or follow you
> to Federal Court and end up broke and crying that you
> have no money to disgorge or repay restitution ..You are
> not leaving by choice ..you have been exposed!!!!!!"[5]

In August 1999, Elgindy was hit with a two-week suspension, one of the heaviest SI gave out before terminating a membership. His alleged transgressions, according to a message posted on Silicon Investor, included

> "personal attacks, vulgarity, advertising, and posting
> too much on a single thread."

Of course, this message couldn't have come from Elgindy. His posting privileges were suspended. But it came from the next-best source, his wife. Not coincidentally, Mary Elgindy joined SI at the time her husband got hit with his two-week hiatus. She wrote that

> "he misses you all as much as you will miss him, by the
> way please bookmark me since I will be on here regularly
> and although I dont know a whole lot about what he does,
> he does talk in his sleep, and I take copious notes."[6]

On her newly minted SI member's profile, Mary Elgindy listed her college degree as a

"Phd of A@P"

and described her investment style as

"Whatever anthony says is good."

She certainly proved to be a less combative poster than her husband. In connection with one stock, she wrote,

"I'm just the messanger and I'm quickly ducking out of the line of fire , so please be nice."

When an Elgindy critic suggested that

"you might want to start asking about visiting hours for the nearest federal prison for Mr. Know it all,"

Mary Elgindy simply responded,

"Please don't post any more messages to me. Thank you."

Part of her online time she spent chatting with the girls.

"Maybe we could do some shopping!"

she wrote one female poster who turned out to live nearby. When another woman wrote,

"Me and my girlfriends down here in NYC just hung a big sign out our window that says 'Bring Anthony Back to SI,'"

Mary's response was,

"Alright! thats awesome you go Girl!"

However, Mary Elgindy's Silicon Investor career lasted only about two days. Then her membership wasn't just suspended, it was terminated—along with her husband's. Tim Luke, another prominent online poster, started a thread to discuss the taking out of Tony and Mary.

> "Why why why would someone please tell me why . . . i
> can't take it anymore,"

wrote Luke. A whole new online brouhaha was brewing.

Then Jeff Dryer interceded in response to an overture from Elgindy. Invoking the privileges of a co-founder, he reinstated the Elgindys. To Anthony, Dryer wrote,[7]

> "You're funny, scary, and informative all at the same
> time . . . quite a package. . . . . . I don't want there to
> be a war between you and SI . . . If I close my eyes and
> look back later, maybe everything will be ok, I hope."

Elgindy returned to his Silicon Investor haunts and exulted,

> "There is still justice on SI."

Well, at least for twenty-four hours. Then Elgindy and his wife were booted again. This time, the new bosses of SI, the officials of Go2Net, intervened and overruled Jeff Dryer. In return for the tens of millions of dollars worth of stock he and his brother received, Dryer discovered that he really had given up control of his baby. "I don't make the decisions anymore," Dryer says, looking back on the incident.

Elgindy didn't take the reversal quite so philosophically. In a message on his private e-mail service, he asked each of his followers

> "to post publicly, a demand for JuSTICE!!!!This is Dis-
> crimination and Political in nature!!!I aim to Sue GNET
> for discrimination!! and for damaging my reputation and
> my members and those who follow my trade call on SI and
> who have been injured these last few days!!!"

Go2Net did, however, take an unprecedented step by breaking its own rule of never discussing disciplinary actions against members. Silicon Investor's managing director, Bryan Burdick, posted a message announcing the Elgindy ban. Burdick said terminating Elgindy was

> "an extremely difficult decision."

He said that Go2Net was tempted to make an exception to its rules to keep someone who

"has clearly been a popular and prolific contributor to SI. I am sure that he will be missed."

But, he says, it was decided that such an exception would ulti- mately undermine the operation's integrity.

"I am confident that this post will not win me any pop- ularity points,"

he added.

He was right. More than fifty people responded to Burdick's message. Almost all of them were critical of SI and supportive of Elgindy. "BIG mistake" . . . "bad move" . . . "SHORT GNET." (GNET is Go2Net's symbol.)

One of the messages came from Elgindy. Though he could no longer post on Silicon Investor, his response to Burdick was passed on by a supporter who could. Reading Burdick's message,

"I felyt as if I were reading my own obituary,"

Elgindy wrote. Much of Elgindy's message read like a eulogy, albeit an unedited one.

The trader told of how he had hoped

"my experience on Wall Street, witch is a corrupt and dirty place & where one person will galdly eat your heart out for a 1/16 of a point, woule aid others. . . . . . . I was hoping to bring a new honesty to the internet. One that withstood the test of time.. In that I failed, I let my passions get the best of me, I let my own frailties overcome the goals I had set. . . . . BUt ,onething is certain.. Wall Street wont change ..unless my message is carried out on by each and everyone here.. spread the message and do not let it fade.. I will continue on my work, for I believe that there is no more an honorable way to make a living than by uncovering fraud and scammers..

> Undoubtedly there will be a dramatic increase in
> such activity here on SI , since I am banished from
> this place. . . . . . I chose SI, because it had some
> rules and some structure, I wil not take this oppurtu-
> nity to attack anyone at SI. . . . . May
> God Bless you and yours and may peace fall upon
> you."[8]

At least one SI member took this message to heart and picked up the fallen staff. He was a mysterious figure who joined Silicon Investor at the time Elgindy was banished. In his Silicon Investor biography, he listed his occupation as

> "The KING Of Short Sellers."

He didn't give his age or hometown, other than to say,

> "I am located right behind every Criminal."

His online name was A@P Trader.

In an early e-mail, the newcomer wrote that

> "I have known Anthony practically all my
> life. . . . . . I have his permission to offer guidance
> here in his abscense, and I taught him much of what he
> knows. . . . . . Please Book mark me as well as keeping
> the sacred Anthony@Pacific Moniker forever bookmarked.
> I will mainatin this role until he returns or until
> all scams dissapear from the earth."[9]

Of course, one immediate suspicion was that behind this new masked man was the Man. A@P Trader insisted he wasn't Elgindy. But it was a tough sell.

> "Anthony, this has to be the most severe split person-
> ality disorder I've ever witnessed,"

wrote one skeptic.

> "You smell surprisingly like Anthony,"

wrote another, though it has never been proven that smells (even from White Castles) travel over the Internet.

As it turned out, the A@P Trader didn't have to hang around long—certainly not until the last scammer dropped. For within a few weeks, Silicon Investor had yet another change of heart on the subject of Elgindy.

While SI officials couldn't quite bring themselves to allow him back, they decided they could allow the membership to allow him back. So, they announced they would put Elgindy's return up to a vote. SI even started a message board to discuss the matter, with the opening message from a slightly battered Bryan Burdick. In recent weeks, Burdick wrote, he had been hearing from members about the Elgindy termination. The reactions, he wrote, ranged from support to

> "Bryan, You're a complete moron! Who the hell put you
> in charge!?!?"

So, SI came up with

> "a (potentially) brilliant idea [that] could com-
> pletely backfire in our faces,"

Burdick wrote. But, he added, the plan at least had the distinction of apparently never having been tried on the Internet before.

The new Elgindy-vote discussion site attracted over 1,500 messages.

> "Well, I understand why Tony would want to come back
> to SI. It is the best message boards for stocks out
> there now. . . . . . However, once that ban button is
> pushed it can't be taken back, IMO,"

wrote Daniel Miller, a.k.a. the Whiz Kid. Miller had attained his own Internet following as a stock picker and a good deal of publicity because he is only a teenager. Elgindy periodically tried to prove that Miller a) is not a teenager, or b) is a teenager but his father is doing the stock picking. Either way, Elgindy didn't like Miller.

But Miller raised a good point. Elgindy's desire to be reinstated, and SI's desire to find a face-saving way to take him back, underlined the developing economics of the Internet stock-discussion world. For Elgindy, SI is a major media outlet that allows him to get his messages across to potentially tens of thousands of active traders. For SI, Elgindy is a draw. And more than ever, the name of the game is attracting eyeballs. For advertising dollars and other remunerative things follow the bouncing retinas.

Finally the vote results were announced. Those in favor of the return of Elgindy numbered 435. Those opposed totaled 268.

```
"I'M back,"
```

Elgindy announced. Having been through this trial, he called for a higher level of online discourse.

```
"The drivel needs to end,"
```

he wrote.

It's a sentiment easier typed than done. That same day, an e-mail message described one company as

```
"utter stinky and smelly junk from the depths of Hell,
for your finacial ruin. eat and you will puke."
```

The writer was the newly re-enfranchised Anthony@Pacific.[10]

CHAPTER

THIRTEEN

BY 1999, THE INTERNET had become, for all practical purposes, an officially designated epochal event in the stock market.

"Today, you can hardly pick up a newspaper, turn on a television, overhear a conversation, or talk to a friend without mention of the Internet. It has done nothing short of change the way our world works and the way our nation invests," says SEC chairman Arthur Levitt in a May speech at the National Press Club.

In a speech a month earlier at the same location, Richard Walker, head of the SEC's enforcement division, likens the Internet's impact to the invention of the printing press and the discovery of electricity. Other senior government officials make similar impressed sounds about cyberspace.

It's almost impossible to find a major business or news publication that hasn't done multiple major pieces about online investing. "The history of investing is replete with manias," observes a cover story in *U.S. News & World Report*. "But few can top the frenzied pursuit of Internet stocks."[1]

A *Forbes* magazine cover story, titled "Amateur Hour on Wall Street," notes that seventy-three Internet companies have business losses totaling $1.5 billion. Yet, collectively, they have a stock market value of $115 billion. The article lays out a few other numbers. Some 7 million investors have online accounts. That number is expected to rise to 17 million by 2001. "Each day a 5-million-strong mob of on-line investors is proving that when it comes to stock picking, might makes right," writes *Forbes*. The magazine predicts that within five years, 50 percent of U.S. households will own stocks compared with 33 percent in 1999 and 20 percent in 1990.

A cover story in *Business Week* about the "Investor Revolution" asks a question that is weighing heavily on the minds of about 600,000 generally very fat and happy Americans: "Who Needs a Broker?" On the cover is a chimp holding a newspaper and staring at the stock tables. "Three years ago, it was an almost invisible blip. Two years later, it was hard to miss. But the major brokerage firms continued to ignore the exploding phenomenon of online trading. Today, online trading has caught Wall Street's attention with a vengeance," says this article.

Before the year is out, the biggest Wall Street brokerage firms are announcing plans to open online trading operations. What will happen to the compensation—and jobs—of tens of thousands of brokers becomes a stay-tuned-next-week question.

The most widely noted conversion comes at the nation's biggest broker, Merrill Lynch & Co. Besides its size, Merrill's embracing of online trading is noteworthy for the critical things the brokerage giant has said about the practice in the past. In 1998, the *Wall Street Journal* quoted Merrill's head of brokerage operations, John Steffens, as saying that "the do-it-yourself model of investing, centered on Internet trading, should be regarded as a serious threat to Americans' financial lives." As it turns out, the financial lives in greatest danger just might belong to Merrill and the other doyens of Wall Street.[2]

The media are covering almost every aspect of online trading. Readers are being educated in the strengths and weaknesses of online brokerage firms, individually and generally. There are stories about the frenetic pace at scores of day-trading rooms around the country, where individuals—an estimated 5,000 nationwide—congregate to do rapid-fire trades and rarely hold a stock overnight. A story by author Neal Gabler in the *Los Angeles Times* ruminates on the rise of the "Net-setters," who are the successors to the glamorous jet-setters of the '60s. Only in the "topsy turvy world" of the Internet "could unprofitable businesses turn into market favorites and nerds turn into Net-setters," writes Gabler.[3]

There are pieces explaining the ins and outs of stock-trading software and the differences between Internet "discussion" sites and Internet "chat" sites. A discussion site, such as Silicon Investor or the Motley Fool, involves posting pre-written messages on the electronic equivalent of a bulletin board. A chat room involves writing the message on the bulletin board as you go. Since dozens of people or more are often in a chat room at a given time, it's a little like trying to carry on a conversation at a crowded party. As disjointed as discussion-site writing can be, chat-room chatter often reads like an unedited letter put through a Cuisinart. Yet, thousands of investors visit chat rooms. Some of the rooms are free, others charge for entry. On their private websites, Park and Elgindy, for example, have members-only chat rooms.

Meanwhile, companies are promoting courses to teach people how to use the Internet to trade stocks. "You Can Become a Millionaire on Regular Pay," says the headline on a circular from Online Investors Advantage (which happens to be owned by Zia-Sun Technologies, the company that is suing Elgindy's online friend Floyd Schneider, a.k.a. The Truthseeker). The document goes on to say that "people just like you are getting rich working from the comfort of their homes, starting with little capital, and using easy to learn cyber investing strategies," which Online Investors Advantage will be happy to teach—for a price.

For the interested, Online Investors Advantage holds free informational seminars where a motivational speaker provides more details about the riches that can be mined in cyberspace. I attend one such meeting, along with a few dozen others at a hotel near the Los Angeles airport. The smooth and engaging speaker keeps us entertained for over an hour. He talks of bull and bear options, group rotation, profit timing, and of course, the stochastics.

The man adds that all he has told us is merely a tempting—and useless—taste of the inside dope of Internet stock trading. The real stuff can be found in the two-day course offered by Online Investors Advantage. The regular price for the course is $3,995. That's a bargain, he assures us, given the potential profits. But anyone willing to slap down his or her credit card this night can have those likely life-changing two days for just $2,995. And a spouse can learn along for just $500 extra. When the meeting ends, more than half a dozen people head to the back table to exercise their Amex. Millionaires on Regular Pay. (In an interview, a ZiaSun spokesman says that thousands of satisfied customers have gone through the training course and there have been almost no complaints.)

By 1999, Internet stock fraud, too, has come of age as a certifiably serious problem. In March, the U.S. Senate's Permanent Subcommittee on Investigations holds hearings on the subject. Along with all the opportunities for legitimate investing, the Internet also appears to be providing swindlers "with equally profound avenues for committing financial fraud," says committee chair Senator Susan Collins. Among the witnesses is Tom Gardner, whose title is given as "Head Fool" of the Motley Fool. In what may be the least accurate sentence of his testimony, Gardner proclaims that "fools do not often get the chance to speak in the U.S. Senate."

The SEC's enforcement chief Walker also testifies. He gives senators a Cook's tour through the land of online stock fraud. He explains touting, scalping, and other terms of art. The SEC's top cop also tells of the sixty-six cases the agency has already brought against alleged Internet stock frauds. One, which he refers to as "The Sweep," involves forty-four defendants and the alleged illegal touting of 235 small-company stocks.

"We have been vigilant in developing proactive and flexible responses" to Internet stock-selling abuses, says Walker. The SEC expands John Stark's little Internet unit to ten people from two.[4]

The agency's online policing efforts are also attracting less complimentary descriptions. For instance, an October 1999 front-page story in the *Wall Street Journal* about online stock trading says that the SEC's "inertia" is often leaving it "on the sidelines while securities markets are embroiled in the biggest revolution since the Great Depression." The *Journal* reports that the SEC hasn't even gotten the funds to purchase computer software that would help it search the Internet for investment frauds. One of the agency's few technological tools, according to the story, is the free Internet search engine provided to anyone by Yahoo!. The *Journal* quotes the SEC's chief technology officer as saying that using Yahoo! to find fraud is like "trying to shoot something a couple hundred yards away with a shotgun."[5]

The SEC isn't the only government body tackling cyberspace fraud. On the morning of April 7, the stock of PairGain Technologies soared by more than 30 percent on news that the company was being bought in a billion-dollar acquisition by an Israeli company.

"Wahooooooooooooooooooooooooooooooooooooooooooooooooooooooo oo!!!,"

writes a trader on the Yahoo! message board for PairGain.

"I knew this day would come!!!!!!!!!!!!!!!!!!!"

So did some law-enforcement officials. There is no planned acquisition. Just a fake story that is made to look like it came from the real Bloomberg financial news service and then is launched into cyberspace to do its work. In June, a twenty-five-year-old North Carolina man named Gary Dale Hoke pleads guilty to securities fraud charges in Los Angeles federal court for concocting the PairGain hoax. In an example of how the Internet can also help catch criminals as well as aid them, the Federal Bureau of Investigation tracks the fake story back along its online journey and back to Hoke, who was a PairGain employee at the time of the hoax. After all his work creating the fraud, Hoke, for unexplained reasons, never tried to cash in by selling any PairGain shares. He is sentenced to five months of home detention, five years probation, and fined about $92,000.[6]

The press takes the opportunity of the Hoke case to point out the dangers of believing things that are posted on the Internet. One of the talking heads about this belongs to Elgindy. The Associated Press quotes him as saying "The Internet has become the world's largest conference call. And plenty of the people talking about stocks have hidden motives for what they're saying."

Of course, truth matters less than timing to some stock traders.

```
"WHO CARES IF IT's REAL OR NOT I JUST SOL(D)...
$3,000! yesss!!!!!!"
```

writes one message poster after word of the hoax begins to surface.

State securities regulators are also trying to crack down on Internet abuses. In July, for example, the California Department of Corporations issues twenty-three desist-and-refrain orders in connection with allegedly fraudulent efforts to raise money over the Internet for film projects. Collectively, the offerings sought to raise over $2 billion, state regulators say. The state department says that its ICE team (short for Internet Compliance and Enforcement) has already found 3,000 websites where investment opportunities are being offered. Of those, 300 are suspicious enough to warrant opening an investigation. "Up to now (the Internet) has been a frontier with a frontier mentality. Now Aunt Minnie is coming in. So the vulnerability of the Internet population will increase dramatically," says G. W. McDonald, the department's assistant commissioner for enforcement, in an interview.[7]

In August, the North American Securities Administrators Association, a Washington, D.C.-based group representing state securities regulators, issues the results of a seven-month study of the day-trading industry. Of those among the public who day trade, 70 percent "will not only lose, but will almost certainly lose everything they invest," the study says. Only about 11 percent of the day traders studied "evidenced the ability to conduct profitable short-term trading," the report says. It calls for more oversight of firms where people go to do day trading, and more disclosure of the risks to would-be practitioners. An association representing day-trading firms calls the findings "not a representative sample of the industry."

Even for successful traders, there can be psychological costs. Jodi Segal-Lankry, the Philadelphia schoolteacher turned Internet trader, says she made $150,000 in 1998, mostly from buying and selling penny stocks. But to do that, she was at her computer terminal from 5 A.M. to 1 A.M., with breaks to take care of her children. The tension was so great that she began to have panic attacks and stomach problems. "It was so crazy," she says.

Finally, for her own sake and the sake of her family, Lankry geared back. "It was cut back the hours or have a nervous breakdown," she says. She is feeling better, but now there is a new problem. "I'm just not making the money I want to" from trading, says Lankry. In a later interview, Lankry says she is still working on finding the best balance between profitable trading and the rest of her life.

Meanwhile, dozens of Internet-related investigations by state and federal authorities bubble along. Gary Swancey still hasn't heard back from the SEC regarding the Midland mess. Ga Bard has gone through his day of grilling under oath by SEC attorneys. He has supplied copies of his e-mail messages concerning Midland, over 5,000 of them. Just putting that packet together took him some three days with almost no sleep, he says.

As the months click past, Swancey waits with a mixture of resignation and anger. All he did was try to help other Midland investors, he insists. But "no good deal will go unpunished," he laments. His position is that if the feds want to sue him, sue ahead. He has nothing left to take, he says. Unless Uncle Sam wants some Midland shares.

As he waits to hear back from the SEC, Ga Bard sets out from his garage penthouse in Kilgore in search of the comeback trail. He has decided that if he gets no respect doing free investor-relations work on the Internet, he might as well get paid for it.

Swancey has started hiring himself out to small companies for investor-relations work. He additionally has offered to do website design for the firms. And, if necessary, he can probably fix the air conditioner or heater. He vows he won't be a typical happy-talking PR man to investors. "I am not a smooth-talking touter," he says. "I am blunt, just tell it like it is."

His first client is CNH Holdings, Inc., a little energy and environmental company based in Swancey's temporary hometown of

Kilgore, Texas. Swancey has been a fan of the company since early 1998, when he started a Silicon Investor discussion site about it. After the Midland debacle, he came to Kilgore to do website work for CNH and stayed to do investor relations. CNH officials are "just good folks, good country folks," says Swancey. On his Internet postings about CNH, he has begun to add at the end of each message the phrase, "Paid IR in cash and 50K in stock option." That's an option to buy 50,000 of CNH, Swancey explains. Full disclosure, he says.

If he was looking to CNH as a respite after Midland, he has been disappointed. Part of the problem is the similarities between the two companies. CNH and Midland have looked at doing some of the same business deals and had some of the same officials. CNH even announced plans to buy Midland's restaurant and bar in Las Vegas, though the deal fell through. CNH's outside counsel on regulatory matters is Mark Pierce, the sometimes Midland officer who is being sued by the SEC. Pierce has also served as CNH's corporate secretary. Swancey says he isn't bothered by such connections.

Others are, including Ga Bard's onetime online buddy, Big Dog.

> "Give me a break. The same people, the same tired,
> failed acqisitions. Where does it end?"

asks Big Dog in one e-mail message. He provides his answer in another message:

> "If it smells bad it usually is bad."

In a series of e-mails back to Big Dog, Ga Bard sounds like a man suffering the arrow's shaft of ingratitude from a former pupil.

> "DO your worst that is fine with me. You have taken on
> the top day traders on line for the king's crown and
> you have it. Me I am going to continue on. . . . I have
> lost a lot of money to you and your picks based on
> your real info too. . . . . You have made a ton
> of money on me and some losses too. No one is perfect
> not me not you not anyone I know of. Especially in
> this arena."[8]

Next in the critic's parade is the man Ga Bard once considered *his* mentor. This poster's online name is Alan Markoff, a.k.t.s.a. (also known to Swancey as) the "Internet God." Early in his Internet wanderings, Swancey says, he encountered Markoff and was quickly taken by the man's online "style, his persona, the way he carried himself." Swancey was also impressed by Markoff's discussions of religion and ethics and his ability to debate stock "bashers." By Swancey's recounting, he became an avid, almost blind follower. He bought when Markoff recommended buying and sold when Markoff said sell. He claims that Markoff even supplied him with the text of online messages, which Swancey gladly sent out under his Ga Bard moniker. Markoff "would order me to do something and I would do it without question," Swancey wrote in an e-mail message on Silicon Investor. All this seems incongruous for a man who himself preaches the need for independent investment thinking, but Swancey says he became less dependent on Markoff as he began to get his own feel for the Internet stock-trading world.

Swancey's falling out with Markoff apparently began with disagreements following the 1998 Midland debacle. By 1999, Ga Bard seemed to have replaced blind obedience with something closer to blind rage for his onetime mentor.

At about 5 A.M., New York time, one April morning, Markoff posted an e-mail message criticizing a CNH news release as being "misleading at best." Swancey's name was listed as the company contact on the release. In subsequent e-mails, Markoff also complained of having

> "been hammered with this God routine for some time now."

As for CNH, he pronounced that

> "from my perspective it has all the earmarks of another investigation."

> "Oh look at this Markoff has resurfaced . . . :-),"

responded Swancey with sarcasm and a smiley. He defended the accuracy of the press release, and in his own series of e-mails, had a few unfriendly things to say about the man he once called friend.

> "LOL . . . The INTERNET GOD has spoken . . . all bow to
> the infamous scalping GURU" . . . . "do be do
> be doooo. Hey GOD have written anyone's post lately???"
> . . . . "you throw mud it comes back . . . and I am
> JUST getting started to. do be do be doooo."
>
> "Why don't you learn how to be civil,"

snapped Markoff.

Civil war seemed a little closer to Swancey's mood.⁹

> "OH for 9 month the Internet God CLAN has been any-
> thing but civil . . . Now I am showing the internet
> what you are about and now you want me to be civil.
> LOL,"

he wrote.

After just two often tumultuous months, Swancey quit as the investor relations representative for CNH. He says that while he likes and respects CNH officials, he decided that perhaps the company was looking at one too many of Midland's old business ideas. For a man still under SEC scrutiny, Swancey decided that was not a good connection to have.

CNH president Gerald Pybas says the aborted restaurant/bar deal occurred before he was in management. He says he looked at getting the company involved with DF 144 but decided not to proceed.

Swancey moved back to his native Georgia from Texas, though he didn't go back alone. "I went to Kilgore and found a sweetheart. Her name is Elizabeth," he says. The two met via the Internet when Swancey, ever energetic, tried to organize a local social club via computer. They corresponded, then talked on the phone, and finally met.

He wooed her. He gave her his poetry books. She read them. He showed her his pool-shooting prowess. She confirmed his stories of beating guys one-handed, using a broomstick instead of a pool cue. Each day he sent a different flower, and a dozen roses on Friday. She says she was overwhelmed, embarrassed, and flattered by all the attention. They married. "I got very, very lucky. Women like this supposedly don't exist," says Swancey.

But beyond domestic tranquility, the frontier of cyberspace always beckons. Where there are lessons to teach, battles to fight, and demons to exorcise.

In the spirit of his moniker, Swancey started a discussion thread dedicated to Shakespeare.

```
"Shakespeare was a man with pen in hand wrote, some-
times in a mere 14 lines, the truest of visions thus
arriving at the heart of some of today's demographic-
economic problems,"
```

wrote Swancey in his opening message. With the hope of eventually discussing all of The Bard's work, Ga Bard posted a Shakespeare sonnet. "I would appreciate it if we could stay focused," he wrote. Not a problem. Through the first two months of the site's existence, nobody responded.

Ga Bard also started a discussion thread dedicated to larger-company stocks. He called it "Ga Bard Goes Big Board." Part of the aim, he wrote, was to try to invest with "a bit more safety factor" than penny stocks provide. While a bigger hit than Shakespeare, this new thread also never really caught on. It sometimes went weeks without anyone posting a message.

Plus, Ga Bard's own heart still seems to belong to the rough-and-tumble world of small-company stocks. Much of his Internet writing is still focused there. After all, there are so many people to educate, so many issues to address. There is the problem of the

```
"sheep/zombies"
```

buying stock while the

```
"PHantomites"
```

are selling, leaving the aforementioned buyers (a.k.a. average traders)

```
"no way to get out.... .without losing their royal
backsides."
```

He campaigns against those who play the

`"short & distort"`

game. This, Swancey explains, is the opposite of the pump and dump game. While the P&D crowd manipulates up the price of a stock, the S&Ders use similarly slimy tactics to drive down a stock price. In Swancey's opinion, S&D is worse than P&D because it sometimes destroys legitimate companies.

Swancey put together an online essay about the short-and-distort "scenario" that includes his outline of the seven stages of "the deadly art of stock manipulation." Among the short-and-distort weapons are POS and PAS. Though POS usually has a scatological online meaning, in the Bard's lexicon it stands for Purposely Omitted Syntax. Its companion, naturally, is Purposely Added Syntax. Of course, for manipulators the prime directive is "above all control the message boards," writes Ga Bard.

Admirers have posted this and other bardian essays on message boards around Silicon Investor—with credit, of course, to Ga Bard. Thus, the word goes forth.

As always, Swancey is ready to do battle with "bashers" and "nays" on the Net. He spars with Jeff Mitchell, the merry prankster and Janice Shell ally from Connecticut, over a little mining company whose share price has gyrated from pennies to dollars to pennies again. Swancey likes the firm's prospects a whole lot better than he likes Mitchell.

> `"You know you only here to make purely intentional and`
> `malious posts to harm the image of a corporation.`
> `Besides you are a peanut with no credibility anyway,"`

writes Ga Bard.

However, Swancey eventually comes to have questions about the mining company, spurred in part by the discovery that the firm might have connections to a convicted swindler.

> `"I am out of here . . . learned my lesson and this one`
> `to ridiculous to even talk about anymore. Just another`
> `BS OTC stock,"`

Ga Bard writes.

He evidently can't leave soon enough for some. When he posts an additional message, with a last few observations on the stock, another trader writes,

"Geez GaBard, how many encores does it take for you to leave for good!!!"

For Ga Bard, there may never be a last encore as long as his fingers have strength and his modem is willing. Like Johnny Appleseed, he still has many places to visit and much work to do.

"For three years now, I have tried to teach people to watch out for the dangers of the internet. The secret inside tips, the great connections, the diferent hypsters and bashers that dominate the boards, the eogtistical GURUs the stock runners,"

Swancey wrote in October 1999. But the ground remains treacherous, he warned.

"You do not always know who the enemy is either. TRUST NO ONE NOT EVEN ME."[10]

CHAPTER FOURTEEN

JEFF MITCHELL HAS BIGGER Internet headaches than just Ga Bard. So does his someday-we'll-have-to-meet friend and ally in Milan, Janice Shell. For them and others, the Internet turned uglier in 1999.

For months they had been in running e-mail wars over the value—or lack thereof—of various companies. None was nastier or more bizarre than the fight over Amazon Natural Treasures. Amazon Natural is involved in "importing, developing, manufacturing and selling products derived from plants grown in Brazilian Amazon Rain Forest," according to a filing by the company with the SEC.[1]

The company has more than a hundred different "phytogenic" products for people. Phytogenics is a fancy way of saying the products come from plants. While the company says it strongly believes in the efficacy of its products, it acknowledges in its SEC filing that "there is no scientific evidence to establish that the products are safe or beneficial for human consumption." Amazon Natural is based in Las Vegas, a city once dubbed "The Green Felt Jungle" by authors Ed Reid and Ovid Demaris.

The company has its coterie of fans, who helped push its stock to above $3 a share on the Bulletin Board, where it trades under the symbol AZNT. But by early 1999, Amazon Natural shares were down to about a buck each and heading lower.

Company officials knew whom to blame for the decline. "This drop was caused by unscrupulous stockbrokers shorting AZNT stock," said an Amazon Natural press release. "We, the stockholders, must fight back and stop these unscrupulous shorters. . . . With the help of ALL the stockholders, we will be triumphant!"

Later, Amazon Natural was even more specific—and threatening—about its alleged tormentors. In a June 1999 filing with the SEC, the company said it "is preparing to file suit against Janice Shell and numerous others for utilizing Internet chat rooms to defame, slander and libel" Amazon Natural. Additionally, Shell and company have been seeking to "malign, harass, cyberstalk, defame, injure and annoy," according to the filing. The future defendants illegally shorted securities and conspired to "commit illegal shorting of non-securities," asserted the company.[2]

It didn't elaborate on what constitutes "non-securities," which is a term that doesn't crop up much in the securities business. One Shell online ally jokingly wondered whether Amazon Natural was "accusing people of shorting bed sheets." In a December 1999 interview, an Amazon Natural spokesman said that the reference to non-securities was probably just a typo. In February 2000, Amazon Natural filed suit in Las Vegas federal court against Shell, Mitchell, and several others.

Shell and Mitchell—who deny doing any trading in Amazon Natural stock—argue that the firm's problems are self-generated. Some were outlined in a July 1999 piece by reporter Jason Anders in the interactive edition of the *Wall Street Journal*. The story related how Amazon Natural at various times has announced big—and so far unfulfilled—plans for products such as a cream protection against AIDS and a chewing gum that starts to whiten teeth within three minutes of chewing. (The story doesn't quote the company release announcing its Amazon "HAIR GROWTH FORMULA" that "penetrates deep into the mammalian skin layer." The release adds that natives have been using the formula for centuries "and to date you cannot find a 'bald' Brazilian Amazon Indian.")

The *Journal* story also quoted a company forecast that sales in 1998 would reach $75 million. Sales actually reached $392,061 and produced a net loss of $4.8 million. In the story, Amazon Natural president Michael Sylver said having to battle Shell and other critics had kept the company from reaching its growth goals.

Online, the Amazon Natural fight had all the biting and clawing of a jungle cat fight. More than 30,000 messages were posted on the Amazon Natural message boards at Silicon Investor and Raging Bull. Many of the exchanges were insulting, vituperative, and sometimes simply sick. Many of them involved Shell or Mitchell battling with defenders of the company. Each side seemed to have an utter contempt for the other.

> "U really are one sick depraved 2-bit stock hustling
> old lady,"

and a

> "chain smoking unemployed dung heap,"

wrote a poster called Pugs in messages to Shell.

> "Brain transplant letting you down, Pugs?"

asked Shell.

> "Those things from mice don't last long, I'm afraid."[3]

Usually, she gave him less credit than that for intelligence.

Shell's adversaries do their own DD on her in hopes of finding hidden economic motives for her attacking Amazon Natural. Pugs writes of running a credit report on her and finding five different names attached to her social security number.

> "This has implications imo , with 5 aliases. . . reason-
> able people can question how it is you make money so you

can bash stocks all day and night. Do these 5 aliases
have anything to do with how you might be paid ?"[4]

asks Pugs in one message on the Amazon Natural discussion
board at Raging Bull. For good measure, he adds that

"It is YOU that is at the core that all is wrong"

in the over-the-counter market for stocks.

Shell writes back that

"the information's wrong. I find it amusing to watch
you chase your tail and make a fool of yourself."

Big Dog's online buddy, Cavalry (a.k.a. Jesse Cohen), was
another early AZNT fan who went after Shell. He wrote that his
research showed that Janice Shell is actually a stockbroker from
Georgia whose middle name is Diane. He also predicted that Amazon Natural's plans

"to bust the shorts will become a text book case"

and result in the stock soaring to $25 a share.

"Oh God, Cav, you ARE pathetic,"

retorted Shell, who noted that it would be difficult to be a Georgia
stockbroker while living in Milan. Plus, she added, her middle
name is Louise.

In an interview, Cohen says his message about Shell being a
Georgia stockbroker was done in jest. "I was just messing with
her," says Cohen, adding that "everyone knew" Shell lived in Italy.

Well, not everyone. Pugs insists that Shell is really living in
the Sacramento, California area. When I mention in a phone interview with him that I have called Shell at a number in Italy, Pugs
isn't impressed. He says it's easy to have one's real location
shielded by forwarding calls through another location. He and others have found a Janice Shell employed at an entity in Sacramento
that does governmental human resources work, such as giving
entry exams for police and fire departments. However, a

spokesman for that organization says that its Janice Shell isn't involved in Internet stock-discussion boards and is "feeling harassed" by the attention she has received from the online set.

> "Shell, I noticed you posted right thru the New Year,
> Milan time, but was nowhere to be found New Years',
> Sacramento time. . . . .gee Shell, wonder why,"

wrote Pugs. Shell says that she greeted the new millennium at her computer—in Milan. (In its suit, Amazon Natural listed addresses in both Italy and California for Shell.)

Then there was Icabod. The person behind this moniker clearly was an Amazon Natural fan, who predicted in a discussion board message that one of the company's products

> "by far will outsell every other single product in the
> world combined."[5]

Icabod exhibited a peculiar venom toward Shell. First, Icabod posted an "intercepted" e-mail purportedly written by Shell in which she admitted she had driven down the price of Amazon Natural stock so she could buy large amounts of it and then profit when the price inevitably rebounded. The e-mail also had Shell saying she used and loved Amazon Natural products.

> "Icky, you moron,"

wrote back Shell.

> "You're so anxious for me to express a favorable opin-
> ion of this stock that you're prepared to make one up."

Then icky turned ugly. Soon this person was posting seemingly solicitous e-mails concerning Shell's health.

> "WE ARE VERY VERY SORRY THAT YOU HAVE CANCER. TAKE
> CARE OF YOUR SELF." . . . "I DO NOT CARE WHAT YOUR DOC-
> TOR SAID. AS YOU TOLD ME ON THE PHONE. THERE IS ALWAYS
> HOPE." . . . "THE BEST THING FOR YOU TO DO IS GET ALL
> STRESS OUT OF YOUR LIFE."

Shell vehemently denied having cancer or ever talking on the phone to Icabod. She did jokingly suggest that the explanation for Icabod's strange message might be found in the rain forest:

"TOO MUCH SUPER GUANO CAUSE HALLUCINATIONS
LOLOLOLOLOLOL!!"

Shell's denial seemed to disturb Icabod—or Icabods.

"WE DO NOT UNDERSTAND, YOU ARE THE ONE THAT TOLD US THAT
YOU HAVE CANCER. IF YOU ARE NOT TELLING THE TRUTH , YOU
ARE A VERY BAD PERSON."

Shell kept another Icabod e-mail message that appeared to have been erased by Silicon Investor censors as having finally passed the bounds of postability. It read, in part:

"YOU MUST BE TAKING TO MANY CANCER DRUGS . . . . . . THE
STREET TALK, IS THAT YOU JUST LIKE THE DRUGS. HOW ELSE
COULD SOME ONE SPEND 24 HOURS A DAY ON THE INTERNET
BASHING A COMPANY . . . . THE DAYS OF THE JANICE
SHELL GAME ARE O..V..E..R.
!!!!!!!!!!!!!!!!!!!!!!!!!!!!!!!!!!!!! . . . . LETS,
HAVE . . . . . S. . . . .E. . . . .
. . . . X. . . . . .WITH ALL
THE CHEM,S IN YOUR BODY YOU MUST BE A GOOD
???????????"

Not long after the cancer messages, Icabod stopped posting on Silicon Investor. Shell says his membership was terminated. Silicon Investor officials won't comment. Icabod, whoever he or she is, can't be located for comment.

In e-mail messages and interviews, Shell has said she suspects that Icabod is actually Amazon Natural president Mike Sylver.

"Now Icky—or should I say 'Mike'?"

she wrote in one message.

The Amazon Natural spokesman says Sylver isn't Icabod and the company doesn't know who is.

Indeed, Sylver says, he has been the target of some pretty sick characters, himself. In an August 1999 affidavit filed in a Nevada state court in connection with a dispute over ownership of some Amazon Natural stock, Sylver says his firm has been the "victim of an ongoing stock shorting scare, which stems out of Vancouver, British Columbia." As a result, the company hasn't been able to raise money and can't "pay any of their creditors nor buy supplies to run the day to day operation."

At the Sylver household, money has been so tight that "my wife has not gone shopping for groceries in over three months. We are eating can goods from our cupboards and handouts from friends and family members," the affidavit says. What's more, Sylver says, "I have been shot at, ran off the road, harassed, intimidated, extorted" by the "illegal group of stock shorters and manipulators."

The names of two alleged securities-law violators showed up in the Amazon Natural saga. In one corner was John Fasano, who began to do investor relations work for Amazon Natural—until critics discovered that he was under indictment (and eventually convicted) in a stock fraud case in New York federal court. The Amazon Natural spokesman says the company severed ties with Fasano after learning about his legal problems.

Fasano plans to appeal the conviction, says his attorney Martin Jay Siegel. After conferring with his client, Siegel says that Fasano doesn't wish to answer questions about Amazon Natural.[6]

Then there is Richard Marchese. And Rick Marcasse. And Ric Marcasse. And Dante and Roger and Calvin and, of course, four-legged Errol.

All these figures are characters in a little cyber-melodrama revolving around Shell and Amazon Natural. It's the kind of strange saga tailor-made for the Internet where lives play out across a computer screen and where someone doesn't necessarily have to be real to exist. As time passes, Shell begins to wonder whether "people" that she had corresponded with and come to care about were merely mirages on a computer screen, characters in a bizarre hoax.[7]

As Shell began her work on Amazon Natural she says she was contacted via e-mail by someone using the name Zorro. Zorro seemed very knowledgeable about the affairs of Amazon Natural and began passing information about the company to Shell. He then began signing his messages as Don Diego Dey La Vega, which was almost identical to the "real" name, Don Diego De La Vega, of the Zorro character.

Over time, Shell learned more about her mysterious friend, from him and others. She was told that his real name is Dante Dey La Vega. One message from his e-mail address was just signed "Z" and was preceded by a cryptic but rather ominous-sounding one-liner, apparently referring to Amazon Natural's president Mike Sylver:

"TIC TIC TIC TIC TOC MIKE SLYVER—DOA. Z."

In e-mails to Shell, Dante was described as a Mexican native living in Vancouver, British Columbia. He was a millionaire and master swordsman. He had a softer side that he shows to Shell.

"I just wanted to thank you for being so nice to me all this time. You know I am the last of the Dey La Vega family. . . . . We shared our passion for beautiful women. It was a passion not a lust. Making love to a woman was to be like a warm breeze on a cool night, poetry, Shakespeare philosophy and the arts,"

he wrote. Shell says she became fond of her online Dante, though they never met or even spoke on the phone.

Then, Dante was gone. Shell received an e-mail from him in September 1998 saying that he was heading into the hospital the next day for cancer treatment. A few days later she receives word that Dante has died. Jeff Mitchell recalls what a shock the news was for his friend. Shell says she was told she would get Dante's sword as a keepsake but has yet to see it.

A man that Shell knows as Richard or "Rick" Marcasse of Manhattan Beach, California, delivered the news of the death via telephone. She met Marcasse through Dante. Marcasse, too, became a mysterious figure in her life. Like Dante, he seemed to know a lot about Amazon Natural. Shell believed he was involved in shorting Amazon Natural stock.

On the stock-discussion boards of Amazon Natural, others also had thoughts about Mr. Rick. Pugs, the Amazon Natural fan, argued that Marcasse is actually Richard Marchese, a securities scofflaw with an impressive file of newspaper clips. In the 1980s, Marchese helped found Power Securities, a fast-growing brokerage firm that specialized in penny stocks—until regulators stepped in. Eventually, Power closed. A 1989 *Wall Street Journal* story quoted then New York state attorney general Robert Abrams as saying that records showed that Power took advantage of clients by marking up stock prices and charging commissions as high as 50 percent. A story that same year in *Business Week* estimated that "some 40,000 investors had lost at least $200 million in what regulators think was one of the biggest hustles yet in the penny-stock trade." In those stories, Power and Marchese denied wrongdoing. According to a 1993 *Denver Post* story, Marchese also helped federal law-enforcement officials arrest a major penny-stock swindler. The swindler had "fled" the country and Marchese "lured" him back to a place where authorities could nab him, according to the *Post* story.

Marchese, himself, was acquitted of federal fraud charges in 1996, according to SEC records. Those records also show that in early 1999, Marchese settled SEC civil charges that he had "engaged in repeated fraudulent conduct" while president of Power. Without admitting or denying the SEC's allegations, Marchese agreed to be barred from any association with a brokerage firm or any participation in a penny-stock offering.[8]

Are Marchese and Marcasse the same man? Shell seems to be of two minds. Early on, she chides Pugs online for coming to that conclusion. However, in later phone interviews with me she says she believes there might well be only one Rick.

Not true, says the man I talk with during a late December 1999 phone interview. Jeff Mitchell, Shell's online buddy, has passed on to me the phone number for Marcasse. I leave a couple of messages on an answering machine that gives no hint as to its owner's identity. In the second message, I mention that I am planning to mention Rick Marcasse in my book. About 9:30 P.M. one evening I get a call back.

The man on the other end of the line tells me that his last name is Marcasse. He gives his first name as Ric. No "k." He acknowledges knowing and communicating with Shell and Mitchell. He says Dante "was a very nice guy." But he says he isn't the Marchese of Power Securities and has never been involved in trading Amazon Natural stock—though he adds that several people seem to think he has. He says SEC officials had even contacted him, asking if he had traded the stock. He says he assured them he hadn't.

I ask him what he does for a living. "Semi-retired business-man," he replies. I ask for a little more detail. "Consultant for the government," he adds. Later in the conversation, he says he does "classified" work for the government. Details are, of course, classified. I ask him if I can record our conversation. He says no. He tells me he is selling his place in Manhattan Beach—which is located on an expensive stretch of beachfront property known as The Strand—and will make London his home. Much of his work, he tells me, is in Europe.

I try to find Richard Marchese, the former Power president. I reach his ex-wife in Las Vegas. She tells me she doesn't know his whereabouts but does hear from him occasionally and will pass along my interest in speaking with him. She says her former spouse did, at one point, live in Manhattan Beach.

I eventually do hear from a man identifying himself as Richard Marchese. In two messages left on my answering machine and one brief, angry phone conversation, he says he is responding to calls I made to his former wife trying to find him. He tells me to stop calling. "We are not involved in any of your situations," he says and hangs up before I can ask any questions. He doesn't leave me a number to call back.

When the SEC announced its settlement with Marchese, it said his last known location was Manhattan Beach. SEC records show that when Marchese was deposed by the agency in 1998 he gave his address as a location on The Strand. The street number that Marchese gave the SEC is the same one that Mitchell and Shell have for Marcasse. However, the listed owner of that particular piece of property is neither Marcasse nor Marchese.[9]

When I reach the listed owner by phone, he acknowledges that a man with the name that I ask about did rent the house but has moved out. The owner says he can't recall the spelling of his tenant's name and declines to look it up. He explains that confidentiality concerns keep him from talking further about the matter.

When I visit the address, I find a beautiful Spanish style house with a balcony and what looks like a separate guesthouse separated by a landscaped patio. It is right on the beach. My friend who lives in the area estimates that the house would sell for at least $2 million. But nobody is home.

Along with Dante and Rick, Roger and Cal also entered Shell's online world. In his phone conversation with me, Marcasse describes Roger as "my gentleman's gentleman." Roger also served up e-mails to Shell.

So did Cal, short for Calvin. In one e-mail, Cal told Shell about himself and Dante:

"One time a young man broke into Dante's home to rob it. Dante for some reason was asleep in his favorite chair in his living room. As the thief made his way to the dinning room with his flash light he was met by a man with a sword in his hand which was now pointed at the young mans throat. I don't know if the young man was more scared by the sword at this throat or the cold cream that was plastered all over Dante's face! I think it was the cold cream. As I'm sure you can guess that young man was me. Dante scolded me and although I am not well educated he taught me what it was to be a human being. He saved my life. Instead of calling the cops he cooked me breakfast (he was a master chef) and then offered me a job running errands for him all over town. He paid me well and then made me send money to the people I had previously stolen from. The list was sorta long. Boy, I miss him. He was my friend and my Dad."

Cal contacted Shell after Dante's death and told of Dante's feelings for her.

"Since you two met he has had passion in his heart, he
fenced like he was 20 years-old again. He was a champion in real life and although he wouldn't admit it he
was a real life Zorro,"

wrote Cal.

"Always he thought of you and only you. I know you are
interested in what he looked like, he was built like
the TV actor Chuck Norris only with Jet Black hair a
touch of gray on the side."

Cal and Rick wrote about each other in e-mails to Shell. Those
messages tell of Cal temporarily moving into Rick's house while
preparing for college-entrance exams. An e-mail from Rick said
that Cal

"might be smarter than we think. He just can't focus
on reality. Errol is his world. I feel for him."

For his part, Cal told Shell that

"Rick knows everybody. In his house he has pictures of
him on Air Force One with Regan, Bush and I think
Ford. His house is covered in photos of him and famous
people."

In another e-mail, he wrote that

"Rick is mean to me sometimes but he has really helped
me alot. He yells at Errol sometimes but lately he has
asked Errol his advice on several matters that deal
with those criminals."

The criminals aren't identified, but Errol is. Errol is Cal's
hamster. But, as described in a number of e-mails, Errol wasn't just
any hamster.

"Errol is in his gym, driving his tank (he hit me in
the butt with a missle this mourning), and just being
a complete hamster!"

writes Cal. Another told of Errol promising to take a bath before going to Rick's house, adding that the hamster

> "wants me to get him a tuxido for dinner but Rick yelled when I mentioned it to him."

Messages from Rick added to the rodent lore.

> "Errol's clothes are bought at Eaton's in the toy sec-
> tion. Cal is extremely handly with a sewing kit so I
> take it that he modifies them somewhat,"

said one e-mail.

Another told of finding

> "Errol in my private gym watching aerobic videos on
> my big screen. Cal says not to disturb him because he
> is embarrassed about his weight problem. And yes
> today I hear Errol's tank firing mortar shells and Cal
> taking cover behind the couch as I try to ask him how
> the studies are going. Be advised that Errol is
> inside the tank looking like George S. Patton in uni-
> form which I am positive he is in. Calvin has the
> nerve to tell me that Errol is not mature enough to
> handle a firearm. What the heck is a tank? Ah, the
> joys of life and we are worried about Michael
> Slyver?"

Like Dante, Rick seems to have occasional problems spelling the last name of Amazon Natural president Mike Sylver.

Then, messages from Cal to Shell stopped. One from Roger, the butler, informed her that:

> "Calvin was arrested and deported. He came to the com-
> pound and tried to break in. The security service
> arrived and contacted local Manhattan Beach Police.
> Good bye Mr. Calvin. He had a rather large knife on
> his body. Luck for him Rick wasn't home. There would
> have been no Calvin left."

E-mail messages from Cal described Marcasse as a former professional football player in Canada and made up of

"about 300lbs of muscle."

In our phone conversation, I ask Marcasse about Cal. He describes him as someone who lived with Dante and might be reachable in Vancouver. My efforts to find him there are unsuccessful.

Shell sends me the accumulated e-mails after I talk to Marcasse. I try to reach Marcasse by phone again. I leave messages with the same non-informative answering machine. I say that I need to talk with him about e-mails and addresses and what's in a name. I don't get a call back.

With all this and more—including a bizarre shopping excursion to find just the right blanket for Errol and the even stranger reported death of a hamster—coming to her through the ether, Shell says she is left to wonder who and what is real in this beachfront stretch of the online coast. If all these characters don't all exist why is someone going to the effort of alternately entertaining and tormenting her? In an e-mail to me about all this, Shell writes

"I don't think I've been involved in anything weirder
in my life, and of course I'm still not at all sure
what was ever going on."

Part of whatever was going on included an online figure named SHAREBEAR. In messages on Raging Bull, SHAREBEAR is self-described as a retired lawyer, whose stock holdings include Amazon Natural.

However, his main beef with Shell involved a little Internet company in Rancho Cucamonga, California, called Hitsgalore.com, Inc.

SHAREBEAR started out relatively mildly by declaring that he and fellow shareholders were planning to sue Shell and Mitchell, though he put the threatened litigation in rather apocalyptic terms.

"Get ready bashers you're about to be exterminated,"

SHAREBEAR wrote.

His messages—posted on the Hitsgalore.com discussion site at Raging Bull—got progressively more threatening and personal. (Indeed, they can no longer be found on the Raging Bull site. However, Mitchell kept printouts of some of them.) In one message, SHAREBEAR described Shell and Mitchell as "animals" and added,

> "Who elected them Dictators, CASTRO. Remember what happened to Che after he left Cuba? He was executed by his own soldiers."

If the mention of executions was aimed at getting attention, it succeeded with Mitchell.

> "Sharebear, OK, if your intent was to intimidate me, fine, you win. My wife reads over my shoulder and you now have her petrified for the sake of my two innocent children,"

Mitchell wrote.

> "Yes, living in the street can be intimidating Jeffery,"

SHAREBEAR shot back. SHAREBEAR later said Mitchell would be left alone—if he agreed to never again post on any major stock-discussion board. Mitchell kept posting.

But SHAREBEAR saved most of his animus for Shell, whom he calls a "deceptive witch" and more.

> "JANICE SHELL, YOU COMMON PERSON WHO SEEKS TO BE ABOVE ALL. PROVE ME WRONG! I HAVE E-MAILS TO ROGER AND CAL EXPLAINING YOUR PAST DUE RENTAL, THE EVICTION NOTICE YOU WILL NOT OPEN AND THE MITCHELL PLEA FOR HELP BECAUSE YOU ARE GOING TO KILL YOURSELF. PROVE ME WRONG. I WAS GIVE THESE DOCUMENTS AND I HAVE A RELEASE FROM AN INDIVIDUAL WHO SENT THEM . . . . . . SHELL GAME OVER? YOU BET IT IS!"

SHAREBEAR also accused Shell of taking payoffs on Amazon Natural and, for good measure, of engaging in weird sexual practices. In another message, SHAREBEAR claimed to have received a

"package"

of information from a

"young man who lives in Canada."

Shell says SHAREBEAR did seem to have gotten possession of some private e-mails that went to Cal. She says Cal became angry with her and no longer communicates. She says she isn't sure how the messages got to SHAREBEAR.

For Shell, the Hitsgalore.com saga also included litigation. According to the suit filed in Tampa, Florida, federal court, Shell and several other Internet posters have engaged in "a nationwide CYBERSMEAR campaign." In discussion-board messages, they have falsely portrayed Hitsgalore.com as being engaged in "illegitimate, illegal, dishonest, fraudulent, and criminal business operations," the suit charged.[10]

Hitsgalore.com has seen its stock ride a roller coaster on the Bulletin Board. Trading under the symbol HITT, the stock in 1999 has gone from $4 a share to over $20 and then down under $2.

Shell, who is the lead defendant in the suit, had a number of allegedly offending posts, including one where she wrote,

"How do you feel about con men. . . ..? That's what the
FTC thinks Dorian Grey, oops, Reed, is."

Dorian Reed is Hitsgalore.com's co-founder, chairman, and majority shareholder.

Shell says the suit against her is meritless. In the continuing Shell travelogue, the suit says she is a "resident citizen of the state of Texas." Court filings in the case show that the company tried to find Shell in the Lone Star state. A process server even visited a trailer park in Clute, Texas. Shell wasn't there. Shell joked in an e-mail about being

"back in the trailer park this week."

Curiosity drove one Internet message-board participant in Texas to visit the trailer park. It was only forty-five minutes from her home, she says in an interview, adding that she, too, didn't find Janice there. Hitsgalore.com attorney Carl Schoeppl says he is now convinced that Shell is living in Italy and he is working on having her served with the lawsuit papers there.

Does the FTC think Dorian Reed is a con man? In 1998, the agency filed a complaint against Reed and others in connection with a company selling business opportunities over the Internet. The FTC alleged that the defendants made "false and misleading" statements about how much income the business opportunities would produce. A federal judge in Baltimore ordered the defendants to pay $613,000 to customers. Reed denied wrongdoing and said he is trying to settle the matter.

Though not FTC-related, Shell buttresses her low opinion of Reed by noting that in 1992 he spent ten months in federal prison for wire fraud. In an SEC filing, Hitsgalore.com says the conviction didn't involve securities—perhaps something of a comfort for company shareholders. Reed didn't return phone calls requesting an interview."[11]

Hitsgalore.com has also had problems with its outside auditors. In a filing with the SEC, the company says one outside auditor wouldn't let its audit report be used by the company because of Reed's association with Hitsgalore.com. Concerns over management made another auditor "unwilling to be associated with the financial statements" of Hitsgalore.com, according to a company SEC filing. In public statements, Hitsgalore.com defended its management and its actions and said it was "hard pressed to understand" the auditors' qualms.

Hitsgalore.com wasn't the only entity to sue Shell in 1999. Indeed, as the year progressed, companies began using litigation to hit back at their Internet adversaries. At one point, Shell sent out a message that seems only half-joking, reminiscing about the not-so-distant past:

```
"Sadly, the fun may be over. Nowadays they just sue
you, don't bother to offer you a 'dirt nap'. Damn.
Nothing's the same anymore."
```

The other suit against Shell—as well as Mitchell and a third Fly By Nighter named William Ulrich—involves FBN Associates' April Fool's gag for 1999. The associates kicked around various ideas for that year's prank. "I wanted to start a 'My Dog Spot Picks Stock' site," says Mitchell. "Let him pee on the stock pages and what he hits we would buy."

Instead, they came up with Webnode.com. In an April 1 press release, Webnode.com announced that it had been granted an exclusive contract by the U.S. Department of Energy to raise $4 billion by selling to the public 40 million "nodes" on the "new countrywide state-of-the-art fiber optic Next Generation Internet to replace the existing copper backbone." Webnode.com's motto was "Don't Just Use The Internet . . . Own It!" The company had its own website, of course, and an impressive-sounding parent company. BZE International. BZE, the press release said, is "a recognized worldwide leader in e-commerce," whose projects include work in currency arbitrage and armaments deployment.

The creators watched as their April Fool's baby took off. They say over 1,000 people sent in e-mails to the website expressing interest in Webnode.com and its upcoming offering. Being a hoax, no money was ever taken or any nodes sold.

Wired News, an online news magazine, treated the Webnode press release as real and published a story about the supposed Energy Department contract. When the hoax was revealed *Wired News* magazine published a correction and congratulated the pranksters on their creativity.

Business Wire was much less forgiving. Business Wire is one of the major services—PR Newswire being the other—for disseminating financial-news press releases. The Webnode creators paid Business Wire its fee and the release was sent out.

In late April, Business Wire filed suit against Shell, Mitchell, and Ulrich in federal court in its hometown of San Francisco. The complaint charged the defendants with violating trademark laws, fraud, breach of contract, defamation, and conspiracy. "Their false and misleading descriptions and representations, have caused and continue to cause irreparable injury" to

Business Wire, the suit said. This complaint, at least, did place Shell in Milan.[12]

In a response filed in the case, the three defendants denied any wrongdoing. They said that their prank never tried to collect any money from investors. They used Business Wire, they added, as part of "legitimately exercising their First Amendment rights in trying to educate the public about Internet investment scams—and in trying to show that just because a press release is distributed through a major company it is not necessarily true." The three added that they are being sued because "they embarrassed Business Wire."

Shell is outraged that Business Wire is suing them but has never taken similar action against *real* companies that put out press releases with false or outrageous claims. She is particularly incensed—when she isn't laughing at it—by the case of Uniprime Capital Acceptance, Inc. This Las Vegas, Nevada-based company owned automobile dealerships. But in June 1999, Uniprime was part of a remarkable medical announcement made over Business Wire's HealthWire service.

Uniprime, through a majority-owned research company, issued a press release announcing "a major step in the fight against the human immunodeficiency virus (HIV)." Tests on infected patients in Madrid, Spain, of the firm's "Plasma Plus" formulation showed a "complete reversal from the immune system of the HIV infection, with no reintroduction of the virus after a period of almost eighteen months," according to the release.

The man behind this remarkable event, said the press release, was a Spanish native named Alfred Flores, who was "an honor graduate of the University of Madrid as well as a graduate of the University of Colorado (and) has been doing research into the area of immunology for the past 15 years at his own laboratory" near Lisbon, Portugal.[13]

Following this press release, Uniprime's stock soared on the Bulletin Board. It rose more than tenfold in price to nearly $8 a share as millions of shares change hands.

Not surprisingly, the startling announcement and subsequent stock action attracted more critical attention. Tony Elgindy, for one, noticed. A car dealer finding a cure for AIDS? To his calculating mind, there could be only one response: short the hell out of Uniprime. He was soon tapping out online messages to that effect.

The SEC also took note. In July, the agency said it was suspending trading in Uniprime stock "because of questions regarding the accuracy of public statements by Uniprime to investors concerning, among other things, a product developed by a subsidiary for treating human immunodeficiency virus (HIV)."

Uniprime, at least initially, seemed unbowed. In an August 6 press release, disseminated on Business Wire, the company said it "has strengthened its resolve to seek a medical or pharmaceutical partner to carry on the work of Mr. Alfred Flores."

However, things soon took a turn for the worse for Uniprime and Flores. On August 13, the U.S. Attorney in Manhattan announced that Flores had been arrested on securities fraud charges based on the press releases that "falsely claimed to have developed a cure for AIDS." The federal prosecutor's office also said Flores would have had difficulty doing research in Lisbon for the prior fifteen years, since he "was incarcerated in Colorado from 1983 to September 1992 following his conviction for murder."

Shortly after this announcement, the SEC announced that it was suing Uniprime and Flores in New York federal court for securities fraud in connection with the AIDS releases. Among other things, the SEC said it could find no evidence that any patients in the Madrid hospital were ever treated with Plasma Plus.[14]

Flores has pleaded not guilty in the criminal case. When the SEC filed its still-pending suit against Uniprime, the company's law firm issued a press release denying the charges.

For Shell, the irony of all this in relation to Business Wire was delicious if not particularly tasty.

> "I mean, they sue US but perhaps won't sue a company
> peddling a phony AIDs 'cure'?"

she wrote.

Shell and her fellow defendants received encouragement from other cyberspace voyagers. One admitted admirer of the three started a Silicon Investor message board and called it "Business

Wire Falls for April Fools Prank, Sues FBNers." This person wrote that Business Wire "apparently has no sense of humor." Elgindy and Shell even traded e-mails concerning the possibility of him helping to underwrite the costs of defending against the suit.

However, Business Wire and the pranksters eventually settled the suit. Mitchell's insurance company agreed to pay Business Wire $27,500 to cover some of its legal costs. The defendants also agreed not to put out any more bogus press releases on Business Wire.

Business Wire executive vice president Cathy Baron Tamraz says her company is "satisfied" with the settlement. "We have a great reputation and don't want anyone messing with it," she says. Tamraz adds that she "can't speak" to the specifics of the Uniprime matter.

With the lawsuits and the likes of Icabod and SHAREBEAR, Shell admitted that she is having a harder time finding things to laugh about.

> "Frankly, I'm finding unlooked-for notoriety not all
> that amusing,"

she wrote in one online message.

> "This is getting pretty rough, and I'm not enjoying
> it. There are some real crazies . . . . and
> they'll stop at nothing. I've always wanted an inter-
> esting life, but this may go a bit too far."[15]

As it turned out, the craziness in cyberspace would go a lot farther than litigation and ugly threats.

CHAPTER FIFTEEN

ON JULY 29, 1999, Mark Barton, with a pistol in each hand, walked into two Internet day-trading rooms in Atlanta and opened fire. He killed nine people and then shot himself. Authorities later discovered he had already murdered his wife and two young children. He was also the prime suspect several years earlier for the bludgeoning death of his first wife and her mother, though he was never charged in those crimes and denied responsibility.

In the weeks prior to his shooting rampage, Barton was an Internet trader at the two day-trading rooms. Other traders dubbed him the "Rocket" for his vocal exuberance, reported a *Wall Street Journal* story on the tragedy. Evidently, trading had not been going well for Barton in the days before his murder spree. After the killings, authorities would find a note from him in which he stated his desire to "kill as many of the people that greedily sought my destruction."

Not surprisingly, reams are written about the rampage and the world of day trading. A *New York Times* story quotes the Motley Fool's Tom Gardner. Gardner, a fan of a longer-term and less frenzied investing approach, says that while day trading can't be blamed for Barton's madness, "I do think there's a casino mentality to it that would tend to draw somebody who was very intense. It makes sense that the outcome of that intense personality and intense failure would compound the likelihood of this kind of behavior."

Stories talk of the high failure rate among amateur day traders as well as the possible need for more regulation and safeguards at day-trading rooms. Barton acquaintances tell of him having been a Scout master and active in his local church. Gun-control advocates cite the Barton shootings as one more reason for tougher gun laws.

Alan Abelson, a well-known Wall Street columnist for *Barron's* magazine, complains that the day-trading phenomenon is being "fed by the mindless mewlings of TV pitchmen and gee-whiz accounts in the public prints of programmers, potato-chip salespersons and grease monkeys who quit their jobs and found riches and happiness in a few hours of daily speculation." Abelson wonders what might happen "should this great bull market end in tears and a dizzying descent, leaving a scorched financial landscape in its wake. Those consequences would be particularly severe because everyone and his grandmother is in the market."[1]

In the immediate aftermath of the killings, the Internet stock-discussion world is full of messages about the murders. Elgindy writes that, thinking of the victims,

> "my heart goes out to their families especially their
> children.. May You all rest in Peace."

In another message, he says that the murders

> "personify why I take my security seriously and why
> noone knows at what minute some one will snap . . . or
> for what reason . . . Insanity."

But life and Internet trading soon resume their normal rhythms. For most people, the killings, like almost all killings, quickly become faded headlines.

For Elgindy, life remains a whirl of picking stocks to short and picking fights—or at least not shying away from them.

"You have never been right about anything,"

he writes to one trader.

"You are a liar,"

he tells a second.

"You are one of the most unstable personalities I have
ever seen in my life,"

he informs a third.

And, of course, his thoughts come back to TokyoMex, whom
Elgindy variously refers to as "Tokyo Joke," "Tokyo Joker Hype,"
and "Tokyo Criminal." The two fight it out online over various
stocks with Park being long, Elgindy going short.

Like TokyoMex, Elgindy is branching out. His private website
is humming along—"Trading Against the Dark Side of Wall
Street," its home page proclaims. There is, of course, his August
short-sellers seminar in San Diego. He begins offering personal-
ized, one-week courses in trading at $5,000 per person. By the late
fall of 1999, Elgindy says one or two traders a week are coming to
his new San Diego-area office for the course.

In the wake of his travails with Silicon Investor, he starts his
own stock-discussion operation and calls it "The WallStreetStand."
Membership is free and its website promises to be the place
"Where you come to really find out about the market."

Elgindy says he keeps no ownership in the new site. He gives
chunks of the equity to friends and to subscribers to his private
website. A big piece goes to the man who designed and will operate
the website. WallStreetStand

"is my Gift to the net,"

writes Elgindy.

In short, the short-selling world of Tony Elgindy seems to be
moving along quite nicely. Then, on October 27, he posts a rather
extraordinary message on his original Silicon Investor discussion
thread, Anthony@Equity Investigations. It reads, in part:

"I want to apologize to any creep and or crim I have
offended , it was never personal. My scam fighting days
are over."[2]

Elgindy's sudden retirement announcement is prompted by
the brutal murder of two stockbrokers, Alain Chalem and Maier
Lehmann. The two men were found shot to death on the marble
dining room floor of Chalem's million-dollar mansion in Colts
Neck, New Jersey. According to one news report, the forty-one-year-
old Chalem was shot five times in the head and once in the chest
by a semiautomatic weapon. Lehmann, thirty-seven, took four bul-
lets from the same weapon.

News reports said that the authorities suspect the killings might
be tied to the work of the two men, who operated a website promoting penny stocks. But hard leads were scarce. Local prosecutor John
Kaye told the *Associated Press* that "this is a definite 'whodunit.' "

The mystery set some of the inquiring minds of the Internet
racing. Janice Shell started a Silicon Investor discussion site dedicated to digging into the murders. She named it "Whodunit? Two
Stockbrokers Murdered in Jersey; No Clues."

The site quickly attracted hundreds of messages. The postings
ranged from copies of news stories about the killings to computerized background records on individuals and companies associated
with the victims. Scenarios for the murders were laid out. There
was speculation about whether a bald man (Chalem) would wear a
baseball cap with a business suit. The posters guessed possible
motives, discussed what the victims wore, and gave suggestions on
whom the police should question. One poster even took the idea of
investor rights to the extreme:

"Well, all i can say, harsh as it may seem. if the
killer or killers were scam victims,then i hope they
never get caught."

Shell said she hoped all the work would turn up information
helpful to the authorities. Even if nothing comes of the work, she
added, it is a ripping good mystery.

SCAM DOGS AND MO-MO MAMAS

But one that is a little too close to home for Elgindy, even though the crime took place a continent away from his house. As he explained in his online farewell message, the murders revealed

> "the very real world of Wall Street: not that cute
> picture painted on CNBC. To all those who know me ,
> and all those I know, I knew Al very well, by our
> work together several years ago uncovering scams. now
> he has forever been silienced.. May he rest in
> peace."

In an interview that same night, a clearly shaken Elgindy said he believed the murders were a "mob hit" related somehow to Chalem's stock-market activities. And he didn't have any intention of being the next victim. "I am not going to jeopardize my life for this shit. I have a wife and three kids," he said.

Seeing no reason to understate the severity of it all, Elgindy later wrote that

> "yesterday those bullets silenced not only Al but
> every other person alive. This is too crazy for me, we
> are now killing brokers and traders.. Sorry but ,I
> want to see my kids get old and I want to be done with
> this market. A@P, saying adios Wall Street, I'll just
> trade privately.. no more beef from me."

Elgindy even posted an apologetic note on the message board of a company that he had been favoring with such missives as

> "Criminal Activity.. Must halt!!"

But now a chastened Anthony@Pacific wrote,

> "I would like to take this oppurtunity to apologize
> for comments I may have made and those I did make as I
> passionately berated the Compnay. In no way Do I want
> to have any hard feelings exist.. I wish you all the
> best of luck, in your attempts at recouping your
> investments, or at maximizing current gains."[3]

Not surprisingly, some didn't immediately believe Elgindy's words. One trader who blamed the short seller for all kinds of investor losses wrote,

"you created a Frankenstein and now expect to put it
to sleep with a simple apology."

And Elgindy's Public Enemy Number One took a moment to savor his rival's discomfort.

"2 PENNY,, STOCK,, SCAMSTERS GOT MURDERED,,GUESS A DOG
GOT THE MESSAGE,"

wrote TokyoMex in an e-mail to Societe Anonyme members. Park attached part of Elgindy's e-mail announcing the end of his scam-fighting days.

Some doubted that Elgindy, whatever his words, could really stay away.

"I find it hard to believe that his ego can keep him
from being out front here with all of us,"

wrote one such person, but added,

"we'll see."

It didn't take all that long to see. A few days after the murders, the shock and fear diminished, Elgindy was back to throwing onlinr bombs.

"Really quite a crappy componay,"

wrote Elgindy about one firm. Another company he described as "trash" while a third was a "turd" that "will have blackened and crusted over" within a few months.

But in the life of Elgindy, there always seems to be some new turmoil. For example, his posting privileges were again suspended, though this time the penalty wasn't from Silicon Investor. Elgindy had run afoul of WallStreetStand, the very stock-discussion operation he started. He said the new management objected to him calling someone an "asshole" online. In late 1999, Elgindy had an acrimonious breakup with his lawyer, Matthew Tyson, over operation of the private website.

Around the same time, news hit the Internet discussion circuit about a problem that posed a much more real threat to Elgindy than online censors or fears of assassins. A message addressed to Elgindy but posted for all to see on Silicon Investor announced that in searching a database of criminal-court cases, the following had been found:

```
"CRIMINAL DOCKET FOR CASE #: 99-CR-109-USA v. Elgindy

AMR IBRAHIM ELGINDY defendant . . .

Pending Counts:

18:1341 & 2 - MAIL FRAUD AND

AIDING AND ABETTING . . .

No details given - what's this about?"
```

What it was about was that a federal grand jury in Fort Worth, Texas, had indicted Elgindy in connection with his collecting disability payments several years earlier. While Elgindy "claimed that he was emotionally unable to continue performing his duties as a stockbroker," he actually went to work for Bear Stearns at $30,000 a month and continued to collect disability checks, according to the indictment. He allegedly also worked for a second firm while on disability. If convicted, Elgindy could be sent to prison.[4]

Elgindy denied guilt and said that taking any disability payments not due him was the result of a misunderstanding and not malice. He said he plans to go to trial.

Elgindy has known about the disability-payment investigation for some time. He says that he had hoped that his cooperation with federal investigators would help ameliorate any problems in Texas. Elgindy says that's why he asked the U.S. attorney's office in San Diego to write the letter, outlining his cooperation. He adds that the recipient of that letter—whose name Elgindy had blocked out on the copy he gave to me—was the prosecutor in Fort Worth. But the indictment came anyway.

Besides, Elgindy wrote back to his online inquisitor,

"[I] never claimed to be an angel."

In another message, he said,

"My past is colorful, my experience is what gives me experience to be more effective at what I do."

In a third missive, he wrote

"I have been at the bottom of Wall Street, and I have seen stuff that would make you ill. I bring that experience unfiltered and raw. . . ..This is the very last dark cloud hanging over my head. . . . I feel confident that I will give it my best shot to win, and the rest is in God's hands period."

In the meantime, Elgindy added,

"back to fighting scams on Wall Street."[5]

CHAPTER

SIXTEEN

"I COULD MAKE YOU MORE MONEY in a month than you will make from this whole book."

Big Dog makes this offer as we sit next to each other at the bar of TJ's Pub, a.k.a. Jimmy's Place. The a.k.a. is courtesy of a new owner who doesn't want to drop the original name of this Haledon, New Jersey, watering hole. It seems fitting that Big Dog's favorite hangout has a moniker.

It's the evening of Friday the thirteenth of August 1999. TJ's is long and narrow, full of people, noise, and smoke. It's a neighborhood bar. Bev's behind the bar, busy pouring.

Nichols helps keep her busy. Big Dog is working down another Big Dog. Big Dog, the drink, is a sixteen-ounce glass with ice and two or so shots of Polish vodka topped with cranberry and orange juice for Vitamin C. Bev's cash register behind the bar even has a button labeled "Big Dog" to ring up another for Nichols. The button gets a workout.

This evening Nichols is working on about his sixth Big Dog. He occasionally takes a break by downing a shot glass of hundred-proof peppermint schnapps. I'm nursing my own small nursery of Dewar's on the rocks. I don't try to keep up with Big Dog drink for drink. Years earlier, I learned the hard way—from a sleazy copier salesman with a turbocharged liver—about the dangers of trying to match shot glasses with somebody I was interviewing. Trying to keep up with a four-hundred-pound source is, I know, utter madness.

Still, I've had enough Scotch that I wouldn't want to have to drive the barstool I'm sitting on. Big Dog assures me that he doesn't feel even a buzz yet. Perhaps, I think, it's the fruit juices and the peppermint.

Everybody at TJ's seems to know and like Nichols. Why not? He is friendly, boisterous, and generous. "Let the games begin!" he shouts as we walk in that evening. Many in the crowd roar back a greeting. He is a nice guy to have around. Besides being good company, Nichols regularly buys shots for others at the bar. His largesse is helping one regular patron nearby build a pyramid of empty shot glasses on the bar. The structure is already three stories high. The builder looks to be about the same.

Big Dog has been a celebrity since the first time he stopped by for a couple of drinks and left a $50 tip, says bar owner James Garruto. Little wonder that when Nichols tries to get Bev's attention, he rarely has to try twice.

Nichols pays his bills with a roll of bills that he keeps in his pocket. The wad doesn't look any larger than a hand grenade and probably isn't as heavy—presuming Ben Franklin doesn't have a weight problem. A thick rubber band holds the greenery together. Big Dog says he likes to keep between $5,000 and $10,000 inside the band. Don't leave home without it.

But back to making *me* rich. Nichols explains that he can give me some stock tips, help me set up an account, offshore or on, and school me in some of the nuances of the successful Internet trader. Besides being lucrative, it isn't even all that much work, he assures me. I thank him but tell him that I suspect that I'd make a lousy stock trader, even with a Big Dog guide.

Nichols shrugs, sips his drink, and tosses me the kind of

quizzical glance look you might give a guy who insists on walking past a crisp hundred-dollar bill on the sidewalk. He can't quite understand how someone could stare at riches in the palm of his hand and not close his fingers.

In recent months, Nichols has been keeping his fingers busy grasping opportunity. After being booted from Silicon Investor, Nichols started his own Internet website, called Capital Financial Consultants.

> "We at Capital Financial Consultants are committed to
> bringing you the best in up and coming companies. We
> will bring you the movers and shakers as we discover
> them. 'Together we will build the cream of the crop,'"

wrote Nichols in his online mission statement.

Cream aside, Nichols's bread and butter remains small-company stocks. Thanks to the Internet celebrity status of Big Dog, Nichols was hired by several little companies to do online investor relations. His clients include an aspiring restaurant chain, a seller of disposal bathing kits and a maker of plastic shipping pallets.

For his work, Nichols received hundreds of thousands of shares of their stock. While some of those shares fetched only pennies apiece, others rose into the dollars and cents each. Suddenly Nichols's net worth moved into the millions of dollars. He began turning some of this paper wealth into paper you can wrap a rubber band around. Nichols sold hundreds of thousands of dollars worth of stock. Suddenly he has more money than he has ever seen before.

(He also has a few bruises. Some of his small-company clients "stiffed me" on promise stock payments, says Nichols. One company official went so far as to give him a certificate for 1.4 million shares of stock. The only problem, says Big Dog, the certificate turned out to be bogus. It didn't actually represent shares in the company. Nichols shrugs off such losses as part of the game.)

At the same time, Nichols has been moving closer to a dangerous line that separates the enthusiastic amateur stock picker from the professional tout. Generally, securities regulators cut the amateur a lot more slack than the pro in what can and can't be done without violating the law.

Nichols now has to worry about making adequate disclosure concerning any compensation he receives from companies. Dozens of people around the country are being hit with lawsuits, injunctions, and monetary penalties for failing to satisfy the SEC on this matter. As a paid professional, Nichols is open to more scrutiny from regulators about what he says and how he says it.

Nichols says he is aware of the dangers and very careful to obey the law. He remains an enthusiastic proponent for his stocks. Consider this January 10, 1999, Big Dog recommendation for a voice-recognition technology company called Preferred Voice, Inc., which trades on the Bulletin Board under the symbol PFVI:

> "It is very rare that we put out an urgent buy alert, but in the case of PFVI we feel the time to buy is right now. As you will witness tomorrow, this stock price is headed straight up from here. This company at this level is so undervalued that buying now just about guarantees a 200% to 500% gain."[1]

In a disclaimer, Nichols revealed that he had received 60,000 shares in the voice-recognition company for "investment research, investor relations and consulting services." Nichols says this is adequate disclosure. The SEC, at least so far, hasn't challenged him on the matter.

PFVI didn't soar quite as Nichols predicted. At the time of the recommendation, the stock was trading for about $2.35 a share, having roughly doubled in price in the prior week. In the succeeding months, though, it didn't get much above that level and often went far below. Finally, in late 1999, it began rising and by the end of that year had topped $4 a share.

Though Nichols says he received stock in connection with boosting Preferred Voice, he didn't receive it from Preferred Voice. He says his shares came to him from a shareholder who wanted Big Dog to "draw attention" to the voice-recognition firm. Preferred Voice officials say they know Nichols and have talked to him over the phone but add that they have never hired or paid him.

In his online investor-relations work, it was "commonplace" for big shareholders to hire him to talk up a particular company, says Nichols, though he adds that he only talked up companies he believed in. Nichols says he suspects that this increased shareholder activism is a reaction to the SEC's increased interest in the issue of payments by companies to promote their stock. With many small companies nervous about giving shares to online figures such as him, large stockholders have stepped into that void. The big shareholders figure that raising the company's profile can also raise the value of their stake, says Nichols.

After several months of doing investor-relations work for public companies, Nichols decided that his next logical step was to have his own public company. He got together with his old online buddy, Jesse Cohen. Cohen came up with an Internet shopping-mall website. Nichols came up with a public shell. They reverse-mergered them together and voila! iChargeit, Inc. took its place in the pantheon of would-be Internet powers with publicly trading stock.[2]

The reverse merger is a way of bringing a private company public. It's particularly popular with legitimate small business owners and securities swindlers. Generally, in order to sell stock to the public, a company has to register the shares with the SEC. This involves filling out forms. It is often time-consuming and expensive. The SEC sometimes asks lots of questions, which some find easier than others to answer.

Over the decades, thousands of companies have successfully gone through this SEC vetting process. Not all of the companies have been successful in the business world, though. Many of the failed ones don't disappear. They continue to exist as corporate carcasses, also known as shells. Their main asset is the clearance they have received from the government to be a publicly traded company. And in the right hands, that's no small asset.

Enter the reverse merger. A private company, looking to go public relatively quickly and inexpensively, finds a publicly trading shell. There is a lively shell market, if you know where to look.

The shell then "acquires" the private company in exchange for stock. The owners of the private company get so much stock in the shell that they control the combined entity. That's where the reverse part comes in. Instead of the owners of the shell controlling the private company, the owners of the private firm control the shell. Once the deal is complete, the new owners often change the name of the shell to match the name of the formerly private company.

Reverse mergers are a perfectly legal means for a small company to go public. The fact that the process has been used by crooks to minimize scrutiny from regulators is just one of those unpleasant realities of the market.

Besides finding the shell for iChargeit, Nichols shelled out seed money—he estimates about $250,000 in cash and stock—to fund operations. In return, he received over one million shares of iChargeit stock. As a company insider, he was restricted by federal securities law on when he could sell it.

With Cohen as chairman and chief executive and Nichols as president (he later resigned and remained a major shareholder), iChargeit began lining up tenants for its online shopping mall. Early arrivals included a florist, a coffee seller, a consumer-loan broker, and an art gallery. Some tenants were clients of Nichols's investor-relations firm.

Among its marketing efforts, iChargeit buys the Internet domain name "yohoo.com" and links it to the iChargeit website. "Know how many people mistype yahoo.com?" asks Nichols.

As far as iChargeit was concerned, says Cohen, about 200,000 a month who mistakenly came to the shopping mall via "yohoo.com" or "yaahoo.com," which the company also acquired. However, the visitors almost never bought anything, says the iChargeit chairman. Cohen adds that the two domain names were dropped after iChargeit received a threatening letter from Yahoo's attorneys. Something about infringing on the Yahoo name.

Some of Nichols's and Cohen's acquaintances from past online battles visited the iChargeit discussion site at Silicon Investor. They reviewed the pair's Internet pasts in less-than-glowing terms.

"This is your Management, guys,"

writes Shell. Critics also delightedly noted that the initial artist featured at iChargeit's online gallery was Cohen's mother. Cohen responded that his mother was a very accomplished artist.

The stock of iChargeit briefly reached $29 a share, making Nichols a multimillionaire many times over—on paper. However, the stock was soon trading in the single-digit range, often around a dollar a share. Easy come, easy go.

The gyrations in iChargeit shares don't faze Big Dog, though. He figures the stock will eventually come back. Besides, he adds, with the power of the Internet behind him, "I'm not afraid to lose money because I know I can make more."

I use that quote in my *Wall Street Journal* profile of Nichols that runs on April 22, 1999, under the headline " 'Big Dog' in Chat Rooms Takes Wild Internet Ride." It's not a particularly negative piece, though it does include the crack about Big Dog's brain, a Tic-Tac, and a four-lane highway. Mostly the story is about the power of Internet stock trading to transform one man's life and finances.

After the story runs, a strange thing happens. I don't hear a word from Big Dog. After profiles of TokyoMex, Ga Bard, and Anthony@Pacific, each guy calls within twenty-four hours to give his opinion of the piece. But from New Jersey, there is silence.

To a reporter, such silence usually means that the person hates the story and has decided either to a) never talk with you again or b) sue you into the next century. I figure neither of those possibilities augurs well for my future relationship with Big Dog.

Others call me about the story. Several callers are little companies wondering whether Nichols might be the guy to get them attention in the online stock-trading community. One is a person from the firm that makes the "Big Dog" sportswear, looking for a possible marketing relationship that would bring together two dogs.

I call Nichols's number and pass these messages along to his answering machine. I ask him to call. He doesn't.

Finally, more than a month after the story runs, I call Nichols's number and he answers. I wait to be berated. Instead, he is profusely grateful. "That article changed my life," he says. The story brought him a flood of offers to do investor-relations work, seminars, and other profit-making opportunities, including a possible book about his life. But he also talks of being "overwhelmed," of "going into hiding," and of a chain of events that nearly cost him his marriage. He is reluctant to give details. Nichols says that the next time I visit, I have to stay in the guest room of his new home in Clifton. I take him up on the offer.

We rendezvous again at the White Castle. Having missed lunch in Manhattan and having a little time before Nichols shows up, I try a Slyder. I can't say it's tasty, but I could see eating a sack of 'em while strolling through cyberspace. It does sort of slide down.

Nichols arrives in his new Jeep Grand Cherokee. As I get in, it seems the distance between the back of the driver's seat and the steering wheel has grown since my last visit. (Nichols later estimates that his weight now tops four hundred pounds.) It's a hot day and there are drops of sweat on Nichols's face, though the Jeep's air-conditioner is blasting hard. He gives me a friendly hello. We drive off. The steering wheel looks like a child's toy in his large hands.

It's only about a ten-minute drive to his new house, which is in a well-kept neighborhood with lots of greenery. Nichols proudly tells me it's the fanciest section of Clifton.

The three-bedroom house itself isn't large. But it's comfortable, arranged on three levels plus a basement. Up a short flight of stairs from the living room are the three bedrooms in a cluster. Downstairs is Nichols's office, with papers and equipment lying about.

Except for the mess of his office, the house is neatly kept and nicely decorated. His wife, Janice, has been working for months decorating the place. Much of the time, "Mike was away," Janice says. She doesn't elaborate.

The three of us go out to dinner. On the way, we chat a bit about their newfound wealth. They talk of suddenly feeling like they don't have to worry about money. They talk of the freedom of that feeling and the enjoyment of it. But they also hint at how it has turned their lives upside down in ways. "It has been quite a trip," says Janice.

The restaurant is called Don Pepe. "We have to have champagne," Janice says excitedly after we are seated. Mike gives a shrug of assent. "A bottle of the Cristal," he tells the waiter. The waiter perks up noticeably and hurries off. "We had it here last week. It's so good," Janice assures me. I check the menu. I figure it should be pretty decent at $220 a bottle. I put a cork in my plan to buy dinner.

The waiter soon brings back the champagne wrapped in an apology. The bottle isn't yet cold. It has been locked in the manager's office. Just a few minutes in the ice bucket will do the trick, he assures us. Apparently, Don Pepe doesn't sell a lot of Cristal when the Nicholses aren't dining.

During dinner, the conversation drifts back and forth over a subject that has clearly dominated the Nicholses's lives over the past several months: money. Nichols mentions that he recently had lunch with a bunch of guys and picked up the tab. It weighed about $4,400, he says. The champagne there, he recalls, was about $300 a bottle. I quietly sip our bargain bubbly.

The dinner tab comes to about $350. Nichols pulls out his rubber band and adds what looks to be about a $100 tip. The management offers a complimentary round of after-dinner as thanks for our patronage. They obviously don't want to lose the Cristal crowd.

Janice says she's tired and wants to get home to sleep. We drop her off at the house. Mike says he's ready to party. "I often stay up until five A.M.," he declares. I tell him I'm game, but it turns into an early evening. We're home before three.

The next morning, as Nichols sleeps, Janice makes me coffee with steamed milk and chocolate in a cup large enough to double as a home spa. She is a friendly person, easy to like. While I do laps in the cup, she tells me a bit of her life. How she was the seventh of ten children. How she had more siblings than self-esteem while growing up. How for the past five years she has been working on a psychology degree at a local college, trying to better herself and feeling like she has. How she survived a failed marriage, but at least got a daughter out of it who is now in her early twenties. How she met Mike and now has a second daughter. How, even ten years into their marriage, she still dreams of someday having a real church wedding with Mike instead of one before a justice of the peace. I nod, I sympathize, I drink the coffee to the very last drop.

Later that morning, Janice leaves for the weekend to visit relatives. Their daughter is already away for the weekend with a girlfriend and her family. The house is left to Mike and me. It's a very comfortable house. Over the next day and a half, we spend a lot of time elsewhere. By the end of the trip, I'm pretty practiced at spelling TJ's.

We do spend some time in Nichols's downstairs office for a late morning, early Friday afternoon tiptoe through the stock market. As he sits down in front of his three computers, it's about 11 A.M. The markets have been open for ninety minutes.

Nichols now has three computers instead of just one. He also now uses and avidly advocates Level II software for tracking market action.

Using his computers, he trolls the small-stock world looking for companies whose trading volume is up heavily. Unusual volume often translates into price movement and potential profits, he says.

Nichols finds a little mining company whose stock usually trades hardly at all. But this day, over 340,000 shares have already changed hands and the price has more than doubled—to 7 cents a share. "Already gone up too far," he says, adding that he could have played it for a profit, "if I was up when I was supposed to be up." Then he adds, "Doesn't matter."

He languidly works the computer screens. He shows off a little for his visitor. He looks for a small company that has just made an announcement. Pretty much any company will do, Nichols says. He finds an Internet company that has announced a new contract. He buys 1,000 shares at a little over $1 each. Then he starts sending out e-mails talking up the stock.

Nichols has an e-mail list of about 3,000 names broken into two categories. One, with about 700 names, gets his picks first. These are people he considers serious traders. The second tier gets his choices a little later. He only sends out a few e-mails a week these days.

The little Internet company he just blessed soon pops above $1.60 a share. Big Dog could sell his holdings for a quick few hundred dollars. But he decides to let it ride and go out to lunch. After all, he says, it's mostly a demonstration for me. And what's a few hundred bucks?

On the way to lunch, Nichols swings by his bank. He's feeling a little low on cash. I ask how low. Down to about $3,500, he replies. He picks up another $2,500 at the drive-through teller window. He doesn't count it. Too much bother, he says.

I ask him if he worries about carrying that much money around. He laughs the laugh of a very big man whose brother is a cop. Big Dog points out that he is also wearing about $15,000 worth of jewelry: a heavy gold chain, a Rolex, a diamond-and-gold ring. No, he doesn't worry, he says.

While we're driving around, Nichols gets lots of calls on his cell phone. Some calls he answers, some he doesn't. A few he probably wishes he hadn't. "What? I'm not doing anything with it. You drained it," Nichols tells one caller. He hangs up the phone. It immediately rings.

"You going to complain to me because you made money!" Nichols shouts. "You going to complain to me. . . . I made you money and you're complaining. You gotta be outta your mind!"

Nichols hangs up with more gusto this time. I look quizzical. But before he can explain, the phone rings a third time. "Because this is an idiotic conversation for me," says Nichols in response to an obvious question from the other end. "What are you? What? You're delusional." Nichols hangs up again. The phone rings again. It doesn't get answered this time.

Clearly agitated, Nichols explains that the persistent guy on the phone had given him some money to invest. Since making it as Big Dog, lots of people he knows have been asking him for financial help of one sort or another. Nichols says he made a profit for the guy but not as much as the guy expected or needed. Now the man was complaining that he didn't have enough in his account for his bills. Nichols seems baffled by the ingratitude.

Money changes people, Nichols says. It's an obvious enough

observation, though it's one thing to say it and another to experience it. Since word of his Internet success spread, friends—even old friends—have begun treating him differently, says Nichols. Some are suddenly more solicitous, others more distant. He can feel undercurrents of jealousy and envy. He has no shortage of ideas from others about what to do with his money.

One night, we stop by a restaurant for the fortieth birthday party of an old friend from Delaware Avenue, where Nichols grew up. There are well over fifty people at the party. It's a lively and friendly crowd. Nichols says he knows many of them from his childhood.

The party is well along when we arrive. A buffet dinner has been served. Nichols circulates amidst backslaps and handshakes. Some joke about the celebrity stock picker, others ask his advice about the market. One friend says he recently bought some iChargeit stock and asks when it will bounce back. What was your purchase price, Nichols asks. About $2, the man replies. You'll be fine, Nichols assures him.

I talk for a time to another former resident of Delaware Avenue, an older woman with sharp features and short brown hair. She knows Nichols well. Like me, she is drinking a beer and nursing it from the bottle. She talks of the old days on Delaware as a sort of Camelot in Jersey: every neighbor part of one extended family circle. "I never knew what kids were going to be sitting down to dinner" and didn't really care, she says. In a certain way they were all her kids, she explains. She tells me that four generations of her own family are at this party tonight. She speaks longingly of Delaware Avenue and how she would have liked to stay. "But the neighborhood turned," she says. I don't ask her what she means. It doesn't seem necessary.

It's late Saturday afternoon and my visit with Nichols is nearly over. He is kindly giving me a ride back to Manhattan in his Jeep. We are headed to an old alehouse in the Village called McSorley's, where I am going to buy lunch.

During the previous day and a half, Nichols has filled in for me some of the blanks of his previous several months. He has told me about the whirl of parties and events that he was invited to by investor-relations clients and others. One company even had him as its guest at the Indianapolis 500 over Memorial Day. He got to visit the pit area and everything.

He also talks of the downside of feeling flush. Of how he wandered around the country in a sort sybaritic doldrums. How he largely stopped trading or doing much work of any sort, not even returning phone calls. He tells me of how he began drinking again after fifteen years of abstinence. And of how he now plans to lose weight and get his personal and business lives toned up.

(In a subsequent phone interview, Janice Nichols tells me that her husband's long absences sent her into a deep depression and nearly broke up their marriage. While things are getting better, "I never want to go back to that situation," she says.)

"I just wasn't home. I wasn't paying attention," Nichols tells me as the Jeep crawls toward the Lincoln Tunnel through a construction-caused clog. "It has to be the money. I know that it is there and not going to run out any time soon." He pauses, shifts lanes, and continues.

"Everyone thinks money solves everything," he says. "In a lot of ways, it just complicates things. Sure, you got freedom to buy what you want but that's not going to make you happy, believe me. Before the money I had to go to work nine to five, I had to put so much money away. Had to worry about paying the bills. Couldn't just at the flip of a coin go to Indianapolis or go to Florida."

As things stand, "I have no structure in my life," says Nichols as we near the tunnel entrance. "And I am a pretty undisciplined guy."

CHAPTER

SEVENTEEN

As THE MILLENNIUM ROLLS to its close, the Societe Anonyme stock-trading machine is purring along.

SA's Internet website has become a hive of information and activities and even a touch of mystery.[1] A visitor to the Societe's home page finds the shadowed outline of a man holding a brief-case, his back to the viewer. One hand is held up to his forehead as if he is shading his eyes from the sun. He is gazing at a black and yellow vista of three geometric figures, two balls and a cone, which look molten. In the upper left-hand corner of the page, it says "TokyoJoe's Societe Anonyme." In the upper right corner is a button to connect to an online brokerage firm. Framing the picture are words that might seem strange on a stock-trading website looking for members. But then, it is Joe Park's website. The words are:

> "Moments of glory ,,, desires ,,, wealth ,,, in the
> end all an illusion."

Lest a visitor get too introspective—or discouraged—there is another, more upbeat message at the bottom of the page. It reads:

```
"Time Magazine recognizes Tokyo Joe as 'one of the
country's most influential stock pickers.' EXTREME
momentum stock trading for maximum returns."
```

The reference is to Park's inclusion on *Time*'s online list of the fifty most influential figures in the digital-technology world. Topping the list are Jeff Bezos of Amazon.com, Steve Case of America Online, and Bill Gates of, well, Bill Gates. Also high on the list are personal-computer moguls Michael Dell and Steven Jobs as well as AT&T chief executive C. Michael Armstrong.

Park shares the forty-ninth spot with James Cramer, a Wall Street money manager and co-founder of the TheStreet.com online financial news publication. Cramer actually gets first mention in the next-to-the-last spot. Cramer, *Time* says, "has come to personify the tech-fueled bull market he promotes."

The publication calls Park the "amateur counterpart" of Cramer. It adds that Tokyo Joe is "the best known of the bulletin-board stock gurus" and "one of the country's most influential stock pickers." What Cramer and Park say, concludes *Time,* has "been known to move markets—a power formerly reserved for Wall Street analysts and venerable sources like the *Wall Street Journal*'s 'Heard on the Street' column."

Not too shabby for a burrito maker who couldn't make it as a gas station attendant. Now Park's pumping along with Gates and Jobs and Dell. On the other hand, he is only one perch above a busty, forty-year-old, sphinx-like bimbette who in high heels wouldn't rise much above his ankles. Barbie makes number fifty on the list for success in the computer-game world that has transformed the Mattel doll into "the hippest gal in the Digital Age," according to *Time.*

Beyond the Societe Anonyme home page are many spots to visit on the SA website. Some are available to nonmembers. There is the "About Us" page. Sections of it are almost identical to Park's original SA manifesto way back in early 1998, though the spelling has improved:

> "Our membership is growing everyday . . . Our society is
> made up of anonymous members from all walks of life:
> students, laborers, lawyers, home makers, investment
> bankers, NASDAQ market makers, a burrito maker, doc-
> tors, truck drivers, Asians, African-Americans, Anglos,
> Italians, Arabs, Jews, etc. We call ourselves Societe
> Anonyme™ . . . we go for instant gratification. We
> believe that every stock has Unabomber lurking to take
> it down. We take our profit and move on."

Another Societe Anonyme web page open to all is titled "Who is Tokyo Joe?" Venturing here brings a visitor to another shadowed outline, this one of a head and shoulders. The face is just black-ness. The page repeats the question and says, "Click to find out!" Above the head is an ad from a computerized bill-paying service offering to help "pay all your bills in nanoseconds."

Performing the click leads to the same photo, this time show-ing a broadly smiling Park in sunglasses with a white shirt and a red scarf around his neck. Below the photo are links to some of the stories written about Tokyo Joe. Another photo on the page shows Park, in plaid shorts, sitting in front of a bank of personal computers. There are two photos of Park on horseback, looking dapper and competitive. At the top of the page is an ad for Barnes&Noble.com along with a computer link to the bookseller. There is another link to Barnes&Noble in the Societe Anonyme website's online "bookstore," which provides a list of recom-mended readings for traders.

Anyone can also visit the website's page containing dozens of glowing tributes to Park from SA members. Another page discusses the upcoming, first-ever Tokyo Joe trading seminar, which was held in December 1999. The cost for the day of teaching from Tokyo Joe and others is $1,000.

Off-limits to the public are pages where Park's stock picks are kept. Private stock-message boards are also only for SA members.

Park has also begun a Societe Anonyme charity fund where he urges members to donate some of their stock-trading profits to the needy. To help raise money for the charity, he has begun an auction of special Societe Anonyme coins, featuring a bull on one side and a bear on the other. On each side is the message "We're the New Blood." Coin number one sells for $5,400. In an e-mail, Park promises the winning bidder that

> "I will do a wonga tonga on the coin and send it to
> you."

Of course, there is also a website page available for anyone wanting to join Societe Anonyme. Basic membership is $100 a month, which gets you Park's daily e-mails and access to most of the private Societe Anonyme website. Premium membership is $200 a month, which allows one into the live stock chat room at Societe Anonyme.

By the fall of 1999, Park's membership count for Societe Anonyme is above 3,000. At $100 or more a person, that translates into over $300,000 a month in membership fees.

Park remains the engine that makes all this possible. And he seems to be a tireless motor. Every trading day, and most others, he sends members a stream of e-mails, sometimes a dozen, sometimes two dozen, sometimes more. He writes so many messages that he sometimes has to explain why he isn't writing more.

> "If you have no EMs ,,,, I HAVE NOTHING TO SAY !!! MY
> BIG MOUTH IS RESTING !!!,"

he writes. Of course, Park adds, it could be that your Internet connection isn't working.

His trading philosophy, by now, is almost a mantra: newcomers should paper trade for at least a month before putting any real money into stocks;

> ("It takes 5 seconds to lose $100,000 ,, it will take
> you a life time to save that kind of money at a 9 to 5
> job !!!!!")

read the right books on trading and get the right computer equipment (suggestions for both can be found on the SA website); sell but never buy stocks when the market opens because prices usually surge upward in the first hour and then come back down—

> ("We always sell at open and take the gap .. and we
> always buy around 10 am,")

and that's New York time for all the "schmucks" who keep asking;

> "is it CST ? PST ? or Pakistan time,," . . . "never
> place an open MARKET order,, always put a limit order,,"

limit losses by keeping a standing order to sell a stock if it falls to a given price

> ("Remember ,,always put a stop loss,,); . . . "Learn
> the game folks ,, use your frigging brain." . . . "ONLY
> use the frigging money YOU CAN AFFORD TO LOSE !!!!
> other wise you are nothing but a money whore."

The chant goes on.

The message includes more than a few expletives undeleted. When one SA member objects to Park's use of the term "asshole," Park explains that

> "when it comes to members money ,, hard earned money
> ,, ass hole is too kind ,,when some one screws us with
> bad info ,,."

Park so often uses the term "schmuck" to display his displeasure with one or another person that some SA members begin to use the term on themselves in a sort of vocabulary of self-debasement. As in

> "KING OF SCHMUCKS"

or

> "newbie and schmuck."

One member even puts it to rhyme:

> "Dear stars . . . don't let me be a schmuck

```
Don't let me just rely on luck

Let me trade like TokyoJoe

Can this be my wish, tell me so."
```

A few curse back, though not with much elan.

```
"You make me sick, all in all you may be a nice guy
but you have no clue how to treat people. Fuck you
asshole, die pig,"
```

reads part of an e-mail written by an unhappy former member and passed along by Park. Park also sends along an e-mail from a member listing several stocks he bought that subsequently fell in value. Tokyo Joe does suggest to the disgruntled member that Societe Anonyme

```
"is not for you ,, suggest you go else where,,."
```

Park is now a big enough figure on the Internet to have a problem with online imposters putting out stock picks under his name.

```
"Some one is using my name to scam others !!!"
```

reads one Park e-mail.

```
"SOme one is sending out bogus em ,, don't fall for it
,, tell him to go screw him self ,,"
```

reads another. Tokyo Joe does recommend one possible litmus test of legitimate messages:

```
"A dead give away is my spelling and commas."
```

Park has also risen enough in status to earn a front-page piece in the *New York Times*. The lead paragraph of the August 21, 1999, article read:

Online stock traders, goaded by an Internet chat room leader, commandeered the shares of an obscure company last week, taking it on the kind of roller-coaster ride that veteran traders worry may harm investors and undermine faith in the overall stock market.

The stock in question was Information Management Associates, another Internet shopping operation. In the prior week, the company's shares, which trade on the Nasdaq under the symbol IMAA, rose as high as $14 from about $4 before falling back. During that week, the stock's trading volume was over 35 million shares. In the week prior to the run-up, the volume was less than one million.

Driving this action, according to the *Times* article, was Joe Park, who had been praising the stock, first in e-mails to Societe Anonyme members and then in an August 19 press release on Business Wire. "Tokyo Joe's calls have been uncanny all summer," said the release. (Conversely, Elgindy called the stock a "dead horse.")

The climax in the *Times* story came when the stock peaked at $14 and then "disaster" struck. The chat room at Societe Anonyme went dead. The stock dropped to about $9.50 a share. Though Park later told members a computer server failed, the story said that such loss of connection "was highly unusual, and some traders suspect foul play." The *Times* also reported that later "Tokyo Joe exulted: 'I made over 250k'" on IMAA stock. He presumably wasn't talking about his alphabet collection.

Park was livid over the *Times* story. In one e-mail, he accused the newspaper of "tabloid sensationalism." Attorney James Bjorkman, a top Park aide and chief executive of Societe Anonyme, fired off a letter to the *Times* calling the article a "disgrace" and demanding a retraction or correction. Bjorkman said that temporary connection problems on the Internet aren't at all "unusual" and accused the paper of trying "to create a false impression of nefarious activity." Bjorkman didn't get satisfaction.

But imposters and negative news articles are the headaches of success. For TokyoMex, it has been a remarkable run. When he travels around the country, his followers flock to meet him, in the way others gather to see a movie star or meet a political leader.

One such meeting between Park and members takes place overlooking the Pacific at the Laguna Cliffs Marriott Resort in Dana Point, California. I plan to drive the more than sixty miles south from Los Angeles but figure I won't have a lot of company. For one thing, there is no real program. Park simply will be available in his hotel room from 9 A.M. to noon to meet and greet. Plus, the morning that he has picked is a Sunday morning. Plus, it's Father's Day.

I arrive about an hour early to meet Park for breakfast. I find him lounging at a table outside. Sand and the Pacific Ocean are nearby. Park is dressed in a grayish sweater with a brown scarf wrapped tightly around his neck. White cotton pants lead down to black suede loafers with no socks in between. Though it is still overcast, Park is wearing sunglasses, unusual ones. The lenses are very small, no bigger than a quarter each, and they are suspended with no frames from a bar that runs across Park's forehead.

Sitting with Park is a businessman from Houston. "He is doing our business plan," Park informs me. Business plan for what, I ask.

Plans are in the works to franchise Societe Anonyme Cafés, where people can come to sip refreshments and trade stocks from computer terminals. As an added attraction, there might be a live audio/video feed of Park trading from his apartment "cussing, spitting, calling them schmucks," he says with a laugh. To prove his point, Park spits into a nearby flower bed.

When I mention that he will have to put on clothes if he is to be on video, he laughs again. The Houston businessman gives a questioning look. "I sit buck naked all day long trading," Park explains.

With my own small laugh, I ask Park if he expects Elgindy to visit today. Elgindy lives in the Dana Point area and has been threatening to crash this party. Park practically spits again. Our Texas companion, who is turning into an excellent straight man, asks who is Elgindy. "He carries four guns. He terrorizes companies. He is a cocksucker," says Park. What is there to say after that? (For the record, Elgindy says he only carries one gun, that he only bothers companies that deserve it, and no, he isn't.)

As we sit, Park talks of other plans he has for Societe Anonyme. He wants to start a hedge fund, which is a relatively unregulated investment vehicle for wealthy, sophisticated investors. He wants to turn Societe Anonyme into a public company. There will be stock-trading seminars, online and off, and revenues galore. (Later Park drops the plans for the cafés, deciding he doesn't want the headaches of running restaurants. However, he does add plans to offer online brokerage service to Societe Anonyme members.)

It is nearly 9 A.M. We amble off to Park's hotel room for the meeting. There I get a shock.

Some seventy people show up. They cram into the standard-sized hotel room, fill the small balcony, and spill out into the hall. When Park gives a demonstration of some trading strategies on computers he has brought along, people stand on the beds to crane a look. They at least take off their shoes before climbing on the sheets.

Many have driven a hundred miles or more to meet Park. One woman has flown in from San Antonio, Texas. She says she is a new Societe Anonyme member, made $1,000 in the prior week trading, had frequent flyer miles to burn, and a hankering to meet Park. "I had no reason not to come," she says.

Park plunges into the crowd like a politician at a rally, shaking hands and hugging bodies. He won't be mistaken for Al Gore, though. When a white-haired gentleman approaches, Park gives him a hearty handshake and says, "Hello, old man."

The man presents Park with a brown paper shopping bag from the Trader Joe's foodstore chain. It seemed appropriate, the man says. Inside the bag are two bottles of wine. While Park doesn't appear to have heard of Trader Joe's, he is familiar with wine and seems genuinely touched by the gift. "I'm sorry I called you old man," says Park. Some in the crowd laugh.

After a few minutes of circulating, Park says, "Let's drink champagne." He pours himself a generous glass from the refreshment table. I check my watch. Well, it is 12:10 P.M.—in New York. Park takes a sip. "Two titty girls are coming down soon," he says. That remark evokes more laughter from the crowd. Knowing Joe, I keep an eye on the door.

Park gives a brief speech and introduces Merrick Okamoto, head of a fledgling trading company that's trying to interest Societe Anonyme members in using its new stock-trading software. Part of the reason Park has come west is to meet with Okamoto to discuss the software and play golf.

"I thought I was talking to a Japanese guy on the phone for a fucking year," Joe tells the laughing crowd. Beside him, Okamoto looks about as Asian as George Washington. Well, what's in a name?

"I didn't have the heart to tell him," says Merrick, to more laughter.

"Then up walks this white guy with a gap between his front teeth," says Park

"I'm Japanese in spirit."

"Not under the belt," Joe responds to laughter and groans from the audience.

Before Okamoto starts his spiel, Parks has a few more remarks. "I love you all," he tells the assemblage. "Do not be schmucks. I buy five seconds or thirty seconds before I tell you to. It used to be two to three days in advance. I don't do that anymore since we went corporate.

"I was in a room with my lawyer and the SEC for two days. No one has been scrutinized more than I have been.

"As an immigrant, I want to leave a legacy. Your support has made me happy every day. So just remember. I will never fuck you."

By the end, his voice is beginning to crack with emotion.

For the next two-plus hours, there are no tears. Just the buzz of conversation and the pop of champagne corks. A thin, attractive blonde with short, spiky hair and a low-cut pink sweater tells Park, "I love to trade, but I will have to stop if you ever retire."

"I'll never retire," promises Park.

Another person asks Park about a particular stock. "I will pump it for you next week," Tokyo Joe deadpans, taking a pull on his champagne.

A man approaches Park and hands him his business card. He is a jeweler. "Next time you want to buy a diamond for your wife, call me and I'll get you the best price," he says. Park suggests the man post his card on the Societe Anonyme website message board—offering a member's discount, of course.

After the meeting breaks up, Park and I retire to the hotel terrace for lunch. By now the morning clouds have burned away and it's a glorious California day. Sailboats dot the blue waters below us. At the table are Park's top aide, Bjorkman, and others from Societe Anonyme.

We talk of many things. Park's problem with online imposters. His farm in Walla Walla, Washington, where his parents once lived. The wear and tear of his online life. "I can't believe how this has aged me. I look much older than in February. The SEC, Anthony dog. I wonder if it's worth it," says Park, looking pensive as he munches on fried calamari and Caesar salad. After a moment, he adds "Yes, it's worth it."

After lunch, Park checks out of the hotel for his flight back to New York. We walk out the front door. A long white limousine, courtesy of Okamoto's firm, is waiting to take him to the airport. As we reach the car, Park gives me a quick hug.

Then he's in the limo and the door closes. As the car whisks him away, full of plans for Empire Anonyme, the sun is still high and bright in the sky.

AFTERWORD

WELL, THE WORLD SAILED THROUGH January 1, 2000, and right past the millennium bug with hardly a problem, much less masses of terminally crazed computers littering the landscape. So much for the twenty-first century's first challenge.

The Tokyo Joe stock-trading express hit its own Y2K speed bump, however, only five days into the New Year. At least, Park earned another front-page story in the *New York Times*. This time the headline read: "Stock Adviser on Web Faces Fraud Charges." His travails attracted attention from lots of other news outlets, including a spot near the top of the ABC evening news with Peter Jennings. The nation's more lasting Y2K bug appears to be its ongoing infatuation with the stock market.

The latest media blitz surrounding Park was prompted by a lawsuit filed on January 5 in Chicago federal court. The suit lists as the defendants "YUN SOO OH PARK, A/K/A TOKYO JOE, AND TOKYO JOE'S SOCIETE ANONYME CORP." The plaintiff, listed in no less bold capital letters, is the "UNITED STATES SECURITIES AND EXCHANGE COMMISSION." The SEC investigation of Joe Park finally came to a head.[1]

The nineteen-page complaint says many things about Park,

none complimentary, unless one takes pride in being called a crook. The SEC alleges that Park "engaged in a scheme to defraud members of Societe Anonyme." On "numerous occasions, Park misled those members by failing to disclose or lying to them about the fact that he already owned—and was contemporaneously selling—the very stock he was recommending they buy. In such instances, Park purchased the stock shortly before his recommendation to buy and profited by selling the stock into the buying flurry that followed his recommendation," the suit says.

Additionally, the agency accuses Park of recruiting new SA members "by posting on his Internet web site materially false and misleading performance results." The suit contends Park overstated his gains on individual stocks by as much as 2,000 percent. Finally, in connection with at least one of his on-line recommendations to Societe Anonyme members and others, Park "failed to disclose that he had accepted shares of common stock from the issuer in exchange for recommending the stock."

The SEC suit seeks a permanent injunction against Park that would prohibit future violations of securities laws. It also asks for monetary penalties, including disgorgement of the "ill-gotten gains" obtained from the allegedly illegal conduct. To add insult to injury, the SEC lists Park as being fifty years old, nearly a decade older than the age he gave me. (When I ask, Park says the SEC is correct about his age.)

The suit was filed as Park was flying back to New York from a holiday stay in Barbados. The weeks prior to the Caribbean vacation had been heady days for him. As the market soared in November and December, so did Park's spirits.

> "Societe Anonyme , makes more money in November -
> December, than any other time,"

he wrote in one e-mail to SA members.

> "The irrational exeburance index ,, hits the boiling
> point ,,, I am ready , bring it on ,,"

he wrote in another. Of course, being "personaly up ,, 2600% this year,," in stock trading might help anyone's mood.

He wrote of the planned SATT brokerage operation. "SATT" standing for Societe Anonyme, Tokyojoe Trading. Park sailed through his first trading seminar in New York in December:

> "I was nervous as hell but as soon as I opened my
> mouth ,, it all just came out ,, like a waterfall , We
> had a rocking time."

To his members, he wrote that

> "I love you singularly and individualy,, I have been
> wit you on a long jopurney now."

Naturally, Joe remains Joe—charming and intense, a flamethrower never far from his trigger finger. For those who complain too much about losing money in the market, he has these words of comfort, in the TJ dialect:

> "If your bught high ,, and you are holding the bag ,,
> than you lost,, if you are asking me ,, what happened
> ? then you lost ,, Listen up ~Stocks go up ,, stocks
> go down , ,, use SA rule ,, for last f ing time,, if
> you are a newbie,, learn to trade first ,, And fo rlst
> time ,, I do not have enough money ,, to buy all the f
> ing stocks in this world,, if schmuks sell,,, there is
> notjhing I can do ,, further ,, schmucks,, markets go
> up and markets go down ,, STOP SENDING ME EMS ,, ask-
> ing me what happened ? I DON'T KNOW ~~~~~ !"

At the same time, Park is very optimistic about the future, despite expecting some temporary retreat in stock prices early in 2000. As he soaked up the Caribbean rays, took time to enjoy the view around him and ahead of him, he wrote:

> "Glorious sun rose here today ,, here in Barbados ,,
> burning orange against baby blue skies and Maxfield
> deep blue sea ,, white cream puff , cloud,, so tender
> ,, spread out massive over vast Atlantic horizon ,,,
> it seemed to rise with a purpose and destination ,, a

```
resolute reminder that ,, humanity will triumph ,, and
universe is our home ,,,, Let us use ,, and ride this
new rising sun ,, new opportunties ,,, I see nothing
but , positive signs from here on,,,"
```

Instead, Park flew back to a maelstrom of press attention and charges from the nation's securities cop. Yet, he seemed largely unfazed. By late evening of January 5, he was back in his New York apartment firing out e-mails to members.

```
"My conscience is clean"
```

he told members. Park said that his published stock-trading record is accurate and verifiable, that he has never received any improper remuneration, and that he hasn't taken advantage of his members in his trading activities. So let the SEC try its case.

```
"I believe,, we will set a new frontier, a defining
moment ,, for,, individual traders ,,I welcome the
challenge,"
```

he wrote, tossing in a "R O F L M A O" at the end for good measure.

Others also seem to think that *SEC v. TJ* could turn out to be an important, even a landmark, case. THE CASE AGAINST 'TOKYO JOE' THREATENS ALL GURU-DOM, read TheStreet.com headline about the SEC suit. The story speculates that given the agency's heightened interest in the Internet, more cases against Internet stock gurus could be coming.

In a sign of the status that the SEC attaches to the suit, the agency's enforcement chief Walker is made available for press interviews. "While the Internet has provided a new medium to commit fraud, it has also revolutionized the ability of regulators to respond quickly and effectively," Walker tells the *New York Times*. In the SEC's press release about the case, Walker is quoted as saying "The Internet has witnessed the rapid growth of Web sites run by self-proclaimed investment gurus. Today's action makes clear that we will not tolerate fraudulent conduct or undisclosed conflicts of interest by those peddling investment advice on the Internet."

As Walker's quotes indicate, the SEC has launched a two-pronged assault on Park. One prong is a traditional SEC approach: if you get caught taking money from investors on the basis of telling them lies, you'll get skewered. This is classic antifraud doctrine that has been applied to people whether they communicate by telephone, telegraph, or tell-a-buddy.

The SEC's second line of argument in the Park case, however, has potentially groundbreaking—or, perhaps more appropriately, fence-building—implications for the Internet stock-discussion world. For the agency is also arguing that Park didn't tell others nearly enough about what his own trading strategy and activities were.

Up to now, the Internet stock-trading world has been a pretty wild and uninhibited place where free spirits typed with abandon. The idea that some cyberspace poster—celebrity or not—might recommend a stock and then immediately sell into any price surge probably wouldn't shock anyone who has spent much time hanging around Silicon Investor or Raging Bull or Yahoo!. Reading the message boards tends to breed a certain cynicism in anyone who isn't comatose or Big Bird.

In the Park case, the SEC is arguing that any such cynicism isn't enough protection for the individual Internet investor—at least not for a member of Societe Anonyme. And maybe the regulators are right—especially given that millions of newbies are expected to be flocking to the Net in the coming years to trade stocks and maybe even learn how to trade them. The SEC suit against Park could help set the rules about just how much Internet posters have to disclose about their own trading activities and plans.

Giving the litigation a little extra oomph, people immediately bring the First Amendment into the matter. Park's lawyer Sorkin, the former head of the SEC's New York office, told the *Times* that "We intend to defend against the charges. I would have hoped that the SEC would have dealt with these types of issues such as free speech and the exchange of information over the Internet through regulation and not litigation."

The *Times* also quoted well-known constitutional attorney Floyd Abrams as saying that while the SEC charges "cannot be blown away by hoisting the First Amendment banner," the case "does raise a serious First Amendment issue involving the continued availability of the Web as a place where people can speak broadly in an uninhibited manner about topics, including the stock market."

(Early in the new millennium, Floyd Schneider, a.k.a. Truthseeker, started getting hard lessons in First Amendment issues. The federal judge in the ZiaSun lawsuit slapped him with an injunction against making false postings. In a related state court suit in California, filed by a ZiaSun backer, the judge there also issued an order restricting what Schneider could say on the Internet. The state judge also ordered Schneider to post a retraction on the Internet disavowing press releases he had issued that were critical of ZiaSun. Schneider issued the retraction, though he said in an interview that he still believed the material he had put out about the company was accurate.

In February 2000, Elgindy was invited to the ZiaSun litigation party when he was added as a defendant in the state court suit, which was filed by a ZiaSun investment advisor named Bryant Cragun. Elgindy denies any wrongdoing in the matter.)[2]

In Park's case, his very uninhibitedness might provide some defense for him against the SEC. As a *Los Angeles Times* story on the suit points out, Park hasn't always been exactly secretive about his allegedly abusive stock-trading tactics. The story dredges up that classic Park quote from his 1999 *Money* magazine profile: "Everybody knows that I'm buying before you buy, and I'm selling when you're buying. Otherwise, what am I? A charity?"

While such statements hardly make Park look like Santa Claus in the court of public opinion, they could be very helpful to him in a court of law. For the SEC's power isn't so much over actions as the disclosure of those actions. In the securities world, you can legally do some pretty odious things to investors as long as you tell them about it in advance. One of the central questions in Park's SEC case quickly shaped up to be what did he tell his members and when did he tell them? The SEC suit cites several instances where Park allegedly recommended a stock to members and failed to tell them when he quickly sold his holdings to take advantage of the price surge he had helped cause.

Park realized early on that disclosure—or lack thereof—would be a key issue. He sent out e-mails to Societe Anonyme members asking them to scour their computer files for any of his old e-mails that talk of his trading practices.

> "All the members ,, please send my disclosure em s,,
> such , as I will be selling on to your fat greedy face
> ,, if ou gap up the stock,"

read one Park post-suit message.

He dug particularly hard for some of his old messages concerning a company called DCGR International Holdings Inc. DCGR is a little Boca Raton, Florida, company that sells cigars, food, and skin-care products. According to the SEC suit, Park recommended the company's stock to Societe Anonyme members but failed to tell them that he later "was given 100,000 shares of common stock in DCGR . . . by an agent or representative of DCGR at the request of DCGR," says the SEC suit. Park allegedly sold those shares on the same day he received them—at a profit.

In a January 6 e-mail to SA members, Park acknowledged receiving shares but had an explanation. He wrote that DCGR stock at the time

> "was trading at 6 cents,, their friging pr firm sent it
> ,, as thank you ,, it was sold at 4 cents and used for
> charity."

In another e-mail on the subject of this alleged undisclosed compensation, Park had different numbers but the same message:

> "As for comoensation,,fukk disclosure was made,, also
> dcgr was 8 cents,, at the time ,, sold at 6 cents and
> used for charity."

Park was quoted in a Bloomberg news story that he got $4,800 from the sale of the stock and donated it to his daughter's private school.[3]

In my own incomplete personal archive of Park e-mails stretching back to July 1998—when he added me to the Societe Anonyme mailing to aid in my reporting about him—I don't have any message that refers to him receiving 100,000 shares of DCGR stock. Of course, that doesn't mean he didn't send one out. I do have other messages from him about the Boca Raton cigar company as well as notes from interviews. If he was a paid tout for the company, he wasn't your run-of-the-mill happy-talk booster.

In June and July of 1998 he wrote about a trip he was planning to take to visit the DCGR's Florida headquarters—with the company picking up the tab.

> "Whole trip is paid by DCGR so nothing will be lost
> out of my pocket,"

Park wrote in a June 19, 1998, message posted on the DCGR discussion board at Silicon Investor. Though he came back from the Florida trip with a buy recommendation, he was soon something less than an enthusiastic company backer. In an e-mail to Societe Anonyme members, Park wrote,

> "No more silly pennies,, !!!!!! DCGR was my last penny."

That e-mail was sent on July 19, two days before the SEC says he received his 100,000 DCGR shares.

When I interviewed DCGR's president Don Platten in September 1998 as part of my *Journal* profile of Park, he said he had come to believe that Park is a "hype and dump guy" and regretted having courted him. Platten acknowledged having paid for Park's trip to Boca Raton but didn't mention anything about stock.

When I interviewed Park in the fall of 1998, he told me about buying DCGR shares and then selling them after roughly doubling his money. He shrugged off the fact the DCGR shares later fell in price. Eventually, he added, "penny stocks always go down. That's why they are pennies." However, Park didn't tell me about the free stock he received—a fact that evidently nagged at him after the SEC suit was filed. In a post-suit message to Societe Anonyme members, Park wrote:

"Had I known ,,,,,, that ,, we will be this big ,, I
also , want to extend my personal apology ,, to John
at Wall Street Journal ,, for not having more for-
tright ,, again ,, I had no f fing idea,, where we were
going , I really thought ,, that ,, I will just make
my f you mone and that was that ,, Well I know now."

In an interview with me shortly after the SEC suit, DCGR
executive vice president Isadore Roth said the stock was given to
Park by a company shareholder in hopes of encouraging the Internet celebrity to back the stock. Roth declined to identify the shareholder and said DCGR management didn't know about the
payment at the time it occurred. He noted that the SEC hadn't
charged the company with any wrongdoing.

Not surprisingly, others have opinions about the SEC suit.

"A@P ..Vs Tokyo Blow

after 10 rounds Tokyo Joe takes a hard fall!!!!!!!!!!!!"

Tony Elgindy posted this message shortly after news of the
SEC suit hit the wires on January 5. For the rest of that day—and
after—Elgindy was almost giddy as he threw more punches at
his foe:

"TOKYO JOE>----CONFIRMED AS BEING PAID TO TOUT
STOCKS!!"

(Well, accused anyway.)

"A@P<--->Puts Tokyo Joe Inthe Gutter!!!!!!!!!!!!!!!"

"TOKYO<----->—GETS NUKED!!!!!!!!!!!"

Besides instant analysis, Elgindy offered some tentative predictions:

"TJ is gonna Go BK

[as in bankrupt]

```
and run like a butt head and Crim case follows.. I m
hearing several count INDictment from New York ..Plus
I hear a Organized Crime connection.. Doesnt look
good.."
```

In a later phone interview, he stood by his prediction of an eventual indictment against Park based on the evidence as he saw it. After all, he said, didn't he correctly predict months ago that the SEC would sue Park? As for the organized-crime mention, Elgindy acknowledged that was just speculation on his part. (Or perhaps wishful thinking.)

Elgindy also expressed a willingness to do more than just comment on Park's travails.

```
"Attention all memebers of the now defunct Socitie
Anonymie please contact me if you would like to be
lead plaintiff in a class action suit."⁴
```

A volunteer who claimed to be a former member of Societe Anonyme almost immediately contacted Elgindy.

```
"I would love to be lead in class action suit,"
```

this person wrote. (Park says Societe Anonyme is very much alive.)

Others have opinions about the Park case and, being Internet mavens, aren't bashful about posting them.

```
"Good the scum bag deserves it,"
```

wrote one.

```
"I call dibs on his Porsche Carera when the Fed auc-
tions it off. Ggggg,"
```

wrote another, who clearly preferred Drive to Park.

```
"Tokyo Joe , you are going to jail you piece of
garbage!"
```

volunteered a third, though this writer did add,

```
"Why don't you join him anthony?"
```

Indeed, with his Texas criminal trial for alleged disability fraud looming ahead of him, Elgindy remains a lot closer to a federal prison cell than Park, who still only faces civil charges. While Elgindy insists he will take no plea deal and will defend himself to the fullest, it's clear from talking with Elgindy that his criminal case weighs on him. How could it not? He faces the possibility of being separated from family and friends. Not to mention Internet service.

Elgindy does take some grim comfort from the belief that his alleged crimes—perhaps even Park's alleged wrongdoing—are peanuts compared to the ongoing outrages being produced in the wood-paneled citadels of a certain lower Manhattan thoroughfare.

```
"Its all a big scam..BUt then they are really really
rich and we are just regular people.. ... The Big
Firms are guilty of the same things TJ is .. .. .The
scam Known as Wall Street goes on . . ."5
```

Park found comfort from his loyal fans.

```
"So far,, support ems out number , hate ems ,, 120 to
5,"
```

he wrote on January 5. He sent out a sampling of both to SA members:

```
"You probably pocket all the charity money too,"
```

read one of the more printable comments from critics.

```
"I think the secs allegation are absurd,"
```

wrote a backer.

```
"No scam on your part and i will testify to that,"
```

offered another.

```
"I feel so lucky and am very proud to be your friend,"
```

added a third.

But between the days of energy and bravado are the dark, uncertain hours that come even in cyberspace. On the first weekend after the SEC case was filed, Park was up late on Saturday night. As with most of his waking hours, he was at his keyboard. At a little after 11 P.M., he tapped out a long message of thanks and apology to many people. This, in part, is what he said:

> "Yes,, I made mistake ,, a human nature,, and I accept
> it as a new stepping stone ,, a landmark case ,, where
> ,, they bit a wrong dog ,, a rabid dog ,, Just remem-
> ber,, I always have said , be 75 % truth ,, 25% BS ,,
> and god will open he door for you ,,In my case,, more
> truth than BS ,, ... And my hart,, my spirit ,
> and my body ,, my skin,,even ,, has changed a hew,, a
> tone , of purpose,, a tone ,,, of indeed ,, we are at
> a virge of ,, new era ,,, Call me Joe Hefner from now
> ,, call me Joe Nader from now ,, I always have been
> known as Joe Schindler

[Park has long been a fan of Oskar Schindler, the World War II industrialist made famous by Steven Spielberg. Hef and Ralph seem more recent additions.]

> ,,Good night and my love to you all ,, and your family
> ,, Remember,, I speak ,, your languange,, a red neck
> tongue with southern drawl .. in a population 40,000
> like Walla Walla ,, where my farm is ,, my inheri-
> tance,, I speak the language of constipated academia,,
> as well as ,, able to walk off the face of several
> prime ministers,, but , no mater how I speak ,,,, the
> essence ,, is always ,, truth ,, and sharing of human
> experience,, money follows those who love life,, it's
> a natural progression."

With that said, Park's mind started turning back to the tasks ahead.

> "So far,, I see no unabombers,, this weekend ,, and ,,
> expecting , more rally begining of the week ,"[6]

he wrote at the end of his late-night message. A few hours later, just before 5 A.M. Sunday morning, Park was back at his computer, back at work.

In the hazy dawn of a new century, it's anybody's guess how long Park and all his personas will remain at the keyboard and as a force on the Internet. The government can be a fearsome foe, and when it targets someone it usually gets that someone, one way or another. Like Tyrannosaurus Rex, Uncle Sam might not be the smartest or nimblest of creatures, but he does have a lot of teeth.

Yet even if this Park is, so to speak, paved over by the feds, other Tokyo Joes will follow. And other Anthonys and Janices, Ga Bards, and Big Dogs when those particular Internet icons fall or fade. The new ones might not be as charismatic or outrageous or weirdly likable as the originals. Sequels rarely are.

But millions of investors have come to the Net and millions more are on their way. This migration is already changing the way Wall Street works and the way people invest. While sucking in more people, stock trading is also picking up speed. A front-page story in the January 15, 2000 issue of the *New York Times* quoted an investment study finding that investors in 1999 held a given stock an average of only eight months compared with two years a decade earlier. The holding period for the fifty most heavily traded Nasdaq stocks averaged a mere three weeks. This more rapid turnover was fueled, according to the *Times*, "by the rapid-fire trading mentality" of day traders that is "seeping into the overall market."

The Internet has certainly brought its own Pandora's box of worries and woes to the world of stock investing. If nothing else, it's impossible to feel unalloyed enthusiasm for any invention that makes it easier for con artists to paint their canvasses.

Yet, it isn't hard to root for the success of this Thing. As someone who briefly played at being a Berkeley radical before becoming a *Wall Street Journal* reporter, I can still remember that dinosaur bone of a phrase from the '60s: Power to the people. I think I even chanted it a few times way back when there were two Vietnams.

Well, the Internet is bringing power to the people. Power that was long concentrated in the hands of a relatively few professionals in and around Wall Street is being spread across the fruited—and sometimes fruitcaked—plains.

Like any great moves to democratize a corner of the world, this one is messy and isn't always moving forward. The landscape will probably look particularly ugly when the stock market has its next great downturn. On the other hand, the pre-Internet stock market had some pretty ugly moments, too. Various panics and crashes over nearly two hundred years didn't get their monikers for the fun and profits they brought to investors or the nation.

Many pundits wonder how much of this Internet investing craze is just that: a craze that will soon join the Y2K bug on a cobwebbed shelf of history. Maybe it will fade. But it seems more likely that this particular mania has some mileage in it. Lots of people may just decide that they like having more knowledge and power and responsibility over their own financial affairs—even if they get mugged sometimes as a result. To put it in Internetspeak, the eyeballs just might stick.

For one thing, the Internet offers anybody who wants it—be he burrito maker, bard, or boob—a shot at something at least as addictive as making money: the chance to be *somebody* in the eyes of somebody else. Given the weird nature of the Net, you might never know exactly who are your admirers or hate mailers and whether they are around the world or around the corner. Or next to you in bed. In some ways, that's part of the allure.

Besides, where else in this land of opportunity can a man grab at the brass rings of fame and fortune while sitting in his living room, unshaven, teeth unbrushed, buck naked as the day he was born?

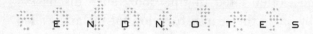

Three major online stock-discussion operations were principal sources of material for this book. They are Silicon Investor, Raging Bull, and Yahoo!. For those with Internet access and interest, these sites can be reached at the following addresses:

Silicon Investor: techstocks.com
Raging Bull: ragingbull.com
Yahoo: finance.yahoo.com

At the home page of each site, one can dredge up all kinds of information about a given company, ranging from the stock price to news releases to financial filings with the SEC. Thousands of companies have had discussion boards set up about them. These boards, as well as other information about the company, can generally be found by typing the company's stock symbol into the site's search engine. The sites also have directories for those who know the name of the company but need to look up its stock symbol. As a general rule at these sites, if you are searching for a discussion board, click on links that say "discussion" or "stock talk"or "message" or any abbreviation, such as "msgs."

Some discussion sites aren't dedicated to a single stock or

even to any issue related to stock trading. At Silicon Investor, the online operation most often cited in this book, such discussion sites can be found by using the search function for the area called "Stock Talk." For example, type in the phrase "Tokyo Joe's Café" and any discussion site whose title contains those words will pop up. Information about individual posters, including their online autobiographies, can be gleaned by typing a person's online name, such as Ga Bard or Big Dog, and searching the "People" area.

Messages on individual discussion sites are numbered and archived by the date and time they arrive. So if you are looking for a message from a specific time, you can search back to that period. If you have a specific message number, you can usually enter that number in the search function at the site, which will then produce the missive.

The following notes contain cites for many of the Internet messages quoted in the book. In some cases, I have given specific message numbers. However, message numbers are sometimes changed by system operators. If a message can't be found by its number, it can usually be found by its date and time.

PROLOGUE

1. The numerous Internet messages—along with many, many others—regarding JB Oxford can be found at the Yahoo! message board for the company, stock symbol JBOH, during the period of late January through the first week of February 1999. Some of the messages cited came from the Silicon Investor and Raging Bull boards for JBOH for the same time period.

2. Observations about Oxford offices are from a visit by the author in early 1999.

3. Material on Irving Kott's background came from various news articles, including "How a Top University Unwittingly Became Stock Promotion Bait," *Wall Street Journal*, April 27, 1984; "Beverly Hills Firm's Stock Offer Is Similar to Major Fraud Case Investments," *Los Angeles Times*, December 18, 1993; and "Convicted Swindler Is Securities-Firm Consultant." *Wall Street Jour-*

nal, May 3, 1995. Information also came from a March 28, 1988 decision by the Ontario Securities Commission, titled "In the Matter of Tricor Holdings, Inc."

4. Material on Rafi Khan came from reporting by the author for a January 28, 1994 story in the *Wall Street Journal,* "Broker Khan's Associations Scrutinized," that was co-written with Rhonda L. Rundle. The SEC case against Khan was filed July 30, 1998, in Los Angeles federal court, case no. CV–98–6143. The criminal case settlement with Khan was announced in a press release from the U.S. Attorney's office in Los Angeles on July 6, 1999.

5. The brief history of stock markets and investing frenzies is drawn from several books and articles. My favorite of the books is *Extraordinary Popular Delusions and the Madness of Crowds* by Charles Mackay. Besides having a nifty title, it is one of the great books ever written on financial follies and frauds. Originally published in the mid-nineteenth century, it was reissued in a 1980 edition by Bonanza Books, New York. This edition contains a foreword by financial journalist Andrew Tobias that offers an intriguing alternate title. Tobias wrote that when a Harvard Business School professor first told him of the book, he heard the title as "Popular Delusions and the Madness of Krauts." Probably not a big seller in Germany. Other books that I found valuable on the history of investing were: *The Big Board* by Robert Sobel (New York: The Free Press, 1965); *A Short History of Financial Euphoria* by John Kenneth Galbraith (New York: Viking, 1993, reprint); and *Wall Street: A History* by Charles R. Geisst (New York: Oxford University Press, 1997). Material on the Klondike was largely drawn from the very readable *The Klondike Fever* by Pierre Berton (New York: Carroll & Graf, 1985, paperback).

CHAPTER ONE

1. The e-mail messages from Park, including his stories from Mexico and Unawatuna, were sent out to Societe Anonyme members. Park was kind enough to include me on his daily e-mail list for Societe Anonyme members in order to help obtain material for the book.

2. Park's Egyptian travelogue was appended to the July 8, 1997 story "CyberCache: TokyoMex, a Fool's Fool, Lives Larger than Life" in TheStreet.com.

3. Park's posts on Tava/Topro can be found on the Tava Technologies discussion thread at Silicon Investor during the months of August and September 1997.

CHAPTER TWO

1. The danger of market orders was laid out in "Schwab Settles With Investors Over IPO," *Wall Street Journal,* March 11, 1999.

2. The messages concerning 800 Travel Systems, IFLY, can be found on the Tokyo Joe's Café/Anything Goes discussion site at Silicon Investor for April 5 and April 6, 1998, as well as on the Yahoo! discussion board for IFLY on July 12 and July 13, 1998.

3. Park e-mail regarding the party went to Societe Anonyme members.

4. "The Naked and the Dead (Legendary Manhattan Strip Club, Scores)," *Playboy,* February 1, 1999.

CHAPTER THREE

1. Quotes from Park's early Societe Anonyme mission statement come from a copy saved by the author.

2. "Dolphin Pulse Charge Engine Technology Offers Solutions to Auto Companies to Improve Both Power and Efficiency" press release from BAT International that ran on Business Wire on January 5, 1998.

3. Park's messages about BAAT can be found at the stock-discussion boards for the company at Silicon Investor and Yahoo! during the period January 12 to February 8, 1998.

4. "Rentech Announces Second Quarter Results," PR Newswire, May 15, 1998.

5. Park's March 3 message and the messages from others, including

Big Dog, can be found at "Tokyo Joe's Café/Anything Goes" discussion site at Silicon Investor, which for a time went by the name "Dog House." There are two other Tokyo Joe's Café sites at Silicon Investor. One has the title "Tokyo Joe's Café/Societe Anonyme" and the other is called "Tokyo Joe's Café/Societe Anonyme/No Pennies." The origins of these two later threads are tied up with the fact that Joe Park has lived an interesting and rather complex online life.

CHAPTER FOUR

1. White Castle's website can be found at www.whitecastle.com.

2. The various messages in the battle of TokyoMex versus Big Dog can be found at the "Tokyo Joe's Café/Anything Goes" discussion site at Silicon Investor between March 6 and March 13, 1998.

3. Swancey's greed formula comes from a message he posted at the AOXY discussion thread at Silicon Investor on November 4, 1999, at 12:22 P.M., no. 588. His message about "shorter slammers" was part of his opening post on April 22, 1998, at the "Georgia Bard's Corner" discussion site on Silicon Investor. That opening message has since been changed and the quote comes from a copy of the previous message retained by the author.

4. A copy of the e-mail from the "Swiss friend" was supplied by Mike Nichols.

CHAPTER FIVE

1. Nichols's WINR message can be found at "Tokyo Joe's Café/Anything Goes" discussion site at Silicon Investor. Nichols eventually gave up the Dog House site and it reverted back to Tokyo Joe's Café. His exchanges with critics can be found at the WINR discussion site at Silicon Investor.

2. Big Dog's messages and replies to him can be found on "FBN Associates—Year 2000/Y2K IPO!!!" discussion thread at Silicon Investor for the period April 26–27, 1998.

3. Information on the Zeigletics hoax came from an interview with David Gardner as well as from the book *The Motley Fool Investment Guide* by David and Tom Gardner (New York: Fireside/Simon & Schuster, 1997, paperback).

4. The various Shell-related discussion threads are all found at Silicon Investor.

CHAPTER SIX

1. Shell's Iomega message was posted on June 5, 1996, on the Iomega board at Silicon Investor. The one mentioning XICO was on the Silicon Investor Xicor board on June 20, 1996, and the Tasty Fries messages were on the Silicon Investor discussion thread for that company, symbol TFRY, in December 1996.

2. "Reverse Splits at Many Firms Spark Outcry." *Wall Street Journal*, November 20, 1998.

3. Shell's story of her freighter voyage was contained in an e-mail to the author.

4. Shell's messages about music, life, and cooking can be found on the "Let's Talk About Our Feelings!!!" discussion site at Silicon Investor from late December 1996 to late January 1997.

5. The Cryogenic Solutions press release referring to "pregnancy suspension technology" ran on Business Wire on January 5, 1998. The company's announcement about the Costa Rican clinic appeared on the same day on Business Wire. Shell's reaction to the clinic announcement appeared on July 19, 1998, on the Cryogenic Solutions discussion thread at Silicon Investor, no. 798.

6. The messages between Shell and Big Dog can be found on the Cryogenic Solutions thread at Silicon Investor on July 20, 1998, as can the contribution of Cavalry.

7. The "PAID TO INVADE" quote is taken from a long message that appeared on the "Welcome to Silicon Investor" discussion site on July 22, 1998, at 7:08 P.M., no. 1908.

CHAPTER SEVEN

1. Much of the material concerning Stark and creation of SEC's Internet unit came from interviews with Stark in late 1999 and early 2000.

2. The *New York Law Journal* piece by Milton S. Gould was excerpted in the December 14, 1986 issue of *Newsday* under the headline "Time for Another Snake-Slayer on Wall Street."

3. Testimony by Arthur Levitt before the Subcommittee on Commerce, Justice, State, and the Judiciary of the House Committee on Appropriations, U.S. House of Representatives, March 18, 1998.

4. I gathered the TRAC data and the material on D'Onofrio's career for a May 12, 1995, front-page profile in the *Wall Street Journal*. Perhaps the first, and best, major piece on D'Onofrio was "Who's Riding This Horse? A Shady Tout Backs an OTC Number," by Diana Henriques in *Barron's* on May 9, 1988.

5. Interviews with Frenkel and Allen.

6. "Securities Fraud: The Internet Poses Challenges to Regulators and Investors," General Accounting Office report, March 22, 1999; "Stock Hustlers Exploit On-Line Services" by Earl C. Gottschalk, Jr., the *Wall Street Journal*, June 21, 1994; speech by Richard Walker at the National Press Club on April 5, 1999.

7. Written statement by Richard Walker to the U.S. Senate Permanent Subcommittee on Investigations, Committee on Governmental Affairs, March 23, 1999. SEC vs. Comparator Systems, case no. 96–3856 in Los Angeles federal court.

8. SEC vs. George Chelekis, et al., civil action no. 97CV–0374 in Washington D.C. federal court on February 26, 1997; Walker quote from "New Effort Launched to Curb Internet Securities Fraud" on Dow Jones News Service, July 28, 1998.

CHAPTER EIGHT

1. Big Dog messages at Silicon Investor on the discussion sites for Cryogenic Solutions and Tokyo Joe's Café/Anything Goes, which was for a time known as the Dog House.

2. Shell message was posted on the "FBN Associates: A Perfect Company" site at Silicon Investor.

3. E-mail messages from Joe Park to Societe Anonyme members.

4. From Ga Bard's initial message of Sept 18, 1997, on creating the "MIDL. . . . A Real Sleeper" discussion thread at Silicon Investor. Swancey posted the message at a little after 1 A.M., further evidence that he wasn't much of a sleeper.

5. The SEC's suit against King was filed in federal district court in Tampa, Florida, case no. 98–2198; the SEC suit against Marsik and Pierce was filed in New York federal court, case no. 97–9303; the information about Midland's frequently changing business lines came from a series of company press releases issued in 1997 and 1998. The release naming Pierce as Midland's president and Swancey as investor-relations contact ran on Business Wire on June 16, 1998.

6. The online kudos for Swancey were posted on the Arcon Energy stock-discussion site at Silicon Investor on June 16, 1998, at 8:32 A.M. and 12:07 P.M. The SEC announced its trading suspension of Midland stock in SEC release no. 34–40331 on August 18, 1998.

7. The message critical of Swancey was posted on the Anthony@Equity Investigations site at Silicon Investor at 2:14 A.M. on October 1, 1999.

8. Park e-mail messages to Societe Anonyme members.

CHAPTER NINE

1. Anecdote about Little's portrait in Sobel's *The Big Board,* p. 40.

2. Messages that Elgindy posted on the Anthony@Equity Investigations site at Silicon Investor on May 6, 1999, and June 14, 1999; Firstwave Technologies press release of July 19, 1999, on PR Newswire.

3. Message on Anthony@Equity Investigations site on July 19, 1999, at 3:01 P.M.

4. Findex.com press release of May 17, 1999, on PR Newswire.

5. For the rundown of some of Reifler's law-enforcement history, see the following SEC litigation releases: no. 14669 on October 2, 1995, no. 14832 on March 4, 1996, no. 14935 on June 6, 1996, and no. 16293 on September 27, 1999.

6. 50-Off Stores suit against Koutsoubos, case no. SA–95-CA–0159.

7. Messages from Elgindy to his private trading group. Copies also provided by Elgindy to the author.

8. Raging Bull messages on Findex.com message board on June 9, 1999, at 5:15 P.M., on June 10, 1999, at 9:46 A.M., and on June 13, 1999, at 1:56 P.M.

CHAPTER TEN

1. Internet exchanges between Elgindy and Park can be found on the Turbodyne discussion thread at Silicon Investor on January 9, 1999.

2. The raid on the Blinder Robinson offices reported by the *Wall Street Journal* on November 21, 1988; Meyer Blinder's conviction was reported by the *Journal* on July 13, 1992.

3. Message posted on Anthony@Equity Investigations site on February 3, 1999, at 12:30 A.M.

4. "Alco Execs Have Seen Trouble," *San Diego Union-Tribune,* May 31, 1992.

5. Interviews with John Fiero.

6. Some of Richards's history with law enforcement can be found in the SEC administrative proceeding file no. 3–3629, dated September 25, 1972, and file no. 3–3826, dated May 30, 1973. His criminal case in San Diego federal court was case no. 97–0387.

7. Details of Elgindy's Ohio licensing woes came from interviews with Elgindy and Gomaa, as well as the June 18, 1997, "Findings of Fact" by the hearing examiner at the Ohio Division of Securities.

8. Elgindy vs. Elgindy, divorce case no. 233–245381–96, filed November 7, 1996, in Tarrant County, Texas state court.

9. Elgindy vs. Bear Stearns, NASD arbitration award, case no. 95–02492; Elgindy's criticism of the NASD was posted on the Anthony@Equity Investigations site on June 14, 1999, at 3:32 A.M., no. 38654.

10. Material about Pitt and Zaman came largely from interviews and other reporting I did for "Prosecutor Explored World of Stock Fraud: Did He Get Lost in It" that ran in the *Wall Street Journal* on October 25, 1996; Pitt's guilty plea in his criminal case was reported in the *Journal* on June 5, 1997. The SEC suit in Los Angeles federal court against Pitt and Zaman was case no. 96–4164.

11. The NASD case against Elgindy was complaint no. CMS950207 and the sanctions were listed in the September 22, 1997 "Decision and Order Accepting Offer of Settlement."

CHAPTER ELEVEN

1. Elgindy posts about USA Talks are on the Anthony@Equity Investigations discussion site: January 23, 1999, at 11:46 A.M., no. 5678; January 21, 1999, at 3:07 P.M., no. 5364; January 24, 1999, at 12:22 A.M., no. 5903; January 21, 1999, at 2:12 P.M., no. 5341; and January 27, 1999, at 10:13 A.M., no. 6576.

2. "I Will be in Anaheim . . ." posted on the Anthony@Equity Investigations discussion site December 2, 1998, at 11:19 P.M., no. 109.

3. "JBOH . . ." posted on the JB Oxford discussion site at Silicon Investor on February 3, 1999, at 11:41 A.M., no. 418.

4. USA Talks press release of December 18, 1998, on PR Newswire. Financial figures are from the company's 1998 form 10-K filed with the SEC.

5. "Portnoy is . . ." was posted on the Anthony@Equity Investigations site on January 23, 1999, at ll:46 A.M., no. 5768.

6. Details of the FTC case against Trendmark can be found in the FTC press release issued June 25, 1998.

7. "I am a nationally . . ." was posted on the USA Talks site at Silicon Investor on January 27, 1999, at 7:36 P.M., no. 112; "very BAD NEWS . . ." was posted on the same site on January 26,

1999, at 12:19 P.M., no. 68; "It will be . . ." was posted on January 27, 1999, at 4:22 P.M., no. 98.

8. Copy of Park subpoena obtained by author.

9. "Wake up . . ." was posted on the Tokyo Joe's Café/No Pennies thread at Silicon Investor on June 2, 1999, at 9:17 P.M., no. 77627; "criminal action . . ." was posted on the same site on March 10, 1999, at 7:48 P.M., no. 60740.

10. "The MOST . . ." post was deleted from Anthony@Equity Investigations thread; "Want to bet . . ." was posted on the Anthony@Equity Investigations thread on July 16, 1999, at 12:22 A.M., no. 41064.

11. "And we will . . ." was posted on the Tokyo Joe's Café/Societe Anonyme/No Pennies thread on March 10, 1999, at 7:10 P.M., no. 60734; "Any one here . . ." was posted on the "Audio and Radio on the Internet-NAVR" thread of Silicon Investor on March 8, 1999, at 4:52 P.M., no. 10766; "I think this . . ." is an e-mail to Societe Anonyme members on January 22, 1999.

12. "SEC Probes Day Traders Web Service," *Wall Street Journal*, April 2, 1999.

13. Nocera's comments about Park can be found in the March 17, 1999 edition of the *New York Times*.

14. "Sabratek Files $90M Suit Vs Online Critic, Publisher," Dow Jones News Service, August 3, 1999.

15. The Pluvia/Elgindy exchanges can be found on the Anthony@Equity Investigations thread on May 4 and May 5, 1999.

CHAPTER TWELVE

1. "Analyst Lends Hand to Refugees Helps 28 to Settle in U.S.," *Chicago Sun-Times,* May 1, 1999.

2. "ATTENTION . . ." was posted on the Anthony@Equity Investigations thread on April 23, 1999, at 4:42 A.M., no. 32247.

3. Silicon Investor history based largely on interviews with Jill Munden and Jeff Dryer.

4. Complete text of Terms of Use can be found at the Silicon Investor website.

5. Park/Elgindy exchange can be found on the Market Gems thread at Silicon Investor on June 6 and June 7, 1999.

6. Mary Elgindy posts can be found on the Anthony@Equity Investigations thread starting on August 22, 1999.

7. "You're funny . . ." message from Jeff Dryer to Elgindy that was supplied to the author by Elgindy.

8. Burdick message was posted on the Anthony@Equity Investigations thread on August 27, 1999, at 9:34 P.M., no. 43474; Elgindy response posted on the same day at 11:41 P.M., no. 43491.

9. "I have known . . ." messages from A@P Trader begin on the Anthony@Equity Investigations thread on August 28, 1999, at 7:24 P.M.

10. "The drivel . . ." message posted on the "Thread Morons" site of Silicon Investor on October 12, 1999, at 1:29 A.M., no. 8695; "utter stinky . . ." message was posted on the "Audio and Radio on the Internet-NAVR" thread of Silicon Investor at 11:38 A.M., no. 24117.

CHAPTER THIRTEEN

1. "The Internet Stock Bubble," *U.S. News & World Report,* January 25, 1999.

2. "Amateur Hour on Wall Street," *Forbes,* January 25, 1999; "Who Needs a Broker?," *Business Week,* February 22, 1999; for information on Merrill Lynch going online, see "Facing Internet Threat: Merrill to Offer Trading Online for Low Fees," *Wall Street Journal,* June 1, 1999.

3. "The Net-Setters," *Los Angeles Times,* June 27, 1999.

4. "Securities Fraud on the Internet," hearing by the U.S. Senate Permanent Subcommittee on Investigations, Governmental Affairs Committee, March 22 and March 23, 1999.

5. "As Huge Changes Roil the Market, Some Ask: Where Is the SEC?," *Wall Street Journal,* October 11, 1999.

6. U.S. vs. Gary Dale Hoke, criminal case no. 99–441, filed in Los Angeles federal court.

7. "State Internet Sweep Nets 'Illegal and Fraudulent' Entertainment Investments," press release from California Department of Corporations, July 28, 1999; "Day Trading Project," report by the North American Securities Administrators Association, August 9, 1999.

8. Ga Bard and Big Dog exchanges can be found on the "(CNHH) C.N.H. Holdings . . . Gas & Oil Service" on Silicon Investor, beginning on June 25, 1998, at 11:54 A.M.

9. Ga Bard exchanges with Markoff can be found on the "A Diversified Environmental Company . . . CNHH" thread at Silicon Investor beginning on April 6, 1999, at 5:09 A.M.

10. "For three years . . ." was posted on Georgia Bard's Corner at Silicon Investor on October 29, 1999, at 9:29 A.M., no. 7082.

CHAPTER FOURTEEN

1. Amazon Natural Treasure's 1998 form 10K.

2. Amazon Natural press release of February 18, 1998, that ran on Business Wire; Amazon Natural form 8K of June 29, 1999, filed with the SEC.

3. "U really . . ." message was posted on the AZNT thread of Raging Bull on September 20, 1999, at 10:45 A.M., no. 6276; "Brain transplant . . ." message was posted on the same site November 4, 1999, at 2:35 P.M., no. 7298.

4. "This has implications . . ." message was posted on the AZNT Raging Bull site on November 2, 1999, at 11:06 A.M., no. 7087; Shell replied at 12:06 P.M., no. 7090.

5. Icabod messages begin on the Amazon Natural thread at Silicon Investor on August 27, 1998, at 2:11 P.M. Messages concerning Shell's alleged cancer begin on the same thread on October 31, 1998, at 8:20 A.M., no. 10162.

6. Story about the Fasano conviction ran on the Dow Jones News Service on July 16, 1999.

7. E-mails from Dante, Rick, Cal, and Roger were supplied by Shell and Mitchell.

8. "New York Accuses Penny-Stock Firm of Fraud in Pricing," *Wall Street Journal,* February 8, 1989; "THE MOST BRAZEN OF THE PENNY HUSTLERS? – Months After a Bust, Power Securities' Scams are Still Surfacing," *Business Week,* November 20, 1989; "Ex-Penny-Stock Figure Gets 3-Year Term," *Denver Post,* February 13, 1993. In the matter of Richard Marchese, SEC administrative proceeding, file no. 3–9817.

9. Marchese gave his then-current address when he was deposed by the SEC on April 3, 1998.

10. Hitsgalore.com Inc. vs. Janice Shell, et al, U.S. District Court, Tampa, Florida, case no. 99–1387.

11. Information about the FTC case against Dorian Reed can be found in FTC press release of March 4, 1998, "FTC Sues Spammer." For additional information on the FTC matter and Reed's criminal conviction, see Hitsgalore.com's form 10K for 1998 on file with the SEC.

12. *Wired News* correction of April 2, 1999; Business Wire vs. Jeffrey S. Mitchell, et al, U.S. District Court, San Francisco, case no. 99–1987.

13. "New Technologies & Concepts, Inc. Announces Major Breakthrough in the Field of HIV Research," June 16, 1999, press release on BW Healthwire.

14. SEC trading halt announced July 22, 1999. SEC release no. 41638; SEC litigation release no. 16252, issued August 13, 1999.

15. Shell message posted on the "XXXXXXX" thread at Silicon Investor on June 25, 1999, 10:17 A.M., no. 2554.

CHAPTER FIFTEEN

1. "Stock Losses Roiled a Volatile Personality, and Slaughter Ensued," *Wall Street Journal,* August 2, 1999; "For Day Traders, a Moment of Silence and Some Soul-Searching," *New York Times,*

July 31, 1999; "Up & Down Wall Street," *Barron's,* August 2, 1999.

2. "I want to apologize . . ." was posted on the Anthony@Equity Investigations thread of Silicon Investor on October 27, 1999, at 6:12 P.M., no. 45850.

3. "the very real world . . ." was posted on the Anthony@Equity Investigations thread on October 27, 1999, at 6:12 P.M., no. 45850; "yesterday those . . ." was posted on the Anthony@Equity Investigations thread on October 27, 1999, at 7:03 P.M., no. 45855; "I would like to take . . ." was posted on the "Starnet (SNMM) Online gaming, sexsites, lottery, Sportsbook" thread at Silicon Investor on October 27, 1999, at 7:13 P.M., no. 8096.

4. U.S. vs. Elgindy, U.S. district court, Fort Worth, Texas, case no. 99-CR–109.

5. "I have been at the bottom . . ." was posted on the AZNT thread at Raging Bull on November 21, 1999, at 9:55 A.M., no. 9581.

CHAPTER SIXTEEN

1. "It is very rare . . ." is from the January 10, 1999, online news release from Capital Financial Consultants.

2. Information about iChargeit came from interviews with Cohen and Nichols and postings on the iChargeit discussion site at Silicon Investor.

CHAPTER SEVENTEEN

1. The website's address is www.tokyojoe.com.

AFTERWORD

1. SEC vs Park, case no. 00C–0049, U.S. district court, Chicago.

2. California state court suit, Bryant Cragun vs. Does 1–50. San Diego County state court, case no. 730826.

3. " 'Tokyo Joe' Park Says SEC Charges Ignore His Blunt Warnings," Bloomberg news service, January 13, 2000.

4. Elgindy posts can be mostly found on the Anthony@Equity Investigations thread starting at 12:53 P.M. January 5, 2000. A few can also be found on the same day on the Tokyo Joe's Café/Societe Anonyme/No Pennies site at Silicon Investor. Likewise, responses from other message posters can be found at the same sites.

5. "Its all a big . . ." was posted on the Tokyo Joe's Café/Societe Anonyme/No Pennies site on January 7, 2000, at 9:44 A.M., no. 116265.

6. Park e-mails to Societe Anonyme members.

What follows is a very informal, very incomplete compilation of Internet stock-discussion terms. Apologies in advance to Mr. Webster.

AFAIK "As Far As I Know." Depending on who is typing, we could be talking millimeters or miles.

AFK "Away From Keyboard." Something that true Internet addicts almost never type when the market is open. A trader needs discipline and a strong bladder.

____ BAGGER As in "two-bagger" or "three-bagger," or even better, "ten-bagger." A reference to a stock that increases two or three or ten times in price. An easygoing word, "bagger" will accept any numeral in front of it. However, traders who seek more bags also face more risks of holding a stock long enough to see it get bagged. Just remember, even Babe Ruth struck out a lot pursuing four-baggers.

BASH; BASHER Bashing is the art of viciously and unprovokedly attacking a fine little company that, if left alone, might cure cancer, lead humankind to the stars, or at least see its stock price double; a basher is the practitioner of this dark art. These terms are usually used by shareholders or other friends of the bashed company. (Antonym: See HYPE; HYPESTER)

BB Bulletin Board. An electronic stock-quotation system operated by the NASD (see NASD). The Bulletin Board is home to thousands of little stocks with lots of potential. Unfortunately, an unknown number are complete frauds whose only potential is to send your investment dollars to a place from which they won't return. However, the Bulletin Board has great potential for Internet acronynmania. As in: "DD that BB POS. EOM."

BLIND POOL A type of investment in which the investor puts in the money and later finds out what business the company plans to be in. (Synonym: A really stupid thing to do with your money)

BRB "Be Right Back." They generally are, unless it's the guy who has just received your check for that can't-miss stock offering.

BTK "Back To Keyboard." AFK's bookend.

BTW "By The Way." A very secondary use is "between you and me," which, BTW, can sound a little silly when you are posting it on a public message board.

CRD The Central Registration Depository. Okay, so regulators for this database of information about brokers and brokerage firms won't win any headline-writing awards. But some of the stories in the CRD can actually make for pretty interesting reading. Residing there are the employment and disciplinary histories of brokers. Though it has limitation, the CRD is a good thing to check before entrusting any of your investment money to a smooth-talking stranger. In some states, citizens can get CRD information through their state securities commissions. CRD information is also obtainable online through the NASD at www.nasdr.com or 1-800-289-9999.

DD/DUE DILIGENCE Doing your homework to learn about a company's operations, prospects, and any criminal convictions of top officers. DD is best done before you buy buy. Unless you don't mind seeing your money go bye-bye. Sometimes used as a verb, as in "I DD'd that stock." Depending on how well the DD is done, could also stand for dumb-dumb.

DT (See TIC/TICK) No, it doesn't stand for delirium tremens, which generally afflicts alcohol addicts rather than Internet addicts. However, downticks are known to afflict stock-trading bulls.

EBITDA "Earnings Before Interest, Taxes, Depreciation and Amortization." A financial measure of a company's performance. Of course, in the roaring Internet '90s, how many people really care about measures of financial performance? Just watch that stock price soar!!!

EMOTICON Here is how one web page dedicated to emoticons describes the objects of its affection:

> A shorthand version of expressing moods has emerged on the Net and together with certain behavioral rules form nettiquette. The shorthand for moods uses standard (QWERTY) keyboard symbols and they are known as EMOTICONS a.k.a. "smileys." There seems to be a never ending supply of these, and they can get rather irritating at times. Applied properly, however, they serve a useful purpose.

There are basic emoticons:

- Happy :-)
- Smile :->
- Sad :-(
- Yelling/Shocked :-O

Then there are more complex ones:

- Net Flame ~~:-[
- Put Your Money Where Your Mouth Is :-$
- Sticking Out Tongue :-P
- Tongue In Cheek ;-^)
- Hung Over: %*@:-(
- Drooling: :-~~
- Vampire With Many Teeth :-E
- Vampire With Broken Tooth :-F

EOD "End Of Day." Usually the end of the stock-trading day, since the sun never actually sets in cyberspace.

EOM "End Of Message." Three little letters that often seem to come not nearly soon enough.

EPS "Earnings Per Share." Well, at least all the hot cyberstocks have shares.

! The seemingly universal punctuation point of Internet-stock chatdom, a spear through the heart of the drab period. And in cyberspace, it multiplies like bunnies!!!!!!!!!!!!!!!!!!!!!!!!!!

FLAME To attack or uncover the dastardly deeds of someone. Always, of course, done with the purest of motives. Unless, of course, done by an evil basher or unscrupulous hypester. Or someone who is just a real pain in the butt.

FOCL "Falling Off Chair Laughing." Depending on where you sit, a necessary prelude to ROFLMAO.

FTSE Usually pronounced "footsie." A stock-market index, it's sort of the Dow of Great Britain, where bathrooms are named "Loo" instead of "John."

FUBAR Like Spam, a survivor of the Big War that Tom Hanks and Steven Spielberg recently refought on the Big Screen. Stands for "Fucked Up Beyond All Recognition," though some Internet posters have changed it to "Fed Up Beyond All Recognition"—perhaps in recognition of living in an overstuffed decade.

FWIW "For What It's Worth." Often less than the writer thinks.

G "Grin" or "giggle," usually. Some posters seem to use it instead of "grrrrr," which is definitely not a giggle. Plural form is GGGGG.

GAP A popular chain of clothing stores, or a quick, relatively large movement in the price of a stock. Such as "Sell that dog on the next gap up." Slang form: GAPPO.

GTO "Go To Zero." Once the muscle-car dream of every teenage boy, it's now the stock-price dream of every short seller and the nightmare of every long.

HYPE; HYPESTER The absolutely most fabulous word you will ever read. Best used by highly skilled and trained hypesters when describing stocks with unbelievable prospects. Emphasis on the "un." (Antonym: See BASH; BASHER)

IANAL "I Am Not A Lawyer." Usually written by someone who plans to give you legal advice anyway.

IDK "I Don't Know." A term all too rarely used on the Net or off.

IEI Irrational Exuberance Index. Also known to some cynics as the stock market of the late 1990s.

IMHO "In My Humble Opinion." The more easily pronounced cousin of FWIW, this term is invariably followed by an opinion, often light on the humble.

k "O.K." Talk about saving keystrokes. Some of the more affectionate message posters may use "k" for "kiss." However, neither should be confused with "K," the stock symbol for the Kellogg Co., that well-known guardian of the SCP (snap, crackle, pop).

LOL "Laughing Out Loud." Roughly the same meaning as ROFLMAO, but briefer. A longer version, contributed by Janice Shell, is LOLOLOLOLOLOLISSIMO!!. Then again, she lives in Italy—unless you believe her critics who claim to have made Shell sightings in Georgia, Texas, and California.

LTHTT "Laughing Too Hard To Type." Obviously not.

LURKER Someone who reads the postings on an Internet message board but doesn't write any. "He lurks in his Lerkim, cold under the roof, where he makes his own clothes out of miff-muffered moof." Thank you, Dr. Seuss.

MM/MARKET MAKER A brokerage firm that publicly lists prices at which it is willing to buy and sell stocks that are traded on the Nasdaq or the Bulletin Board.

MO-MO MAMA Refers to a stock that is quickly rising due to excitement among traders, sometimes triggered by news, Internet chatter, disinformation, and sometimes by the need to be excited about something. Hyphen is optional. Since mo-mo mamas often move faster than the average speeding stock trader, it is easy to find yourself buying just in time to watch the price fall. Thus, the still little-known adage that too often chasing the mo-mo mama can leave you a po-po papa.

MOOF See LURKER.

NASD National Association of Securities Dealers. An organization made up of the nation's brokerage firms and stockbrokers, the NASD helps regulate the markets to insure that individual investors get a fair shake when dealing with securities professionals. And only cynics would suggest that having a brokers' organization protecting investors is akin to having Jesse James guarding the bank vault.

NASDAQ National Association of Securities Dealers Automated Quotations. A computerized stock-trading system operated by the NASD. It includes the stocks of such well-known companies as Microsoft and Intel. It has also been the home to some lesser-known ones that Nasdaq officials would perhaps like the world to forget.

NEWBIE A newcomer to the Internet stock-trading world. Suitable for being hazed and otherwise abused by upperclassmen.

NRN "No Reply Necessary." But what fun would that be?

NYSE New York Stock Exchange. The nation's oldest, most famous, and most prestigious securities exchange. And it knows it.

OIC "Oh, I See." As in real life, usable even if you don't.

OT "Off Topic." Given what passes for consistency on many stock-discussion threads, it's sometimes difficult to imagine how someone can actually get off the topic.

PO-PO PAPA See MO-MO MAMA.

POS Piece Of Something you probably don't want to own—or touch.

PTG&LI "Playing The Game & Loving It." Used frequently as a sort of last name on e-mail messages by a guy named Joe. No, not Joe Park.

PUMP & DUMP The art of convincing others that a stock is a great investment and then selling your shares when the fools start to buy; a.k.a. P&D; a.k.a. ALWTTF, A Lousy Way To Treat Friends.

ROFLMAO "Rolling On the Floor Laughing My Ass Off." Used to express happiness, triumph, or contempt. Used so often that you wonder what Internet traders have left to sit on. There have also been a few alternate meanings proposed for this acronym. Two from Tony Elgindy, one seemingly designed for scam artists, the other for farmers on the Net: Ripping Off Families Laughing My Ass Off and Rolled a Fat Lady Merrily Around Oxen.

SCALPING A trading strategy that involves holding a stock for a short period of time, perhaps only a few minutes, in hopes of selling it for a small profit. Regulators tend to view some examples of scalping the same way that early settlers did.

SCAM DOG A stock that combines the qualities of a "scam" and a "dog," being at worst a fraud and at best overvalued and headed for a fall. An online canine whose bite is often worse than its bark.

SCHMUCK If you don't already know, consult any English/Yiddish dictionary or hang out at a local deli.

SEC Securities & Exchange Commission. A fine group of federal public servants dedicated to the fair and orderly operation of the nation's stock markets. Occasionally powerless in the face of career stock swindlers. But nobody's perfect.

SHORT SELLER A stock trader who believes more in the power of gravity than the power of faith.

SOHF "Sense Of Humor Failure." A too often undiagnosed disease that was carried from the Old World to the Net.

SPAM Posting the same message on many message boards; a.k.a. Stupid Persons' AdvertiseMent. And of course, it's also an all-purpose mystery meat, biting into which is something like buying into a blind pool. (See BLIND POOL)

SPOOS The Standard & Poors 500 index. A widely followed measure of stock-market activity. Great headline potential in a down market: Spoos Spooked.

TIA "Thanks In Advance." Sometimes best given beforehand, depending on what comes back.

TIC/TICK Up or down, which also appears as UT or DT. When a stock moves up or down in price. Like the bug, this tick can draw blood.

TOUTING Basically the same as hyping, except it sounds more British and refined.

UNABOMBER Any unexpected event that severely damages the value of a stock. A TokyoMex term.

UT See TIC/TICK.

WYSIWYG "What You See Is What You Get." Frequently untrue.

YUPPO "Yes," the long way.

Y2K The possibly ultimate computer dating problem you have probably already forgotten about.

Abelson, Alan, 218
Alco International Group, Inc.,
     136–37, 138
Allen, Stuart, 101
Amazon.com, 23, 239
Amazon Natural Treasures, 195
America Online (AOL), 10, 11, 111,
     239
Anders, Jason, 197
Anthony@Pacific. *See* Elgindy, Tony
Armstrong, C. Michael, 239
Armstrong, McKinley, 136–37, 138,
     140, 141, 146
Associated Press, 188, 220

BARD's Trading System (BTS), 58,
     116
Barton, Mark, 217–18
BAT International, 34–40
Bear Down, 161–62, 166
Bear Stearns & Co., 141–42, 223
Bezos, Jeff, 239
Big Dog. *See* Nichols, Mike
Bjorkman, James, 244, 248
Blattner, Kellie, 154, 157
Blinder, Meyer, 135

Blinder, Robinson & Co., 134–35
Bloomberg financial news service,
     187, 255
Books-A-Million, Inc., 23
Brilliant Digital Entertainment, 108
brokerage firms
   bribes to brokers and, 133
   Internet stock trading and, 23
   Level II software and, 20–21, 54
   as market makers, 21, 110
   online trading and, 183–85
   short selling by foreign firms and,
      131–32
BTS (BARD's Trading System), 58
Buffett, Warren, 33
Bulletin Board, 21
Burdick, Bryan, 178–79, 181
Business Week magazine, 184, 204
Business Wire, 213–14, 215–16
BZE International, 213

California Department of Corpora-
     tions, 188
Capital Financial Consultants web-
     site, 227
Case, Steve, 239

Chalem, Alain, 220, 221
chat rooms, 185
   passwords on, 52–53
chat threads, 2
Chelekis, George, 105
CMGI Inc., 117–19
CNH Holdings, Inc., 189–92
Cohen, Jesse (Cavalry)
   Amazon Natural Treasures stock
      and, 199
   Nichols (Big Dog) and, 93, 228, 230
Collins, Susan, 186
Comparator Systems Corp., 103–4
Conectisys Corp., 144–46
Cragun, Bryant, 254
Cramer, James, 239
Cryogenic Solutions, Inc., 61,
      90–93, 106, 111, 112
Cytec Industries, 107–8

DCGR International Holdings Inc.,
   255–57
Dell, Michael, 239
Digitech, 150–51
discussion sites, 185, 263–64
Dog House (chat thread), 51, 52, 63
D'Onofrio, Mark, 143
D'Onofrio, Ramon, 99, 100, 143
Dryer, Brad, 2, 13, 172, 173
Dryer, Jeff, 2, 172–73, 178

Egghead.com, 22, 23
800 Travel Systems, Inc., 24–25, 27,
   110
Einhorn, Irving, 145
Elgindy, Mary Faith, 135–36, 141,
   176–77, 178
Elgindy, Tony (Anthony@Pacific),
   120–61, 167–72, 176–82, 185,
   188, 214, 216, 222–24, 231
   Armstrong, McKinley investiga-
      tion and, 138–41, 146

author's interview with, 158–61
background of, 132, 133–34
Bear Stearns arbitration and,
   141–42
bribes to brokers and, 133
criminal charges against, 223,
   259
FindEx.com stock and, 124–27, 161
gathering of short sellers and,
   128–32, 137
Keyser (Pluvia) and, 164–65
Key West Securities and, 133, 142,
   147, 160
Kosovo mercy mission of, 169–71,
   174
marriage and family of, 135–36,
   141
Park (TokyoMex) and, 30, 130–31,
   153–56, 176, 245, 258
SEC investigations and, 138–40,
   145–46, 151, 152–53, 154
Silicon Investor (SI) comments by,
   119, 120, 129, 136, 148–49, 166,
   218–20
Silicon Investor's suspensions and
   reinstatement of, 171, 176–82,
   222
stockbrokers' murder and, 220,
   221–22
stock recommendations by, 147,
   148–49, 244
stock-trading approach of, 121–24,
   129–30, 131, 159–61
stock-trading experience of,
   134–47
USA Talks.com, Inc. stock and,
   149–53
E*Trade, 22, 56

Fasano, John, 202
FBN Associates hoax, 68–70, 71–72,
   106, 213

Federal Trade Commission (FTC), 151, 212
Feelings thread, Silicon Investor (SI), 85–88
Fiero, John, 137–38
50-Off Stores, 125
FindEx.com, 124–27, 161, 166
First Amendment, 253–54
Firstware Technologies Inc., 123–24
Flores, Alfred, 214, 215
Forbes magazine, 184
Fortune magazine, 11, 157
Frankel, Jacob, 100, 101
fraud. See stock fraud
FTC (Federal Trade Commission), 151, 212

Ga Bard. See Swancey, Gary
Gabler, Neal, 185
Gardner, David, 9–10, 12–13, 33, 71
Gardner, Tom, 9–10, 33, 186, 217–18
Gates, Bill, xxiv, 239
Gibson, Dell, 91
gifts (undisclosed compensation), and stock recommendations, 27
Gomaa, Laila, 140–41
Gore, Al, 37
Go2Net, Inc., 173, 178–79
Gottschalk, Earl, 102

Hitsgalore.com, 209–10, 211–12
hoaxes
   FBN Associates, 68–70, 71–72, 106
   PairGain Technologies, 187
   TechniClone Inc., 90
Hoke, Gary Dale, 187–88

iChargeit, Inc., 229, 230–31
Information Management Associates, 244

Intel Corp., 15
Internet stock trading
   brokerage firms and, 23
   foreign brokerage firms and, 131–32
   hoaxes seen in, 70–71, 90
   market orders in, 23
   Nichols (Big Dog)'s approach to, 54, 59–62, 63–64
   Park (TokyoMex)'s approach to, 22–27
   promise of profits and wealth in, 23, 26
   pumping and dumping (P&D) and, 26
investment fraud. See stock fraud
Iomega, 10–11
   Park and, 11–13
   Shell on, 78–79

JB Oxford Holdings, Inc., xiii–xxi, 4, 149
Jenna (online trader), 163–64, 176
Jobs, Steven, 239

Kaye, John, 220
Keyser, Steve (Pluvia), 162–65
   Elgindy and, 164–65
   SEC investigation of, 162–63
   stock recommendations by, 163
Key West Securities, 133, 142, 147, 160
Khan, Rafi, xix–xx
King, Steven A., 113–14
Koenig, Mark, 41–42
Kott, Irving, xviii–xix
Koutsoubos, Yanni, 125–27, 161

LaStella, Joseph, 35–36, 40
Lehmann, Maier, 220
Level II software, 20–21, 54
Levitt, Arthur, 183

limit order, 22
Little, Jacob, 121
Los Angeles Times, xviii, 162–63, 185,
    254
LOTSOFF Corp., 125
Lozman, Fane (Scanshift), 170–71, 174
Luke, Tim, 177–78

Marchese (Marcasse), Richard, 202,
    203–6, 208
margin, 84–85
market makers, 21, 110, 159–60
market orders, 22–23
Markoff, Alan, 191–92
Marsik, Robert, 114
Mastrini, Mark, 26, 27
Merrill Lynch & Co., 184
message boards, 2, 4, 5, 11, 39, 41.
    See also Silicon Investor (SI)
  bashers on, 93
  Shell's popularity on, 73–75
  Topro/Tava stock on, 14–18
Microsoft Corp., xxiv, 123–24
Midland, Inc., 59, 113–16, 189, 190,
    192
Miller, Daniel, 181–82
Mitchell, Jeffrey, 89–90, 93, 122,
    209, 210
  Amazon Natural Treasures stock
    and, 196, 197, 198, 203, 204,
    205
  Business Wire suit against, 213,
    216
  FBN Associations hoax and, 213
  Swancey and, 194
  TechniClone Inc. hoax of, 90
Money magazine, 26, 254
Motley Fool newsletter, 10
Motley Fool website, 9–10, 11, 13, 33,
    71, 185, 186
Mountain Energy, 106
Munden, Jill, 172, 174–75

naked shorting, 131–32
Nasdaq stock market
  Level II software and, 21
  Topro/Tava trading on, 14
National Association of Securities
    Dealers (NASD), 21, 144, 147
  animosity toward, 142, 146
  arbitration by, 140, 141
Newkirk, Thomas, 101
New York Stock Exchange, 97
  short selling on, 121
  specialist system in, 21–22, 159
New York Times, 217, 243–44, 249,
    252, 253, 254, 261
Nichols, Janice, 53, 232–34, 237
Nichols, Mike (Big Dog), 43–71,
    225–37
  author's meetings with, 44–45,
    51–54, 59–63, 225–27, 232–37
  background of, 52, 55–56
  Cohen (Cavalry) and, 93, 228,
    230
  Cryogenic Solutions, Inc.
    stock and, 61, 92–93, 106, 111,
    112
  Dog House on Silicon Investor
    (SI) and, 43, 45, 51, 52, 55, 63,
    66–67
  FBN Associates hoax and, 68–70,
    71–72
  iChargeit, Inc., venture of, 229–31
  investor-relations work of, 227–29
  marriage and family of, 53,
    232–34, 237
  1998 stock market downswing
    and, 106, 112
  Park (TokyoMex) and, 30, 43,
    45–49, 61, 69–70
  Silicon Investor's suspension of,
    175, 227
  stock recommendations by, 60,
    62, 65–66, 228, 234–35

stock-trading approach of, 54,
    59–62, 63–64, 193–95, 234
Swancey (Ga Bard) and, 56, 58, 59,
    190
Swiss offer to, 62–63
Tokyo Joe's Café takeover by,
    45–51, 58, 61
Wall Street Journal profile of,
    231–32
Winners Internet Network, Inc.
    stock and, 54, 60–61, 62,
    65–66
Nocera, Joseph, 11, 157
North American Securities Adminis-
    tration, 188

Okamoto, Merrick, 247
Online Investors Advantage, 185–86
options, 85

PairGain Technologies, 187
Park, Joe (TokyoMex), 1–44, 185,
    231, 238–62
    author's interviews with, 19–29,
        44, 110, 245–48
    background of, 3, 5–9
    BAT International stock and,
        34–40
    CMGI Inc. stock and, 117–19
    800 Travel Systems, Inc. stock
        and, 24–25, 27, 110
    Elgindy (Anthony@Pacific) and,
        130–31, 153–56, 176, 245, 258
    enemies of, 30
    entry into Internet stock-trading
        world by, 9
    FBN Associates hoax and, 69–70
    Iomega stock and, 11–13
    partying and leisure time activities
        of, 28–30
    marriage and family of, 8
    name options used by, 3–4

New York Times articles on,
    243–44, 249
Nichols (Big Dog) and, 30, 43,
    45–49, 61, 69–70
1998 stock market downswing
    and, 116–19
pumping and dumping (P&D) by,
    26
Rentach, Inc. stock and, 40–42
SEC investigations of, 154, 156–57,
    249–50, 252–61
Silicon Investor (SI) reports by, 13,
    36–37, 38–39
Silicon Investor's suspension of,
    175–76
Societe Anonyme (SA), 31–34, 86,
    108–10, 116, 118, 156–57,
    157–58, 222, 238–44, 246
    stock recommendations by,
        24–26, 27, 36–37, 38–39,
        107–10, 117, 244, 250, 254–55
    stock-trading approach of, 22–27,
        117, 241–42
    Swancey (Ga Bard) and, 58–59
    tip about, 2–3
    Tokyo Joe's Café (chat thread) and,
        2, 42–43, 49–51, 61
    Topro/Tava stock and, 13–18
penny stocks, 134–35, 189, 220
Pfizer, 108
Pierce, Mark, 114, 190
Pitt, Andrew Sturgis (Drew), 142–45
Platten, Don, 256
Pluvia. *See* Keyser, Steve
Portnoy, Allen, 150–51
Power Securities, 204
Preferred Voice, Inc., 228–29
pumping and dumping (P&D), 26,
    194
Pybas, Gerald, 192

Quinn, Thomas, 101

Raging Bull message board, 126–27, 198–99, 208, 263
Reed, Dorian, 211, 212
Reifler, Lionel, 125, 126–27, 161
Rentach, Inc., 40–42
reverse mergers, 229–30
reverse stock split, 79–80
Richards, Melvin Lloyd, 136–37, 138, 139–40
Ross, Brian, 143
Roth, Isadore, 257

SA. *See* Societe Anonyme
Sabratek Corp., 163
Saide, Yesmin, 139
Scanshift (Fane Lozman), 170–71, 174
Schneider, Floyd D. (Flodyie), 165–67, 185, 254
  Elgindy and, 165–66
  TheTruthseeker.com site of, 166–67
Schoeppl, Carl, 212
Securities and Exchange Commission (SEC), 106, 166
  BAT International case and, 34, 40
  Comparator Systems Corp. stock manipulation and, 103–4
  creation of, 97–98
  defections of staff from, 100–101
  Elgindy and investigations before, 138–40, 145–46, 151, 152–53, 154
  Internet enforcement office of, 95, 96–98, 103–5, 186–87
  JB Oxford Holdings case and, xix–xx
  Keyser (Pluvia) investigation of, 162–63
  Midland, Inc. case and, 113–14, 115, 189
  Park (TokyoMex) investigation of, 154, 156–57, 248, 249–50, 252–61

stock fraud investigations of, 4, 98–101, 124, 125, 126, 135, 137, 144–45, 189, 204, 215
  stock-picking newsletters and services and, 105, 156
  USA Talks.com, Inc. case and, 152–53
Segal-Lankry, Jodi, 52, 61–62, 188–89
Senate Permanent Subcommittee on Investigations, 186
Shell, Janice, 72–94, 122, 194, 220, 230–31
  Amazon Natural Treasures stock and, 196, 197, 198–201, 202–9, 211
  background of, 76–77, 81–84
  criticism of, 93–94
  Cryogenic Solutions, Inc. stock and, 90–93
  FBN Associates hoax and, 72, 106, 213
  Feelings thread on Silicon Investor (SI) and, 85–88
  Hitsgalore.com stock and, 209–10, 211–12
  lawsuits and lawsuit threats and, 73–74
  message-board popularity of, 73–75
  sense of humor of, 72, 81, 87–89
  Silicon Investor (SI)'s suspension of, 175
  stock recommendations by, 78–81, 106
  stock-trading approach of, 84–85
  suits against, 211–14, 215–16
  threats made to, 75–76
short and distort (S&D), 194
short selling, 121–22, 124
  Elgindy on, 159–61, 164

foreign brokerage firms and,
131–32
Siegel, Martin Jay, 202
Silicon Investor (SI), 2, 13, 185, 198,
215–16, 263
bashers on, 93
Big Dog's comments (Dog House)
on, 43, 45, 51, 52, 55, 63, 66–67,
92, 106
Elgindy (Anthony@Pacific)'s comments on, 119, 120, 129, 136,
166, 182
Feelings thread on, 85–88
membership fee introduction on,
173
Park's comments (Tokyo Joe's
Café) on, 2, 36–37, 38–39,
42–43, 49–51, 52, 106, 107–10,
117–19, 175–76
rules governing, 172–75
Shell's comments on, 74–75,
91–92, 106
suspensions and terminations of
memberships by, 171, 175–81,
201, 222
Swancey (Ga Bard)'s comments
on, 56, 113, 191
TechniClone Inc. hoax on, 90
Silver Star International, 108
Skruem and Leevum, 72
Societe Anonyme (SA), 31, 86, 118,
153, 156–57, 222
BAT International stock and, 38, 39
creation of, 31–32
membership of, 32, 110–11, 116,
157–58, 241
mission statement of, 32–33
Park on approach and goal of,
33–34, 108–10, 246
Park's stock recommendations to,
238–44, 250–51, 254–55
rules of, 33

Tokyo Joe's Café (chat thread) and,
42–43
Sorkin, Ira, 99, 156, 253
Soros, George, 33
specialist system, New York Stock
Exchange, 21–22, 159
Stark, John Reed, 98, 102
background of, 95–97
memo on Internet stock fraud
from, 102–3
SEC Internet enforcement office
and, 95, 96–97, 104, 105
state government securities regulators, 188
Steffens, John, 184
stock-discussion message boards, 2,
4, 5, 11, 39, 41. See also Silicon
Investor (SI)
bashers on, 93
Shell's popularity on, 73–75
Topro/Tava stock on, 14–18
stock fraud
bribes to brokers and, 133
Comparator Systems Corp. stock
manipulation and, 103–4
criminal justice statistics
(mid-1990s) on, 99–100
Elgindy on, 143
growing concern about, 102
SEC Internet enforcement office
for, 95, 96–98, 103–5, 186–87
SEC investigations of, 4, 98–101,
124, 125, 126, 135, 137, 144–45,
189
state government securities regulators and, 188
tips about, 2–3
stock hoaxes
FBN Associates, 68–70, 71–72,
106
PairGain Technologies, 187
TechniClone Inc., 90

stock market downswing (1998),
106, 111–19
Swancey (Ga Bard) and, 112–13
Nichols (Big Dog) and, 112
Park (TokyoMex) and, 116–19
stock options, 85
stock recommendations
Elgindy (Anthony@Pacific) on,
147, 148–49, 244
gifts (undisclosed compensation)
and, 27
Keyser (Pluvia) on, 163
Nichols (Big Dog) on, 60, 62,
65–66, 228, 234–35
Park (TokyoMex) on, 24–26, 27,
117, 244
Shell on, 78–81, 91–92
stock trading. See also Internet stock
trading
Bulletin Board and, 21
foreign brokerage firms and,
131–32
gifts (undisclosed compensation)
and, 27
Level II software for, 20–21, 54
market makers and, 21, 110,
159–60
market orders and, 22–23
pumping and dumping (P&D) in,
26
specialist system, New York Stock
Exchange, and, 21–22, 159
Swancey, Gary (Ga Bard), 56–59,
189–95, 231
author's interview with, 59
background of, 56–57
marriage of, 192–93
Midland, Inc. stock and, 59,
114–16, 189, 190
Nichols (Big Dog) and, 56, 58, 59,
190

1998 stock market downswing
and, 112–13
Park (TokyoMex) and, 30, 58–59
Silicon Investor (SI)'s suspension
of, 175
stock-trading approach of, 57–58
Sylver, Michael, 198, 201–2, 203,
208
Szczepaniak, Joe, 125, 126

Tasty Fries, Inc., 79–80
Tava Technologies, Inc. (formerly
Topro, Inc.), 13–18
TechniClone Inc. hoax, 90
TheStreet.com, 3, 4, 6, 29–30, 252
TheTruthseeker.com, 166–67, 185,
254
Time magazine, 239
Tokyo Joe's Café (chat thread), 2,
42–43, 49–51, 58–59, 61
TokyoMex. See Park, Joe
Topro, Inc. See Tava Technologies,
Inc.
trading. See Internet stock trading;
stock trading
Transactional Records Access Clear-
inghouse (TRAC), 99, 100
TrendMark, 151
Troyer, Verne, 131
Truthseeker Reports, 167
Turney, Howard, 91
20/20 television show, 143, 151
Tyson, Matthew, 171, 223

Ulrich, William, 213
undisclosed compensation, and
stock recommendations, 27
Uniprime Capital Acceptance, Inc.,
214–15
USA Talks.com, Inc., 149–53, 166
U.S. News & World Report, 183

Walker, Richard, 102, 103, 105, 183, 186, 252–53

Wall Street Journal, xvii, 1, 22–23, 132, 135, 184, 217, 239, 256

  Amazon Natural Treasures story by, 197–98

  Cryogenic Solutions, Inc. article in, 90–91

  profile of Nichols (Big Dog) in, 231–32

  stock fraud articles in, 102, 187, 204

  story on Park in, 4

WallStreetStand website, 219, 222

Walters, Barbara, 143

Washington Post, 32

Webnode.com, 213

Wehner, Charles, 145

White Castle, 44–45, 51–52

Whitney, Richard, 97

Winners Internet Network, Inc., 54, 60–61, 62, 65–66

WiredNews magazine, 213

Yahoo!, 39–40, 41, 111, 187, 230, 263

Y2K problem, 13–14, 71, 249, 262

Zaman, Michael, 143–46

Zeigletics, 71

ZiaSun Technologies Inc., 167, 185, 254

Zumbrunnen, Bob, 172, 175